How to survive anorexia

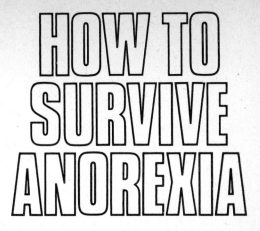

HOW TO SURVIVE ANOREXIA

A guide to anorexia nervosa and bulimarexia

Peter Lambley Ph.D.

Frederick Muller Limited
London

First published in Great Britain in 1983 by Frederick Muller
Limited, London SW19 7JZ

British Library Cataloguing in Publication Data

Lambley, Peter
    How to survive anorexia.
    1. Anorexia nervosa.
    I. Title
    616.8'5206   RC552.A5

    ISBN 0-584-11012-X
    ISBN 0–584–11066–9 pbk

Typeset by Texet, Leighton Buzzard, Bedfordshire
Printed in Great Britain by
Redwood Burn Limited, Trowbridge, Wiltshire

For Dorrian with love

"If she is capable of being a stubborn liar, the anorexic is also capable of a certain stubborn honesty in the sense of being true to herself, the self which has somehow been mislaid and/or starved and which she must find and nourish again. In feeding the body, the wrong part of herself is being nourished. It is the true, the buried self which is in need of real nourishment, and the more the wrong part (the obvious, visible body) receives, the likelier the right part is to remain buried and die of starvation."

Sheila Macleod *The Art of Starvation*
London (Virago, 1981) Used with permission

Contents

Preface

I have never before started a book by telling my readers how it came into existence. It seldom matters and usually the author is the only one involved anyway. But this time things were rather different.

This book was originally conceived of in 1973-74 when it became apparent to my patients, researchers and me that the anorexia nervosa we read about in psychiatric text books was only the tip of an iceberg. Many of the patients I had seen up to then had begun their 'troubles' with the classic form of anorexia, that is the weight-loss and starvation kind, but later became bingers and vomiters, what I then called 'secret anorexia' but is now called bulimarexia. We believed, in fact, that the latter was more prevalent than anorexia nervosa simply because over a two-year period I and my colleagues had seen more bulimarexics than anorexics. Moreover, a good many of the female patients I saw in private practice had episodes of bulimarexia and some of my older patients had been vomiting up their meals for over half a century. Very early on in my practice, then, my colleagues and I were acutely aware of what (we thought) was going on.

I tried on several occasions to publish academic papers on the preliminary results of our early research, but with no success, despite the fact that in other areas of research nearly every paper I wrote was published. Perhaps, I thought, we were wrong. After all some of our ideas were quite unorthodox; one for example required close study of a prospective patient's dental history, a fact that irritated a number of my medical colleagues — 'What does a psychologist want with a dental record?' they would ask, unconvinced of the diagnostic value of rapid tooth decay in detecting a 'secret anorexic'. Vomiting destroys the lining of the teeth incredibly quickly and we had found a way of early detection that helped dentists and patients.

There were other insights, more concerned with psychology and society, that needed exposure beyond the fairly closed world of psychiatry and clinical psychology and so in 1978 I wrote the first of several proposals for this book. By then I was pretty sure that there was a broad need for a survival guide about anorexia and bulimarexia. I felt that there were many ordinary people with varying degrees of bulimarexia as well as many anorexics who had been treated for the condition but remained in one or other state. Parents, doctors and patients themselves needed some idea about how to cope.

However, no one wanted to publish. Publishers felt that there were enough books out on anorexia and that I was writing about a minor aspect of it. After many interviews with editors and a large number of rejection slips, I gave up. I had other things to do.

Not so, however, my agent and sometime researcher Ms. Shelley Power. She believed in what we were trying to do and that the findings, ideas and treatment hints in my proposed book should be widely available. She found that Mr. Anthony White at Frederick Muller Ltd. was of the same opinion and he agreed to publish this book.

As you can imagine, I am grateful to them for this. Why I have gone into this, though, apart from a desire to record my thanks, is because I want my readers to know just how difficult it can be for all of us to get at the truth and make it known in the face of opposition or disinterest. While the material for this book was being put together, things changed markedly. From being a minor area of the anorexia spectrum, 'secret anorexia' or bulimarexia has now become almost a disease in its own right. Articles have appeared in the British and American press expressing shock at the discovery of how widespread bulimarexia is amongst 'normal' people, while almost weekly new evidence is put forward in journals about the numbers of women now coming forward to admit to the habit. *Newsweek,*

Omni, *The Sunday Times* and *The Observer* are just a few of the publications to have given the new illness prominence, showing, I think, just how extensive it is.

To all of us who worked on this project there is some comfort in knowing now, many years later, that we were right. But it is cold comfort. Bulimarexia is not new. It has been around for years. All that is new is the fact that psychiatry, psychology and the media have become aware of it. What worries us is that the underlying methods of psychology and psychiatry will not change, that bulimarexia will become saturated with the same kind of psycho-babble that originally clouded our understanding of anorexia, that the depths of the problem will not be probed and that once again psychiatry and psychology will *tell* patients what to think instead of listening to what they have to say.

I say this, not from a position of arrogance, nor because I consider that my methods are better. As a doctor I had to learn to listen to my patients and to trust their perspective as a viable perspective and it was not easy. This experience may or may not have worked in the sense of producing some of the answers to the problems that lie behind anorexia or bulimarexia, but it has, I think, pointed out where we have to look. Anorexia and bulimarexia are *not* just slimming problems, not just the result of ideas propagated by the media or the fashion industry and not just limited to models and others concerned with being thin. They are problems that may be experienced by all women in our society and as such require a frank and open investigation of the whole structure of modern living.

If this book leaves you with nothing else, I hope it will be with the awareness, at least, that the underlying element in anorexia and its various forms is *fear*. Nearly all of the symptoms we traditionally associate with anorexia nervosa are normal fear reactions carried to the extreme; anorexics are people who have had to learn to live with chronically high levels of panic:

> "The state of being suddenly overwhelmed by fearful sensations constitutes panic anxiety. It is accompanied by massive autonomic responses, both sympathetic and parasympathetic, particularly tachycardia, sweating, dizziness,

dry mouth, hot and cold flushes, diarrhoea, vomiting, sensations of fainting and fear of death. Panic anxiety is indistinguishable from the reaction to overwhelming threat, for example, being threatened with death, but it may occur suddenly without apparent precipitant... We believe panic often has a close biological relationship to separation anxiety."[1]

Loss of periods, excessive verbalization, irritability and anorexia (loss of appetite) itself are other, equally well-known components of panic and fear. What should concern us all is why it is possible in our sophisticated societies for this to happen. And, above all, why to so many women? This book, I hope, will go a little way towards answering these questions, but there is no doubt in my mind that it will only scrape away at the surface. Much more is needed.

The book itself is based on the work that my patients, researchers, colleagues, friends and I have conducted into anorexia. It was, and continues to be, a co-operative effort, begun in Cape Town, South Africa, and continued in Britain and Greece. Although I alone bear the final responsibility for what appears here, many people worked on the project.

First and foremost, my wife Dorrian has been the backbone of much of the effort that has gone into the book. She and my friend, Merle Baum, have provided many of the working hypotheses and insights as well as typing out the various manuscripts. My patients over the years have done more, I believe, than most patients. Not only have they taught me about themselves and about myself, but they have helped keep us on the right track, often against quite formidable opposition. Last, but by no means least, I thank my researchers, colleagues and friends who helped uncover the mysteries of anorexia and took care of a bunch of people who were often difficult. In particular, I thank Stan Rabinowitz, Shirley Jenner, Peter Cooper and Lucinda Suckling for research and

1 Quoted from Donald F. Klein, M.D. and John M. Davis, M.D. *Diagnosis and Drug Treatment of Psychiatric Disorders* (The Williams & Wilkins Company, Baltimore, 1969). See also S. Lesse *Anxiety* (Grune and Stratton, New York, 1970).

clinical assistance, and Dick Kukard (gynaecologist), Marshal Hotz (dentist) and John King (physician) for support and medical back-up.

One last word. I have tried to maintain a consistent use of the word *anorexia*. Where I use the word *anorexia* alone I refer to the general subject matter: not only the familiar anorexia nervosa, but also bulimarexia. Where I use the words *anorexia nervosa*, I refer to the specific condition in which there is loss of appetite and loss of weight. Where I use the term *bulimarexia*, I refer to the specific condition in which gorging of food and vomiting occur.

Introduction

A strange title for a book — *How to Survive Anorexia*. It is that word 'survive' that does it. You would expect, perhaps, *How to Cure Anorexia* or *How to Treat Anorexia* — but 'survive'? 'Survive' has a different meaning; it implies 'scraping by' or getting through a long tough battle in one piece — as in a war movie in which the hero or heroine barely make it through the minefield, or, more appropriately, as in a horror story in which perfectly normal and trusted things continually turn into something terrifying.

The heroine survives — but at what price?

Well, in my experience, many sufferers from anorexia or its related condition bulimarexia live out existences very similar to 'survival' movies, with one difference — they do not survive to live happily ever after. What is worse, in the process of treating anorexics, I have found that by and large those who survive do so by literally fighting for their lives, sometimes against the very people who appear to want to help them: friends, parents, society, even doctors. To survive anorexia, I believe, requires the victim to act sometimes as if she were living in a horror movie; nothing must be seen as safe or to be completely trusted.

Very few people are able to see their lives in this way, and even fewer can literally take on all comers to survive; hence the need for a book with this title. I believe the victims of anorexia and its modern treatment need to know how to get through life, and how to deal with their families and friends, and with society and doctors. In short, they need a 'survival guide' on their emotional travels so that the horror of the illness and its after effects can be faced properly.

"But why?" some may ask. After all the publicity and the books and the magazine articles, surely anorexia is straightforward and curable? Surely anorexia is the slimmers' disease that just needs a bit of hospitalization to bring the silly girl — it is usually a girl, isn't it — to her senses and put weight on her skeletal frame? Is it not just a phase some girls go through, helped along by the silly obsessions they — and the fashion magazines they read — have with being thin?

No! Not really.

Anorexia nervosa is a very, very serious illness, far more serious than most people, including doctors, care to believe. This is so not simply because sufferers can die through starvation (and do, in disturbing and increasing numbers), but because it is a problem that has its roots so deeply and insidiously embedded in the structure of our advanced societies that, by and large, we cannot see them properly.

A little thought soon shows this up. We have known about anorexia for over two hundred years, since the late seventeenth century in fact, but how scientists and lay people alike have thought about it has reflected far more their concern with shunting people into convenient little boxes than with the reality before them. Those terms 'silly girl', 'fashion', 'slimmers' disease' all reflect self-evident truths about anorexia and they have been used since the late 17th century — at least in the Anglo-American world — to define and explain the illness, despite the fact that there are other equally obvious truths about anorexia for anyone who cares to look to see. People have seen anorexia as a *weight* problem, for example because some anorexics lose a lot of weight. It has been seen as an eating problem because some anorexics will not eat. Anorexia has been seen as a *fashion* problem because fashion models are thin and because people, especially women, are encouraged to be thin in order to be considered attractive. Each such theory contains an element of truth and all are easy to be seen. They are convenient, straightforward ways of explaining anorexia, in which the cause and effect are all neatly embodied in the victim: "*She* won't eat and this causes her to lose weight and become anorexic!" At best, this neat analysis is pushed a little further: "*She* doesn't want to eat because she doesn't want to get fat and be unattractive. *She* takes too much notice of what the fashion media say. *She* should know better."

There are two other very important facts about anorexia that are just as easy for all to see as what we have been talking about, but which are a good deal more difficult to explain. They call for, it seems, far greater and more troubling effort, more socially penetrating analysis and are not easily contained in the 'its-her-fault' cycle of explanation.

The first fact is that anorexia affects women almost exclusively. Very few men indeed ever suffer from it and those that do seldom suffer from it in the same way. Women are overwhelmingly more likely to get anorexia than men.

The second fact is that despite the 'fact' that anorexia is a female illness, it has not been easily explained (if explained at all) by the normal range of theories that can usually be counted on to fit this label. These theories have all to do with hormones. Whenever there is a mental illness that only women suffer from (and many somatic ones as well) it is quickly explained by reference to hormones. Not so with anorexia. In fact, in my view, research has shown the reverse. When a woman becomes anorexic she literally forces her hormones to change their function; menstruation for example, a hormone-controlled somatic function, ceases in certain forms of anorexia due to an act of will (or mental preoccupation) rather than any body changes such as weight loss or pathological hormone fluctuation. In short, despite all the research, all the cases seen, and all the public attention, anorexia remains a puzzle. No one really knows why apparently normal girls suddenly refuse food and risk death through starvation, no one knows whether its cause lies in the brain, in hormones, in the family or in personality development. Lastly, and most important, no one knows how to treat anorexia successfully.

If you go over the history of anorexia, or simply look at the conflicting case reports cited in magazines and on television, you will see that hospitalizing anorexics and making them put on weight was initially greeted as the solution to the problem. However, it soon became apparent that many anorexics simply gained weight to get out of hospital, and once out carried on as before. Further, some anorexics learnt to fool everyone by eating hearty meals but later vomiting up what they ate. Very recently, magazine articles in Britain and America, and some research studies, have shown that numbers of women at large use eating and vomiting routinely as a means of keeping their weight down[1]. In the same way that a dragon grows a new head every time one is cut off, people with anorexia nervosa seem able to survive our best attempts to understand and cure it.

Why is this?

Why do women get it? Is it part of 'being female' in the physical sense, having something to do with 'being a woman' — with being more prone to following fashion, being more easily influenced? Has it got something to do with a women's role in our society? And why is anorexia a puzzle anyway?

In science today, the word 'puzzle' is usually reserved for something really big, the mysteries of space for example, or cancer; it hardly seems appropriate to use the word to describe anorexia, something so seemingly straightforward and, on the face of it, curable (nearly all weight-gain programmes used in hospitals work in the simple sense of putting weight on anorexics).

These are essential and very obvious questions you ask about anorexia. When you try to answer them though, you run into problems. Few professional people have really thought very much about why anorexia is primarily a female illness, nor have they gone very thoroughly into why anorexia is a puzzle, nor why it is not easy to treat. Much of the recent controversy about anorexia and its treatment has come from patients themselves and other interested non-professionals seeking to open up the whole matter, and expose both what has passed for treatment and the way anorexics' suffering and the female issues involved are neglected. "If men were suddenly, in the space of one or two decades, to become anorexic, to waste away," they ask, "would not the concern and the focus be very different?"

---

1   See, for example, the study by Yvonne Roberts in *Over 21* (March, 1981). See also *Newsweek* (November 2, 1981) for a review of studies in the U.S. and *Omni* (October 1981). *The Observer* (January 17, 1982) also contains information.

HOW THIS BOOK CAME TO BE WRITTEN

If all that I have written so far interests you, or concerns you, then possibly this book will help you. Instead of looking at anorexia purely as a problem of loss of appetite or serious weight loss, this book focusses on the very questions I have already raised. Why women, and why a puzzle?

When I began to plan writing a book on anorexia, I had to choose how best to get across what I wanted to say. Should it be a kind of formal description of what we know about anorexia and how we treat it? 'We', of course, being doctors in general. Or should it be a book about what really goes on in anorexia — or rather what I, and my patients and helpers, had found to go on in our attempts to understand it and how people (families, doctors, society) react to it?   In 1978, anorexia had become a very topical issue and quite a few books were appearing, written much as I would probably have written them — in a formal style that glosses over the vital questions. I decided then that it would be better to write the second kind of book. People were being informal about anorexia. What they really needed, I thought, would be a book about how to survive for themselves, with or without help. However, at the time no one was really interested in publishing the type of book I had in mind. Everything seemed understood: "all sewn up", in the words of one publisher I consulted. Now, however, things look very different. As I have said, patients, researchers, journalists, television producers and others have tended to take matters into their own hands, and in contrast to the steady stream of straightforward and confident reports of 'cures' published in academic journals, more and more reports appear in the media of failed cases, of people being dissatisfied with the treatment and the explanations that have been offered about anorexia.

This book takes a new look at anorexia from the viewpoint of what life is like for the anorexic before the illness begins, and during conventional treatment. It focuses primarily on *survival*, on helping the anorexic to understand what is happening to her.

The book is based on the work that I and my colleagues (doctors, assistants, patients) have been doing since the early

1970s on understanding and treating anorexia. The questions we asked ourselves as we went along are the ones I will try to answer here. When I began treating, I used the available methods: sent patients to hospital, focused on the conventional explanations just like anyone else; but slowly it became clear that far more was involved. Why only the daughters in a given family? What happened to sons? How did they turn out? What happened to anorexics in their families *before* they became anorexic? How do the families cause it, if they do? What role do mothers play in the formation of anorexia? And fathers? And siblings?

And then there were the terrible contradictions. Look at this list:

> Anorexics avoid food. They hate it.
> Anorexics hate putting on weight.
> Anorexics are very thin people.
> Anorexics are afraid of being pregnant.
> Anorexics are scared of sexuality.
> Anorexics are immature, inexperienced people.
> Anorexics are intelligent, highly insightful and usually from middle-class homes.

And yet daily I was coming across anorexics at variance with these common beliefs. Daily I heard about anorexics being obsessed with food, thinking about nothing else, gorging themselves, toying with their weight, putting it on and taking it off; about anorexics being deeply involved with being female, falling happily pregnant and about anorexics with deep and varied sexual encounters. I met anorexics who looked healthier and fatter than me; and I was overweight! I met anorexics in their teens, in their 20s, 30s, 40s, 50s and 60s. I met single, married, divorced, widowed anorexics. I even met true, fully-fledged anorexics in poor squatter communities in Africa and in the corners of peasant communities in Greece, far away from the affluent middle class suburbs of Cape Town or London, where I also saw them. I saw anorexics who starved themselves to death and others who did not. I saw anorexics who gorged and vomited (now called bulimarexics but then lumped together with the whole range) and those that did not. In short, I saw anorexics everywhere, all with bits and pieces of the various symptoms described in text books but all different, unique individuals with their unique adjustments to their lives. The only thing I can really say they had in common was that they were all female and all suffered deeply.

Not unexpectedly, in looking at anorexia and anorexics' families in depth, and in looking at anorexia cross-culturally and across class boundaries, I evolved a somewhat different view of anorexia to that normally accepted by psychoanalysts and behaviour therapists. For one thing, I discovered that when you see a person suffering from anorexia nervosa you see only a small part of the problem. Behind every anorexic is a long and often tragic history of suffering and distress, not only in the anorexic, but in her siblings and in her parents as well. This is made worse, by and large, by the fact that it is a story not yet told. People in anorexics' families suffer in silence and despair, often for years if not decades at a time without ever realizing how and why. I believe now that anorexia is not limited to pathological cases. I found that many women —perhaps all women — suffer at one time or another from an anorexic kind of crisis. Many get through it and go on to lead healthy fulfilled lives with fully rounded personalities. But many do not get through the crisis easily. Many are crippled by the conflicts involved, and live partial, fragmented lives thereafter, again seldom fully realizing why. Others fail more significantly and become bulimarexics, eating and vomiting, putting on weight and taking it off in endless cycles of rituals that stay with them always. Still others fail hopelessly and slip into severe anorexia and starve themselves to death. Anorexia, I shall argue, is not just a mental illness in which people lose weight, or die. It is, as a phenomenon, a symptom of deep and penetrating social and personal problems that remain largely ignored.

This then is not just a book for anorexics. It is for all women. And of course, it is for men interested in the human condition in general, and in women and their psychology. If we can understand the struggle anorexics go through it will help us all to understand ourselves and our society, for in a very fundamental sense we all suffer unnecessarily in subtle but vital ways just as the anorexic does. The study of anorexia is a study in subtexts, in subtleties, in innuendoes, in the unsaid, and in the unstated. As such, anorexia should concern us all.

HOW THIS BOOK IS ORGANIZED

Much of this book is devoted to exploring what actually goes on in anorexics' families and what actually causes anorexia. The first part of the book concentrates on helping you to understand yourself and those around you. I found in practice that it was vital for my patients to know a lot about what was happening to them in order for them to help themselves. Often, I found that they resisted facing up to the kind of information contained in the first part of the book. For one thing, it was, and is, much easier to accept the conventional clichés about anorexia and to try and control it, repress it or suppress it in any way possible. It was only after time — and sometimes after seeing other doctors or trying other techniques — that patients would begin to accept some of the truth (or what I think is the truth) about their condition. As you will see this was not a question of my knowing exactly what happens, or what to do. Rather, it was a question of facing up to an unpleasant reality and the fact that it is very much up to the *individual* to do something about it. I had my best results with people who had first tried other, more passive methods (hospitalization, drugs, interpretative psychotherapy) in which most of the work was done for them by a doctor. Modern societies tend to encourage passive approaches to mental problems; you take a tranquilizer or you put yourself in the hands of 'the professionals' who fix you up — you can sit back and relax and watch your life being run as if it were on television. When patients have tried this and found that it does not work, they are then ready to help themselves to survive better. These are the kinds of patients I have worked with best. We have formed a team. The latter part of the book, therefore, is devoted to giving you some idea of what to do to help yourself, using my own cases to show you how to go about it and how to think things out.

TO SUM IT UP

I will concentrate first on explaining anorexia by telling you what I think is reliably now known about the condition. Then we will look at what has to be done to survive anorexia, seeing how normal people live and how to set about becoming normal. Lastly, we will concentrate on self-help, on spelling out what you can best do to help yourself.

This book is not meant to replace conventional medical or psychiatric help. It is designed to help you think about anorexia more clearly and to motivate you to take more care of yourself and to ensure that those who try to help you do not make matters worse. It is a straightforward survival guide and I believe it will be the most realistic book about anorexia you will have yet read. Use it to give yourself insight. Use it to penetrate those clichés tossed at you. Use it to make your doctors give you more of what you need and, above all, use it to make yourself believe in yourself and your human and individual rights. Why should you suffer?

Chapter 1

What is anorexia nervosa?

Everyone knows what anorexia nervosa is. It has been written about, read about and talked about more often than almost any other form of mental illness; its victims have been recorded on video, photographed, filmed and interviewed with the kind of frequency normally reserved for film stars. It has even been politicized: many people will remember the outcry when two female members of the I.R.A. were released from prison in Britain because they were allegedly suffering from anorexia nervosa? Some people thought the women were faking — "an illness of convenience, of political convenience" were words I heard used at the time. Others were less sure. Nevertheless, whatever the case, the illness anorexia nervosa is extremely well known by now and the ins and outs of who gets it and how they get it are widely discussed.

Given all this, it should be very easy to present a straightforward definition of what anorexia is. Unfortunately this is not as easy as it sounds. True, much publicity has been given to the condition and many sufferers have come forward and apparently opened up their eating, or lack of eating, habits to the public. Yet, paradoxically, anorexics are by and large an intensely secretive bunch of people. In fact, because anorexics are such a secretive lot, our understanding of quite what it is has had to be continually revised and updated. Anorexics part with information on themselves about as reluctantly as the head of the CIA — more so: he would probably break under torture; not so your average anorexic.

What seems to have happened is that while many people

have suffered from one form or another of anorexia, they have done so, and continue to do so, in secret. Only those who have had to get help or who have been forced to get help have 'come clean', and then only in part. Imagine all of London's anorexics, for example, fitted into the Albert Hall in darkness. Now turn on a pocket torch: you will see only a fraction of the gathering actually assembled there. This is analogous to what happened in the study of anorexia during the 1950s and '60s. A handful of torches were turned on, and focused only on the few people revealed in the tiny area of light. It was only later on, when someone had the bright idea of moving the torch beam around a little to reveal other people, that we saw more. Undiscovered, anorexics, it seems, have an amazing ability to stand still and silently in the dark.

Consequently, when anorexics have revealed something of what is going on, they have had the effect of causing chaos in respectable medical circles, with the result that even quite cherished theories and formulations have frequently had to be thrown away unceremoniously. This of course helps to account for at least some of the confusion and mystery about anorexia in the medical and psychiatric professions.

Look at it this way. In the early days, and right up till very recently, most cases of anorexia were seen virtually on an emergency basis in hospital casualty units; a girl or a woman who had been dieting or had refused to eat for a long period, would collapse or cause sufficient concern to be hospitalized. Not unexpectedly, doctors having to deal with this situation would immediately focus on saving the girl's life *through increasing her weight*. The whole problem then naturally became conceived of as a *refusal-to-eat* and a *weight-loss* problem.

Doctors have treated anorexia nervosa in this fashion for years. When I was training in the early 1970s, we were issued with a list of clearly defined symptoms — mainly to do with weight-loss — that we had to apply before we could consider someone to be anorexic. You might be familiar with some of the conditions on this list which I have summarized:

The patient had to be under 25 years of age when she first had anorexia.

The patient had to have lost at least a quarter of her normal body weight.

The patient had to have a 'bent' attitude towards food. 'Distorted' is the word the compilers of this list used, meaning that nothing could make the patient eat and she would do strange things with food, like hoarding it and handling it unusually.[1]

The patient would have no other medical or psychiatric illnesses that could be related to anorexia.

The patient had to have at least two of the following symptoms: Loss of periods (amenorrhoea), too many fine body hairs (lanugo), episodes of overactivity, vomiting and gorging (bulimia) and lastly, a slowed pulse rate.

All of this seems very specific and straightforward. Imagine my surprise, therefore, when one day — two years after I had qualified and some 18 months after I had begun to do research on anorexia nervosa, working in a hospital with a long history of research on anorexia and supervised by one of the world's experts on the subject — one of the psychiatrists on the staff whom I had been treating for depression for a year, announced to me that she was a secret anorexia sufferer.

I could not believe it. How could she be? She was healthy, vibrant and, moreover, very nicely covered, even curvaceous. How could she have fooled not only me but our world-famous expert who had seen her nearly every day?

"Simple," she said, "I vomit."

Swearing me to secrecy, she told me the following tale which may seem very familiar to you now but which, in 1973, was quite a surprise.

As a teenager at home, she had gone on an extreme diet, had been unable to stop and wound up in a hospital on the verge of death. While upset at how much harm and shame she believed she had caused her parents and all the trouble she had created, she nevertheless was determined to remain thin. So she had taken to vomiting to keep everyone happy. She could eat as much as she liked at the dinner table and thus keep her family happy (who were by then completely obsessed with her eating

---

1 The list can be found in J. P. Feighner *et al* 'Diagnostic Criteria for use in Psychiatric Research' *Archives of General Psychiatry* (1972) pages 26, 57-63.

habits) and then bring it all up later to stay thin. Over time, this had developed into a regular habit and no one had ever found out — right through her years at university.

How many other women, I wondered, were in the same boat: classical anorexics who had developed a secret ritual *after* medical treatment had pronounced them cured? How many women used this fixation on vomiting and food to maintain their weight without ever really needing the attention of a doctor or a hospital?

Well, as we now know, a very large number of women (and some men) do engage in rituals such as this and when these are added to the number of hospital cases seen each year, you can see just how great the problem is. As you would expect, therefore, the problem of defining quite what anorexia is has become somewhat awkward. Before embarking on the definition and explanation to be used in this book, then, let us briefly look at the historical views of anorexia so that you will understand the way in which some doctors, and people in general, are continuing to think about the problem; you will also get an idea of the way the approach of the medical profession has evolved.

A LITTLE HISTORY

As I have said, anorexia nervosa is a fairly widely-used term now, but a few years ago it was barely mentioned in the popular press. As recently as 1960, the term was only just beginning to emerge in the psychiatric literature from the depths of medical practice where it had been confined since the turn of the century. The word 'anorexia' itself was not to be found until recently in the average English dictionary despite the fact that an Englishman was the first to describe accurately the main features of the condition and that English doctors have played a considerable role in developing our understanding of anorexia. It is, however, a word easily found in French dictionaries and has been a term in everyday use in France and in other continental countries for many years. *'Anorexie'* can be found, for example, in the Concise Oxford French dictionary of 1950, where we are told it means 'loss of appetite', but it is not found in the corresponding English dictionary of the same date.

Both English and French words are derivatives of the Greek word ἀνορεξία which has two meanings. Traditionally it means both 'want of appetite' and 'lack of zest for living'. The stem of the word ὄρεξις means 'appetite' or 'mood'. In modern Greek there are also two ways of using the term; καλή ὄρεξη meaning 'eat well' and καλή ὄρεξη meaning roughly 'be happy'. The term 'nervosa' incidentally means literally 'nerves' and is one of the ways in which doctors in the past have referred to problems of a psychological origin.

The fact that the word 'anorexia' is more commonly found in French than in English and that its meaning in French and Greek has a psychological content (rather than the more familiar 'loss of weight' meaning usually put on it by the British) is not accidental. The shift in emphasis reflects the differing approaches to psychological and philosophical problems that have historically separated British from Continental researchers, not only in medicine, but in biology, philosophy, anthropology and even physics. The way in which British and American doctors in the past have understood the condition differs from that of their French and Continental counterparts. Both have been trained in different traditions and so have approached the problem with different preconceptions.

We do not have the time here to go into how these traditions differ in general. What is important is to realize that we have to accept two sources of confusion: the secrecy of the anorexics themselves and the bickering between the various disciplines and schools of medical thought. In other words, from the point of view of someone trying to understand anorexia, patients, as well as doctors and researchers, have confused the picture. While no one minds arguments and differences in opinion in a profession, in this case differences of opinion among the various schools of medicine have not always furthered our understanding of the disorder. Important aspects of anorexia have been ignored for decades at a time and in some instances, deaths have occurred through misdiagnosis. Perhaps the most unfortunate effect of these differences, however, has been the way in which ignorance and prejudice have created sets of misleading myths among the professionals themselves

— the very people on whom the public rely to inform them about illnesses and their treatments.

To add to this sorry picture, anorexia nervosa is one of the rare examples in the history of disease and illness where man's understanding of the condition was actually better some centuries ago than it has been in more recent times. Most medical problems have been better described and better understood as time has gone by, with successive generations of doctors and researchers building on the insights of their predecessors. However, whenever a disorder has fallen between two stools, being neither clearly psychological, nor clearly medical, problems have emerged. Anorexia nervosa, like certain skin diseases and like headaches and migraine, is among those disorders. And like most psychosomatic conditions, understanding of it has been hampered by attempts to place it firmly in one or other camp. This was especially the case in the late 19th century and early 20th century when scientists and doctors everywhere were preoccupied with classifications and with drawing strict lines between mind and body.

Because most anorexics seen by doctors early this century became thin and eventually died, doctors argued that anorexia was essentially a *physical* condition. Death is a very physical fact and it was easy to overlook the much less obvious chain of emotional events that preceded the decision to stop eating. The failure of vital body organs, which directly caused the early anorexics to die, was a physical or a medical problem that required a physical or medical solution. The temptation to round off the whole process by adopting a physical, medical theory about the illness proved too great for many of the physicians who dealt with these cases.

Not so, however, the English physician Richard Morton, who in 1694 was the first on record to deal with anorexia in a rather more perceptive manner. Morton used an apt turn of phrase to describe the only cases of anorexia he saw, one a female and the other a male. Writing in his book, *Phthisiologia* or A *Treatise of Consumptions*, he described the first, a young girl he encountered in 1694, as "a skeleton only clad with skin". Morton treated her by applying "aromatick bags, stomach-plaisters and bitter medicines" such as 'chalybeates and antihysterick waters' (shades of our modern anti-depressant and anti-nausea pills) but without effect. She died three months later after a fainting fit. Morton attributed the cause of her death to a number of factors, amongst them the preceding severe winter and her habit of studying too hard and staying up at night. But he clearly indicated that the root of her problems lay in her psychological condition: she "wholly neglected the care of herself," he wrote, refused to eat and "fell into a total suppression of her monthly courses" — all, it seems, arising out of "a multitude of cares and passions of the mind". Morton's second patient was a young male with some similar symptoms but who subsequently recovered.

The important point is that Morton presented a rather full account of a medical problem in which weight-loss was only one part. He, at least, was clear where the cause lay. Francis de Valagin and Robert Whyatt in their books published separately in the 1760s both mention seeing similar cases also in states of severe somatic distress. They were also amongst the first to note that cycles of overeating and vomiting were central parts of anorexia as well as lack of appetite and dangerous weight loss.

Why is it then, that by the 1950s in Britain and America, 200 years after these early reports, the vomiting, the over-eating, the emotional distress that anorexic patients so clearly manifested had somehow been lost along the way? What is worse, why was it that from 1914 to the mid-1930s, the psychological and emotional symptoms associated with anorexia were almost entirely dismissed as side-effects of an organic medical problem having nothing to do with the mind — an attitude that still persists today in some quarters?

The answer to both these questions lies in the way Anglo-American medical communities responded to the new scientific and materialistic philosophies of the 18th and 19th centuries. In the rush to be as respectable as the natural sciences, such as physics and chemistry, medicine and psychiatry quickly tried to squeeze symptoms and illnesses into categories that were easily understandable 'physically' and could be treated physically. Anorexia was one of the early conditions to suffer at the hands of what we now realize was an unhealthy tendency to minimize the psychological, the emotional and, more pertinently, the controversial, that is, anything that did not fit comfortably into a single category.

It was not until the late 19th century that the doctors in Britain, for example, took more than a cursory interest in anorexia nervosa and when they did, they sought to couch it in anything but psychological terms. In 1868, William Gull published in *The Lancet* of London a description of what he called *apepsia hysterica* found in young women, its main characteristics being severe emaciation and a refusal to eat. At about the same time E. C. Lasegue, a Frenchman, reported on an *anorexie hysterique* he had found in eight patients. The work of Gull and Lasegue was very similar in content, yet the medical professions in Britain and France treated the descriptions very differently.

In France, as in many other parts of the Continent at the time, more interest in emotional and psychological matters was being shown at all levels of academic activity than was the case in Britain or in the United States[1]. So while Janet and Giles de la Tournette, for example, in the late 1800s and early 1900s were formulating theoretical models to help in understanding the psychology behind anorexia, British doctors were sticking to purely medical theories. Therefore in 1914, when a doctor called Simmonds attributed the death of an emaciated young woman to *pituitary cachexia* — a form of brain disease — this provided a convenient way out for physicians wary of dealing with psychological problems in which they had little training and on which they were not able to make much headway.

From 1914 until fairly recently, British and American medical opinion held to this view: anorexia was a medical problem in which, following a malfunction of a part of the brain, the patient lost weight and died. All other symptoms, reliably and correctly diagnosed and described as we have seen since 1694, were ignored. They did not fit into the prevailing opinion so they simply ceased to exist.

This unfortunate mistake was rectified only in the mid-1930s

---

1 Do not forget that practically all the main schools of modern psychiatry and psychology originated on the Continent — Austria, Germany and France in particular.

when some researchers in Britain and the United States gradually accumulated sufficient medical evidence to reinstate the importance of psychological causes in anorexia. By that time, though, not only had large numbers of doctors been trained to think of anorexia as a medical problem but some patients had died suffering from the psychological condition anorexia while being treated for a brain disturbance they did not have. When Anglo-American researchers began to broaden their horizons, therefore, they had to come back to the earliest reports and to the formulations of the Continental medical schools, primarily the French who had followed up Lasegue's work in a different, and in my opinion, more appropriate way.

French reports from the late nineteenth century read as if they had in fact been written in 1980, concentrating on emotional factors, the role of the family and the importance of understanding feelings and insights and so on. They show a sympathy for the condition that has only recently begun to appear in Anglo-American writings.

After a history such as this, as you can well imagine, the present situation is a rather confusing one. Some doctors still adhere to the older more medical theories in which anorexia is seen purely as an organic problem. Others believe the condition is purely psychological, and of course, there is a whole range of theories in between, blending the physical with the mental: some doctors believing that physical or organic changes set off the mental condition, and others believing just the opposite. Needless to say, each theorist has his or her own set of beliefs as to what actually constitutes anorexia nervosa.

Not unexpectedly, what follows is my theory about the nature of anorexia. It is a theory that takes cognisance of the concepts and ideas of both Anglo-American and Continental theorists; moreover it is a theory that takes into account most of the more recent findings as reported by the sufferers themselves about the nature and extent of 'secret' anorexia.[1]

---

1 Please note that although you may assume from the above that I favour French or other Continental ideas about anorexia, this is not entirely the case. Continental ideas, historically, have simply had a broader base of understanding. The theories in themselves may not necessarily be more correct in the long term than Anglo-American ones.

ANOREXIA: TOWARDS A PRELIMINARY DEFINITION

The word 'anorexia' itself offers us no help. In fact it is simply misleading. 'Loss of appetite' describes only some cases of the disorder and only at certain times; it certainly does not describe those people who are trying to diet nor those who gorge themselves and then vomit. How can you gorge if you have no appetite? And, as anyone on a diet can confirm, there is no 'lack of appetite' — the whole battle in fact is to stop your rampant appetite from forcing you to eat. In fact, it is the *inability to control appetite* that leads so many people into vomiting as a form of losing weight.

Let us look instead, therefore, at the question of dieting. In practically all the cases of anorexia that I have ever seen, this has been the starting point irrespective of how it ended up, and it is also the point at which anorexics depart from normal behaviour. So it is a good starting point.

Dieting

Millions of people all over the world go on at least one diet in their lives. There is nothing unusual in that. Most anorexics-to-be start their first serious diet in their teens. A few do not; they go on a serious diet for the first time later in life. What marks anorexics off from ordinary people who diet is the spirit in which they enter the regimen of the diet.

Dieting is not just a means of losing weight. Oh yes, on the face of it, a person diets only to lose weight, but that is not all. Dieting is an exercise in *will*. It is one of the few times in life where you have to put your foot down and *control* yourself. And this is not just a matter of losing weight. Where will is concerned, your whole being is involved. How you do it (that is, how you exert your will) and how well you do it, how doggedly, how variably, all depends on who you are. It also depends on the context in which you carry out this exploration in self-control. Since this is an important point and one that will recur during the course of this book, let us examine it a little closer now.

The social context of dieting

No one lives in isolation. Who we are depends very much on the context in which we live. We grow up in specific cultures that give us different ways of thinking, behaving and existing, according to the accepted values. Individual societies take these differences further and create their own ways and means (institutions, associations) of organizing actions and thoughts. Classes within society — be they based on education, wealth or whatever — further narrow down the range of permitted ways of being; individual families complete the process.

Take dieting. As you can see, a lot of contextual factors have to be in place before you can even consider going on one. For one thing, you have to have access to a regular supply of food. Undernourished people seldom diet: they *live* diets. Also, your community must allow you the right to diet. Some communities do not; it is not forbidden by law but by tradition, with reactions of intense hostility to someone who systematically refuses to eat as much, or as often, as everyone else in the community. Lastly, you must have the *personal freedom* to diet: I know of families who agree in principle to dieting, but in reality make certain that anyone trying it does not succeed.

Looking at dieting in this way rather than looking at it from the point of view of it being a phenomenon among the affluent or the middle classes helps to explain how anorexia occurs. The key is really the context, both social and immediate, of the person trying to diet. When you diet, your family diets with you — at least in spirit. In some poor communities in the eastern Mediterranean, the only wealth is food from a family's own stock; the only way parents have of caring for and protecting their children, or of demonstrating how much they love them, is by giving them food — their only area of competence in a harsh world. To diet in such communities is literally a massive insult to the parents; frequently the more 'modern' children resort to inventing illnesses to justify their anorexia — or lack of appetite.

As you can see, status within the family and in society are key components to the dieting process, influencing the decision to diet and the way in which to go about it. It will be very important to us in this book to look at the ways in which cultures react to dieting behaviour.

The outcome of dieting

You decide to go on a diet (for whatever reason you choose) and so you begin. Let us say that you really have iron determination. You struggle to control your appetite and finally you do it: you no longer feel hunger pangs. Happily you can look at whole tables of food and not be tempted in the slightest. Now, you really have lost your appetite but this need not make you ill. Many people can achieve this quite well and they use dieting to stay healthy and realistically thin. In other words, they do not lose their judgement when they lose their appetite. They know they must eat to stay healthy and do so, selecting carefully and sensibly whatever they think their bodies need.

If, however, you were to lose your appetite and at the same time also lose your judgement about eating, you would very likely slip into the classical form of anorexia nervosa. In this condition you would gradually stop eating altogether, intent on becoming thinner and thinner and you would refuse all attempts to make you eat. Beyond a certain point you would cut off from reality. Your iron determination is so strong that you take over your own life. You believe that only you know what is best for you and you ignore what anyone else says. If you were to eat at all, it would be food *you* selected and believed in, hence the strange food fads of some dieters who become convinced that only peanuts or lemons or carrots or whatever are necessary.[1] If you persist in a too-rigorous diet and for too long, you can enter a state that borders on the insane — you lose contact with reality. Amongst other things, you think you are fatter than you really are and instead of being horrified or shocked by your state, you become proud of

1 These food fads do not come out of the blue. Often the anorexic has read somewhere about a certain food's value and misunderstood the meaning of the report (as do millions of other people). Often reports on dietary matters oversimplify the body's requirements.

your skeleton-like frame and determine to keep it that way. This is now the state of *classical anorexia nervosa*.

The story, however, does not stop there. Purely as a matter of research there are enough questions in the above paragraphs to occupy us for the rest of the book. Why is it that some people lose their judgement with their appetite? Why such iron determination? How does it work? And so on. But for the moment, let us concentrate on the outcome of such a diet. This basic prime act of entering a state of anorexia nervosa can end in four ways:

1. *Return to normal*   For a time, you may enter into a state of anorexia and then come to your senses and make a full recovery. Usually someone notices what is happening and makes enough fuss to get something constructive done. Often, in my experience, a boyfriend complains about how skinny his girlfriend has become, or favourably eyes another (more shapely) female, and the victim takes stock. This kind of 'fuss' is ordinary fuss. Doctors are not called in, hospitals are not telephoned and so on. A lot of things can trigger a 'spontaneous' recovery: a change of boyfriend, husband, or girlfriend, even a change in fashion, or just a change in the weather. Lots and lots of perfectly normal dieters go through this experience then recover and never do it again, quite unaware that for a time they were in a state very similar to anorexia nervosa.

2. *The classical outcome: death*   Suppose you did not come to your senses; suppose too that there was no one to help you. You just kept on losing weight. Well, if you do not eat, you die, eventually. The dangerous irony about achieving this awful finality is that beyond a certain stage, your body actually helps to continue the process of dieting. The more emaciated you become, the more the body slows down to cope: you become more tired, less inclined to help yourself and gradually you sink into a reduced state of consciousness which ultimately shuts you off from contact with the outside world. Beyond a certain point, you stop caring; whether you survive or not depends almost entirely upon the people around you: your parents, friends or doctors.

One of the remarkable things about classical terminal anorexia is the fact that the people in the environment in which these anorexics live tolerate this state of emaciation to such an awful degree without anyone — husbands, parents, friends — really doing anything about it. If you consider that most of the published reports on anorexia involve youngish women, many of whom were living at home and were generally ostensibly well cared for, well educated and so on, it should have suggested to doctors that people around the anorexic show a remarkable ability to ignore physical states. This fact should have played as important a part in the development of the concepts of anorexia nervosa as the weight loss in the victim — but it seldom has. We will come to this point again later.

3. *Typical anorexia nervosa*   Let us assume that you start a diet, and then develop the symptoms of classical anorexia nervosa. But this time, someone notices and does something about it. Before you turn into a living skeleton, your parents or a doctor pronounce you anorexic and you are rushed off to hospital. You wake up in a hospital ward with only one way out: eat until a decent weight is achieved. Your solution is to conform but only in order to get out of hospital. Once away from supervision, you take stock. The shock of upsetting and frightening your parents distresses you. The shock of going to hospital, of having your freedom curtailed, the trauma, humiliation and indignity make you determined never to let it happen again. You are just as determined to stay thin and to keep on dieting. Your solution therefore is to eat enough to keep your parents or those about you happy, to hide your real shape and to continue to diet. This evolves inevitably into episodes or bouts of anorexia nervosa followed by bouts of normal eating, followed in turn by episodes of anorexia nervosa, and so on. During the anorexic phase, you diet drastically but just manage to pull yourself out of it before you enter that 'unreal' phase. Or possibly the comments of those around you do it for you.

4. *The bulimarexic solution*   From what has been said, you can see that the reaction of the people in the anorexic's environment can save or lose the patient's life. But the life-saving process creates another problem: the need to hide the anorexia and so avoid the trauma of being treated. One very obvious way of hiding anorexia is to vomit up unwanted food. Many of my early patients learnt this trick in hospital

where they were locked up in a room and given huge plates of food while a nurse with a scale waited to weigh them at the end of the meal. Solution: eat the meal, be weighed, then go and vomit up the food. More recently, the young anorexics I have come across learn this as a 'weight-trick' from friends at school, or in modelling agencies or just simply from reading case histories in popular magazines.

Whichever way it happens, the following ritual soon becomes established: gorging of food (bulimia) often over periods of hours, followed by vomiting. This cycle can be, and is, repeated *ad infinitum*. I have registered one of my patients going through this cycle up to 36 times in one day.

I think it is true to say now, however, that this pattern of bulimarexia occurs in a widespread way, with or without the trauma of becoming initially a typical anorexic, being hospitalized and so on. Many people wanting to be thin, without the willpower to stay on a diet, simply cheat a little by bringing up whatever they want; it is a simple, easy way of achieving weight control and, in my opinion, is analogous to taking a tranquilizer for 'nerves' instead of going through the pain and anxiety involved in solving the root issue.

The four categories above, then, are the main forms anorexia can take. We will be concentrating on the last two categories: typical anorexia nervosa and bulimarexia. I hope that you have, by now, achieved some 'feel' for the subject and the problem of definition, and that you will understand why I have spent as much time as I have on it, and why I have stressed the importance of *context* in the definition. Just in case there is still doubt in your mind as to the real nature of each of these categories, the next chapter should clearly determine the full nature of each state and whether or not you fit into any one of them.

Chapter 2

How to tell if you really have anorexia

The starting point for anorexia nervosa and bulimarexia is the preoccupation or obsession with being thin, losing weight and dieting. This is the crucible in which the common symptoms of the illness begin to take shape. And as we know, this is also a familiar and a normal one: most people at one time or another try to diet and lose weight. Before we go on to examine what it is about the potential anorexic that pushes her over the fine line between normality and disturbance, we must consider other conditions that resemble anorexia but are not the same thing.

STARVATION

At the simplest and most basic level, it is theoretically possible to confuse the psychological form of anorexia with the similar effects produced by starvation and malnutrition. Many of what were once considered the classical symptoms of anorexia are in fact due to starvation rather than to purely psychological factors. If you deprive perfectly normal people of food, what happens to them reads like any anorexic's normal day: they become irritable, withdrawn and depressed; they become labile (easily shift their moods) and are preoccupied with food — dream about it, plan menus, eat odd things, hoard scraps, gorge themselves if given the chance, and so on.

DIETING AND FASTS

Dieting may produce similar effects to anorexia and so too may fasting for religious and other purposes. So do not automatically assume you have become anorexic if you develop certain symptoms as soon as you start a fast or a diet. Some people react to even mild food deprivation in extreme ways: they panic and become distressed, faint and can even develop minor heart-rate fluctuations, all of which can be frightening and confusing. Unfortunately, doctors also get confused by these reactions on occasion; more than once, in my experience, a doctor has convinced an anxious girl and her parents that the girl was suffering from anorexia when there was no real evidence for this.

ILLNESS

At another level, when a person falls ill with an infection, perhaps, or something as simple as the common cold, it is usual for the appetite to suffer. If the appetite is affected for too long, there will be weight-loss. When the illness clears, weight should be put on as the appetite increases. However, if at the same time as falling ill the person was also in the throes of emotional turmoil and tended to focus on weight anyway, it is possible that the illness could encourage the onset of anorexia. Sometimes, for example, glandular fever can precipitate anorexia in adolescents. So, if you are a parent, watch out for continued weight-loss or lack of appetite after the doctor has pronounced your child well. Much the same goes for gastro- intestinal infections which also tend to crop up in adolescence. They do not cause anorexia, they act as catalysts.

The difference between an anorexic reaction and a reaction caused by illness is that when you are genuinely ill, you cannot eat simply because you feel wretched. By contrast, the hallmark of the anorexic is that the sufferer feels hungry but does not want to eat.

There are certain other serious medical conditions that produce weight-loss and emotional symptoms similar to those in anorexia. Bowel tumours, for example, and peptic ulcers come to mind as do certain disturbances in the brain, particularly if they affect the functioning of the central nervous system. Fortunately these conditions are relatively rare.

AMENORRHOEA

For a long time, amenorrhoea — the loss of periods — was widely regarded both as a classical sign of anorexia nervosa and proof that it was caused by an endocrinal malfunction. Simply put, the anorexic's hormones (which control periods amongst other things) go awry and since hormone control is located in the brain, in the pituatary-hypothalamus region, it has long been supposed that some brain malfunction is responsible.

This is still a widely held view, and in one sense it may well apply; the chain of command, that is, how the brain stops periods, is likely to be through the pituitary-hypothalamus region, but there is not a great deal of evidence to suggest either that amenorrhoea is caused solely by a pituitary malfunction or that it is a *sine qua non* of anorexia. For one thing, men do (in small numbers) develop anorexia and they do not have periods. Secondly, a whole range of intense emotions — anxiety, fear, upset, determination — can cause periods to be delayed for long or short durations and even to be stopped altogether.[1]

To sum up: if your periods do stop, it does not automatically mean that you are beginning anorexia, even if you are on a diet at the time or are concerned about your weight. Think it over carefully and bear in mind the following:

1. It may be purely a series of coincidences; for example, you may have just changed to a different birth control pill which may affect your periods and your appetite.

2. You may have a hormonal problem unrelated to your dieting.

3. You may be going through a bad time in your private life

1 Most female prisoners-of-war in World War II, for example, in studies summarized in P. Dally and J. Gomez *Anorexia Nervosa* (Heineman, London, 1979) developed amenorrhoea almost as soon as they were captured, that is, before many experienced any weight loss due to poor conditions.

which depresses and frightens you — both feelings which can interfere with your periods and your appetite. You may have had a shock to which you have not yet reacted properly.

DEPRESSION

As we have seen, how you react to upset and stress can interfere with a whole range of functions, including menstruation. Depression, a very common reaction, can make you feel withdrawn from life and in the process, you cannot be bothered with eating. One consequence of this is that you lose weight, which may give you the appearance of being anorexic. You may have lost your weight and your appetite for a time but this is only part of the whole picture: the depressed person is generally withdrawn and disinterested in everything, not just food and eating.

This depressed condition is very easily mistaken for anorexia nervosa and some authorities argue that anorexia is caused solely by depression. They base this view on the fact that some depressed people are capable of reaching a state where their weight-loss becomes serious enough to cause death. However, the defining condition, in my opinion, is the fact that the true anorexic sets out to stop eating in a systematic way. The depressive who becomes 'anorexic' does not set out to do anything and we could say that such a person becomes anorexic almost by default.

Then there is the person who has always had a poor appetite, has always been thin and who drifts inevitably into a form of anorexia at one stage or another in her or his life. In most of the cases of this kind that I have seen, the failure to eat and to have an appetite is due to a primary long-standing depression problem in which there is a failure of the will to do anything: to eat, to sing, to drink, to be involved with life and so on. Close study of such people reveals them to have no fixation on weight, on eating, or on anything. There is no joy in their lives, no will, no determination. I would go so far as to say that many of the men considered in the past to be anorexic fit more correctly into this category of depression. The few female cases I have seen differed from female anorexics quite markedly. Some of them — considered to be medically anorexic because of being underweight — actually ate large meals but simply never put on weight.

GRIEF AND OTHER TRAUMA

Sometimes after a shock or upset, such as a death, a pregnancy or a divorce, a person can become anorexic, often for lengthy periods of time, without necessarily taking on all the characteristics, or attitudes to eating, of the true anorexic. For this reason, certain cures based on inducing mourning or upset have had good results: they help to unblock the upset buried within the person; crying and breaking down help to clear up the problem. It goes almost without saying that any of these anorexic-like states can become chronic or serious if they are allowed to persist too long and the underlying upset is not dealt with. Again, however, it is that element of will, that determination to be thin, that is usually missing in these states.

TEMPORARY VOMITING

Just as weight-loss reactions can be a passing phase, so too can vomiting after a meal. Most of us have experienced an upset either during or immediately after a meal and felt sick or nauseous. It may be the result of an argument or simply the context of the meal. Sometimes a person feels anxious when sitting down to a meal with the boss or with masses of imposing people. It is a short step from this feeling of self-conscious anxiety to nausea and to the act of vomiting. We will discuss this more deeply later since it is an important part of the theory presented in this book. However, incidents like this do not constitute anorexia. Of course, if this form of coping with anxiety persists, it does become serious and if vomiting is preceded by over-eating, then the condition does come under the heading of anorexia.

It is all really a question of thinking things out. Have a look at yourself, if you are not sure, and go over the last year in your mind. See if there have not, in fact, been a number of happenings — medical, personal, social — that may have distressed you. If necessary, discuss things with your doctor, or a psychiatrist or psychologist. Do not jump to conclusions: anorexia is a fairly specific event. If you have got it, you will know.

Chapter 3

The key questions

Anorexia seems to come out of the blue. Suddenly, with no hint of warning, a girl goes on a diet and her world changes. Most anorexics can look back and remember almost to the day when things changed, but few can explain precisely how or why it should have been so at that particular time. What is very frustrating is that while we know (by definition) that it all starts with a diet, few people seem able to pin-point why a particular diet worked. You see, most anorexics had tried to diet before, often on several occasions, even before some of them had become teenagers. The question is — why was it that *that* diet worked, the one that pushed them out of normality?

POPULAR EXPLANATIONS

This is the first of several key questions that must be raised about anorexia (and bulimarexia) to guide us in exploring both how it starts and in what kind of context it takes place. A natural starting point for most people who have written or thought about the problem of anorexia is the question: why that diet at that time? The difficulty is that there are a lot of easy answers readily available, but they do not lead very far.

Some authorities have argued, for instance, that it is essentially an adolescent phenomenon. Since most anorexics do start in their teens, they suggest it occurs at that time as part of the general turmoil that adolescents go through. That is, most adolescents go through fads and fashions and show a wide range of behaviour, a wide fluctuation in mood. They become easily obsessed, be it with the opposite sex, fashion or books, music or the cinema, and so it is a simple matter to link up this kind of obsessive behaviour with anorexia, itself a form of obsession. Instead of being obsessed, say, with boys or pop music, anorexic teenagers become obsessed with being thin.

The trouble with this line of argument is that it does not actually explain anything. It simply links two facts together: the fact that teenagers become faddy and obsessed, and that anorexics become obsessed with being thin. The key question is really, why do some girls become obsessed with being thin and turn into anorexics, while others become just as obsessed with being thin but do not become anorexic? And, of course, what about anorexia in women over the age of 20? What the explanation also does not answer, mainly because it is too broadly-stated, is why a specific diet leads to anorexia and why previous diets did not at an earlier stage.

There is a second line of popular argument that tries to overcome some of the loopholes mentioned previously. It suggests that there is (and had been for the last two decades) a massive pressure on women by the media and the fashion industry to conform to a specific image or model of femininity. This image is essentially a thin one and it is propagated by fashion models, pop stars, and dancers, nearly all of whom appear thin and more or less healthy. Adolescent girls — and some vulnerable women — are easily taken in by this image (so runs the argument) and become obsessed with emulating the models, dancers and so on. They believe that success, happiness and acceptance follows on with attaining just such a thin state.

It is an interesting argument and in some respects, I think, a valid one. Teenagers have become exposed to advertising and marketing to an extent never seen before. This does most certainly help to give a direction — or a head to the obsessions — for young people. It provides a certain context, a certain view of life — to be young, fashionable, thin, into music and dancing and so on, is to be 'there'. One can indeed wonder if 9-, 10- or 11-year-olds are ready for this kind of exposure. However, I feel that this and related issues have very little to do with anorexia. Many millions of teenagers are exposed to exactly the same conditions and in exactly the same way. Similarly, millions of women are exposed to exactly the same 'thin-happy' literature as teenagers, and again, in much the same way: repeated stereotyping, repeated valuation of a simplistic view of women and their lives. One may not agree with such literature, one may in fact be extremely bored with it all; one may even feel that it should be controlled or changed. But would changes or controls prevent anorexia? Do women become anorexic from watching fashion shows or reading women's magazines? I think you will agree, the link-up seems both tenuous and shallow. It does not, for example, explain why most people see fashion and its accoutrements for what they are, simply one of many ways of expressing individuality or taking part in communal life.

There is more, however. Assume that the media are at fault. Assume that it is through their actions that thinness and dieting have become vital issues to many millions of people. Why then are so many people overweight? Why do few dieters become anorexic? Those who argue, for example, that the fashion industry is partly responsible for the increase in anorexia, say that the vulnerable adolescent tends to become anorexic because she cannot see the falseness of the 'thin-happy' image. The argument does not explain *why* it is that these anorexics cannot see it, nor why so many more teenagers can. Above all, the argument does not explain why so many millions of people actively ignore the pressure the media puts on them to be thin.

There is one last point that should concern us here. Why fixate on dieting as a way of losing weight? One can also lose weight by exercise, or by cutting down only a little on food. But for most anorexics, the more rigorously they limit eating and the stricter the diet, the better. Few anorexics manage a mild diet. Presumably, if they could, they would not become anorexic. There is a kind of frenzy and despair about the whole business that makes it an all-or-nothing affair. This aspect of anorexia has, again, been by and large ignored.

FRENZY AND OBSESSIONS

Let us put the key questions together now:

> 1. Why did the diet that started anorexia have effect at *that* time?
> 2. Why is there such a concern with being thin?
> 3. Why is there a fixation on dieting and eating and not on other ways of getting thin?

A close look at these questions reveals something very interesting: apart from asking why the diet 'took off' at that particular time in the person's life, each question points to a very specific state of mind. We know there is concern with being thin, we know there is a fixation on eating — or rather, not eating — and a general sense of urgency about being acceptable through maintaining the diet. Something is obviously at stake for the anorexic. But what?

In other words, in addition to the direction of interest (thinness and food) there is a question of the determination with which the anorexic-to-be pursues this direction. There is almost an over-riding obsession with food and thinness as if nothing else matters, as if it is a matter of life or death.

Since we know that food and being thin has usually been of interest to the potential anorexic long before anorexia began, it follows that it is not just the focusing on eating and weight-loss that gets the whole process started, but rather the marshalling of the person's entire energy into an obsession with it. Obviously, if you find something easy to do, such as dieting, it will never become an obsession because you can do it with your eyes closed. Obsessions arise out of something you cannot do but want to do very badly, something you have struggled over for a very long time.

Why is it so important to be thin or to go on a special and successful diet? So important that you become so obsessed with it that nothing else matters? So important that once you have achieved thinness, you cannot, or dare not, go back? In fact, some anorexics would rather die than go back, and others choose a life of perpetual vomiting. The plot thickens.

At this point in their history, most anorexics go a bit fuzzy. They cannot really remember what made it all seem so important, nor what was going on at the time. They also cannot really remember much about their lives at the time, what they were like then or beforehand. So it is difficult for them to answer these questions in any depth. Most case reports state that things seemed more or less all right before the diet, it was only once it had worked that things began to go wrong, that the anorexics felt they could not break the obsession. Those who can remember usually see their dieting as a kind of initiation: it marked the boundary, for them, between being a child and being grown-up. The diet, as it were, cut out all their childishness, gave them a direction and helped them to discipline themselves.

It is clear, therefore, that what we are looking at in that key diet is far more than just the start of a diet. All the indications are that the adolescent girl who becomes anorexic is in a very special state of mind *before*, *during* and *after* the diet, a state that drives her above and beyond the limits of either a normal adolescent fad or a normal obsession. She appears to be in a state of mental frenzy.

What is different about the anorexic reaction is that it is not like other adolescent reactions. Adolescents do have fads, do go through episodes of believing in single or simple solutions to their problems. They do have obsessions. But inevitably, they have lots of fads, lots of fashions and obsessions all co-existing at the same time in their minds. Anorexics tend to have only their dieting and it alone preoccupies them. Moreover, anorexics have a strange way of being teenagers. While you would think that being thin and being fashionable is an attempt to belong to a peer group, to be at one with other teenagers, for the anorexic it is often the *only* way in which they want to belong. Normal teenagers belong by engaging in a whole range of other behaviours including illicit acting-out with drink, drugs, sex and so on, much of which is shared and enjoyed together as a group. For most anorexics, their most important acting-out is done alone and, if they are bulimarexics, in secret. Anorexics tend also not to get involved in the normal shared acting-out that others do. They may try it but it is done in an uninvolved and unexplored way.

Along then with the other key questions that we must answer are these: why is the anorexic driven by such a need to belong;

a frenzy, as it were, to be thin and, presumably, normal? And why is belonging done in this way, as opposed to normal belonging? Nearly every anorexic I have seen has had the same complaint, showing how clearly they recognize these issues: "I don't feel as if I really belong, or am part of things," they say. And in essence, I think this is true because while an anorexic may seem normal, have boyfriends, a career, a job, even be married and have a family, it is all in a deep way simply done for appearance. There is a lack of real contact with the people that occupy roles and positions in their lives and an over-emphasis on the appearance of normality. In short, the same preoccupation, the same logic that leads an anorexic to equate being thin with being happy and acceptable, appears to govern how they behave throughout their lives. It is vital therefore that we probe the beginnings of anorexia very carefully.

Chapter 4

A closer look at the days before anorexia begins

Our first job is to try to understand the frenzy, the force with which the anorexic stops eating. Once we have the motive (as Inspector Maigret would say) we can understand the actual deed better. Why do they throw themselves into a relatively normal act like dieting in such a way? If we could understand that, we would understand why it goes wrong. What we are looking for is something 'wrong', something 'unusual'. We cannot blame the diet as such, even the act of wanting to be fashionable is not wrong, nor is the desire to be thin. It is *how* these things are done that is all important.

If you were a detective investigating the cause of anorexia, even if you were a Maigret or a Kojak, you would pretty soon find that the trail had run cold. You would start, for one thing, by asking the victim and maybe her parents about life at home, in the family, and you would get back this kind of picture:

> "We were — still are — a very close family. A caring family. We, as parents, have done everything in our power to see that our children have never wanted for anything. The family is a very happy one. There's nothing wrong really in any sense of the word."

This is a composite paragraph derived from many interviews with parents. Even victims tend to believe in it, often to the extent that they think they are the black sheep, the ones who let the family down.

Well, you would say, nothing wrong there. So a good detective would double-check these stories. He would go to the family doctor, ask around, talk to other family members, family friends and so on. At the end of the day, he would not have got very far. There might be a comment like: "Helen's father has a bit of a temper, but then, who's hasn't? Perhaps her mother works too hard?" The point is that almost without fail, the families of anorexics are described as close, warm, good, normal people.

So, you are left with the problem: why the frenzy? What drives these women? What goes on in these families?

A GLIMPSE INSIDE THE FAMILY

What I did in the same situation, was to ask my anorexics to help by going over, painstakingly, an average day in their lives *before* they became anorexic, and, if possible, to give names of school friends and so on who could be contacted to add to the information. We then built up a picture based on all this information which we checked against the kind of life led by average people of the same age, school class, area and so on. Here is one example of such a comparison between two women named Helen and Moira. Helen is an anorexic. Moira is not anorexic.

This is a day in Helen's life before she became anorexic:

> 7.30 Got up, not feeling very nice. Helped my mum get breakfast ready for the family. Took my father some tea. Went to school driven by my father. My mother never drove.
> 9.00-3.00 At school. Wasn't too bad. I like most of the teachers. Worked hard and read up on my set books at breaktime.
> 4.30 Did homework.
> 7.30 Supper time. Talked to my friend Mercia about her English problems. Laid table. Washed up. Jane phoned and confided in me about her boyfriend — I gave her advice.
> 9.30 A snack in the kitchen made by my mum.

10.00 Read set books.
11.00 Went to sleep.

Nothing very unusual, a rather boring humdrum life seldom varying much beyond this: a helpful capable girl, as reported by her schoolteachers and her friends. When we compared this with similar reports from a non-anorexic girl of the same age at the same school, we could see the difference clearly.

Here is a day in Moira's life:

8.30 Struggled to get up after mother had to call me twice; missed breakfast to catch the bus so I could see Mark (boyfriend).

9.00-3.00 At school. OK day, worked in history, which I like but messed around with Dawn and George in English which I don't like. Dawn was sent to the headmaster. At break, we (the girls) had a big talk about the school romance and I found out that Mandy also likes Mark which I don't think is very funny at all. She's much prettier than I am.

4.00 I phoned Mark and he's coming round tonight — or maybe not.

5.00 Did some homework and watched T.V.

6.00 Had supper early before my folks — nervous about Mark. What if he likes Mandy? Phoned Dawn to talk about it — supposed to be doing my homework.

9.00 Mark came and we went out for coffee.

12.00 Came back late — my dad is furious but it's O.K.

Helen did go out with boys but not in the same way as Moira. Her relationships were all carefully supervised by her parents, with 'decent' boys; they would meet only on a Saturday and always go to somewhere posh or grown-up. There was little outside contact during the week.

The difference between these two reports are quite stark. What stands out is, firstly, that Helen was far too 'good', too home-orientated and led basically a very formal life laid out for her by her parents: and, secondly, that there was no hint of rebellion, not a murmur. Overall, a very depressing picture.

Intrigued by these differences, I asked anorexics and

non-anorexics much more about their home-lives and again compared their replies.

Question: What do you talk about at home?

> *Anorexic*: "Mostly we talk about how lovely it is to have a family. We talk about my parents' relatives a lot and about what they're doing and we visit each other a lot too. We don't have many real friends outside the family and our relatives. Oh, and we talk a lot about my parents' work —you know, the problems they have and so on."

> *Non-anorexic*: "We don't talk all that much. Mainly about politics and maybe sport. And big things that come up, like assassinations or whatever. We get pretty excited about our summer holidays and we joke a lot. My dad tells funny stories sometimes. My mother is quite clever and likes to argue with my brother."

It is difficult to give full details here; I can just try to give some idea of the important differences in family life. The family life of an anorexic such as Helen is extremely insular and inward-turning: everything focuses on the family and relatives. There is a tight sense of unity and a relative lack of concern with what is going on in the outside world. Moira, on the other hand, in common with many of the people in her sample, barely knew some of her relatives and cared even less. She was much more concerned with what was happening around her at school, with her boyfriends and so on. Moira did not really know what exactly her father did, let alone what his problems were at work. He may have spoken about such things at home but she seldom listened to her parents' conversation. She had her own life to worry about. Here are some other questions I asked:

Question: What did you like most about your life?

> *Non-anorexic*: "Well — I'll have to be honest and say —boys! I loved 'em. Then, maybe music, going out, of course. Yes, and dancing — I loved dancing."

> *Anorexic*: "Mostly what I liked was always in the future —almost a dream, like being famous, married, or whatever."

Question: What did you like most about home?

> *Non-anorexic*: "Oh — nothing really. It was all right. I

didn't think about it much — I mean, it was there, wasn't it? I liked it. I loved my bedroom, I loved the nights in the living room when we'd all watch telly or something. When we were on holiday, I loved playing games on the beach — you know — it was nice."

Anorexic: "I don't think there was much to like about my life before I became anorexic. It all seemed so black, so hopeless. I was so depressed (still am). I suppose, really, when you come down to it, I liked eating best. Supper time. Oh yes, I liked it when my parents did things with me — like took me shopping with them or bought me something. It used to make me glow all over — as if they really cared about me."

Question: What about going out and having fun?

Anorexic: "It was OK. But you know, I was always nervous — in case it went wrong — say, the guy didn't like me or I didn't fit in or whatever. Actually going out was always a bit of a nightmare. I used to get tense about it days before, and of course everyone in the family knew, and I think my mum was even more tense than I was. It was a whole performance with everyone on tenterhooks. All I used to think about when I was on a date was to get home and have something to eat. In fact, looking back, I used to eat all the time before I was anorexic. Always had something in my mouth. It made me feel nice."

You can feel from these taped extracts that the non-anorexic girl leads very much a life of her own, with the family as a kind of secure base that she takes for granted. The anorexic girl, in contrast, lives almost entirely for and with the family, venturing out only occasionally to do things set up by the family, and to do them, one feels, with great trepidation. There is no sense of *self*, of a growing individual beginning to explore the real world. Instead there is a sense of fear, of dread and depression. I spoke of these findings to Helen, the anorexic we met earlier in this chapter, at a much later stage and she had this to say:

"Looking back, yes, I can definitely say the *dread* is the key word. I was two people: the one my family and everyone else knew, and the other one inside me — the one no one knew. Not even me at the time. It was crazy. To my parents and to the teachers, I was sensible, mature and confident. Always obliging, understanding, thoughtful — people trusted me, relied on 'good ole' me. And for years, I believed all this myself. In fact, I was brought up believing it so I never really knew anything else. But inside me, I was something else all along. A tiny frightened timid mouse. It began when I was about 13, 12; up till then I'd been kind of ignorant about the world. But at about 12 or 13, I began to realize that I was sooner or later going to have to tackle things like boys and growing up and responsibility and so on. And then it began. I couldn't sleep through worry. I worried about everything: whether or not I'd be all right at school, whether I'd pass exams, be good enough on dates. And I was so scared. I was scared of the dark, of going out alone, of people. I hated it and I must have clung to my family, but not so they'd notice. I never told anyone about this. God forbid. I didn't even admit it to myself. Oh no, I was cool and sophisticated and confident but inside, terrified, absolutely terrified. In a kind of numb, endless way. I think my parents used to find me irritating, you know, a puzzle. I used to whine a lot and want to be with them and of course they were always busy with their own problems and things more important than me... but I never did it openly. I sort of began to use things like eating and having presents as a way of calming myself down. Maybe in fact the eating was the only way of blocking my fears? Maybe that's why I used to eat such a lot before I became anorexic.''

Helen is telling us a great deal about the quality of her existence before she became anorexic. Most anorexics in fact would probably admit to similar feelings of dread and anxiety in their lives both before and after they became anorexic. Here is Maureen, for example:

"I think I was rather more aware than Helen about the 'split' within me, between what my parents wanted of me and what I was in reality. In fact, I lied continually. I lied to them, to my friends, to everyone including myself. It sounds silly now but I would set out deliberately to fake things to keep my parents happy. 'How was the date?' they'd ask. 'Oh fantastic,' I'd say, 'we went here and we did this and so on...' — all of which was partially true but I'd have hated it — he would have bored me or I had felt lonely, out of my depth and worse, he would have talked me into sleeping with him — all on the first date. I would be disgusted with myself because I couldn't say no. I couldn't cope with anything. So I lied to them and to myself. I told myself it happened to every girl, that we were really going to get married — after one date! — that he loved me and so on. But you see, I would never talk to my parents, confess, ask their advice. All they ever gave me was bullshit — clichés, pats on the back, 'everything comes right in the end...' With them, I felt I had to succeed the first time or else their world would cave in.''

One of the consequences of this lying, as Maureen calls it, was that she never went through the normal process of trial-and-error, never was properly experienced by starting on a small scale then building up:

"I was — we were all — thrown in at the deep end. From my first date, at fourteen, it was a serious business. Marriage was even mentioned — marriage! Not in so many words, of course, but the hint was there and they watched the guy like a hawk as if it was the love-match of the century. Instead of just being relaxed and letting me handle it, they turned it all into a farce. The same went for everything. If I or my sister failed an exam, it was moped about for weeks. We daren't fail at anything in case we upset our parents. I mean, they were so tight about it all. Since I had no one else to talk to, I had to resort to putting on a bold front and frankly lied all the time. I couldn't tell them anything, or my friends at school. To tell them would have been so humiliating. They looked up to me. It was OK for them to screw things up but not for me.''

The important point to bear in mind here is that the kind of life Maureen and Helen are describing did not just happen over a period of months or just over going out with boys; it built up over several years. Here is what Gayle had to say:

"I think I'd always told untruths. Or rather, I always did what I was asked but hid how hard it was for me. For instance, as a child I'd always done well at school. O.K. And it was nice; everyone would say how clever I was. But the truth was I was a bit slow at school. So what I did was I used all my spare time to do my schoolwork. I would try to learn everything off by heart, and I would copy out my homework twice to be neat. Everyone thought I was fantastic, gifted. When I got to secondary school, though, I simply ran out of time: there was so much to do I just couldn't learn it all off by heart. And what was worse, the environment at school changed — they didn't want you to learn it — they wanted you to think about it, to be creative. Think? I'd never thought in my life. I was frantic. I'd be found out. Luckily I developed anorexia and everyone forgot about my schoolwork and in any case after that, I could blame it all on the illness anyway."

What does this all mean? And how does it relate to anorexia and to that first diet? What does seem to be suggested is that anorexics as children are far too concerned with their families and their family's problems than they should be. When a child is very small, the focus of their world certainly is entirely on their family. Of necessity mother and father (and relatives) protect and shape their existence in a very monopolistic way. But in normal families, this slowly but inevitably gives way, from the age of five or six onwards, to the demands of the outside world: of school and friends. By the age of 11 or 12, this in turn is supplemented by an intense interest in the world of friends, so that in adolescence and onwards, children can build up their own lives, free of the limits imposed by their own nuclear families.

What disturbed me, and what came through in my interviews with Helen, Gayle and others, was the way they automatically did what their parents wanted. It never occurred to them to protest or even complain. It never occurred to them that other children worked much less hard, had to lie less, hide less and lived lives of their own.

What seemed to be happening in these households was that the parents of the anorexics were putting tremendous pressure on their children to do well, to conform, to manage well outside. They seemed to watch them obsessively and, most important, to turn a blind eye to weakness, stress, upset or failure. Everything seemed so serious, so formal. Life was a matter of working hard, doing everything correctly with little room for anything else. From an early age, anorexics had to learn to hide their 'childishness' (failures, trial-and-error experiences, fears and so on) and to put on the kind of front their parents approved of or needed. Not for the anorexic, running to mummy or daddy in tears for comfort; no being held when frightened nor comforted when upset. Anorexic children were encouraged instead to be grown-up and mature; to think, act and be like adults from a very young age.

Moreover, in place of the childish actions, which in normal households take up and occupy a lot of the family's time, the concern and focus of the child in anorexic households, I discovered, is overwhelmingly on the needs, wants and feelings of the parents. Most of this can be felt by the anorexic, though perhaps not in so many words, but she is constantly aware of her parents' anxieties and problems in an overwhelming way. And it all adds to the general distress of the anorexic; she has to live with her own unhappiness and that of her family. There is in fact a deep desire in the anorexic's mind to 'save' her family, especially her parents; to solve their problems and make them happy. Most anorexics worry endlessly about their parents and whether they will be all right. In fact, they have been conditioned or 'primed' to do this for years. One corollary of the neglect of the anorexic's childish needs, is that the attention that should have been given to them —as a normal growing child — is retained instead by the parents. The child is taught to focus on them, their problems and their anxieties. Naturally enough, the way the anorexic has been treated conditions the way she thinks about the world.

This is very important. The growing child should be taught a balanced mode of thinking about himself or herself. A child goes through a period of intense self-interest and then later learns to add in the interests of others. The parent who uses a child for his, or her, own ends tends to create a lopsided balance, so that instead of the child thinking, for example, "I want that sweet," she automatically thinks first, "Does my mummy need the sweet?"

This kind of thinking becomes all-pervasive, and the child neglects herself in exactly the same way as her parents do. Instead of thinking: "I am feeling frightened about something, I'll call my mummy or my daddy," the child thinks: "I am frightened, but my mummy and my daddy look so upset that I won't say anything. I'd better keep quiet." It can progress to physical illness too. Instead of attending, for example, to early signs of illness, of being run-down, overtired, overworked, over-anxious (and it is just as easy for an eight or nine year-old to be overworked as it is for a managing director) the child teaches herself to ignore these signs in favour of continuously over-attending and watching mummy and daddy for signs of their distress and displeasure. There are many other corollaries of this factor which we will deal with later; one major one is that such parental neglect and its resultant self-neglect create a huge and crippling backlog in the child of unresolved childhood problems (fears, anxieties) that have to be gone through systematically before an anorexic can recover properly. The time was simply not spent on the child and her problems and it is difficult to make it up without help and without an awareness of this backlog.

What I am getting at is that anorexics tend to see their worlds predominantly through their parents' eyes. As a result, they also see themselves not as individuals with rights of their own — including the right to grow up properly — but in terms of whether or not they are useful or helpful to their parents. There is very little room ever to think about their own needs or demands or to think outside the emotional and cognitive framework set down for them by their parents.

If you look at the quotes in this chapter, especially at Helen's, you can see plainly some of the results of this process. All of them note a panic, a terror, a fear of what for normal young people are routine events, such as schooling, going out, growing up. Certainly there is anxiety present in each of these things for any normal child, but it is usually temporary or easily overcome through 'belonging' — getting on and doing things. For an anorexic such as Helen, all her normal childhood experiences — being afraid of the dark, and everything else children have anxieties about — had to be experienced alone and in secret. There was no tolerance of such behaviour, no reference for it in her family, and therefore no learning of how to manage fear, anxiety and so on. There was not the security that we all need at some time or another, to be able to fall back onto a mother or a father figure; instead, simply an over-whelming sense of how much one has to carry on one's own. Anorexics grow up having no emotional or cognitive time for these needs.

What is worse, most anorexics sense this. They sense their neglect, their inability to cope with ordinary things. They sense their aloneness. As they approach their teens, there is a growing apprehension and, as Helen described, a tendency to whine and cling. This happens, I believe, because the girl wants to remain in safety at home where she is but an acolyte; I believe she also feels the first inklings of her parents own insecurities and inabilities to cope with things outside the family. Yet she increasingly has to do more outside the family, alone. Her lack of confidence, her inability to cope with fear and anxiety and her lack of personal growth all mount up and she clings, trying to force her mother or father to protect her, to go with her, to make it easier. They react to this by being cold and formal, and inevitably, the anorexic feels she is being pushed out to cope once again on her own. You can detect the traces of all this in Helen's quote.

As a matter of interest, some authorities have spoken about the anorexics' distorted sense of their physical presence; for example, they tend to see their bodies as being bigger (fatter) than they really are. My own view, to sum up what we have just been talking about, is that this distorted sense of self goes much deeper than the physical: throughout their upbringing, anorexics have a distorted view of life, of their own worth and value and of their own personalities.

The previous findings were the results of the early detective work I undertook to try and broaden my understanding of the days before anorexia began. On their own, however, these facts were not sufficiently penetrating to provide realistic hypotheses about how or why anorexia as such developed. Why, did these children not break down differently under pressure? Migraine sufferers, for example, are reared under much the same conditions as anorexics: the same pressure, the same denial of the right to be childish. Under pressure, their bodies begin to show physical stress in the form of nausea, travel sickness and headaches. If they remain unattended, they become organized into a migraine pattern. So why do some people, under the same pressure, become anorexic instead?

When I had just begun to study the childhood patterns of migraine sufferers, nothing was clear about how the context of their families helped to shape their migraine. Indeed most authorities dismissed family contexts in favour of neurological ones. Slowly, however, over time, it became apparent, through the kind of examination reported here, that parents in fact applied subtle but virulent pressure on their children, in much the same way as the parents of anorexic children. [1]

I had to go further into the families of anorexics, into how the parents and the other children lived, before I could pinpoint specifically how it all happened.

PARENTS

How do the parents of anorexics live? How do they see the world? What is the context of their lives? To begin with, from interviews and discussions with parents, what emerged as a matter of course and was uniform throughout every interview, was a tremendous fear and anxiety about life. Without exception, each parent had an extremely submissive attitude to reality, to themselves and to their place in the overall scheme of things. That is, they themselves felt that the world was hostile and frightening, a place in which they had barely managed to survive. Anorexics' parents in fact fixated continuously on how tenuous was their hold on life despite evidence to the contrary; very few of the parents had struggled very much, most were well-off, all were comfortable and some

1 My findings on migraine children can be found in Chapter 8 of *The Headache Book* (W. H. Allen, London, 1980). Interestingly enough, as you will see, many of my anorexic patients had headaches, nausea and travel sickness as children too, and sometimes continued well into adulthood.

had done very well in life and held major positions at universities, in industry, commerce or the arts. And yet their conversations were full of accounts of personal slights, imagined insults, storms-in-a-teacup, most of which are part and parcel of everyone's daily round, but in the eyes of these parents deeply upsetting.

We found that the parents of anorexics tended to use the home as an outlet for their own feelings of personal inadequacy. For instance, they seldom expressed anger or upset outside the home, at work or with relations or friends. On the contrary, they had reputations for being 'nice people', 'self-contained'. But they would often go home and let out their pent-up emotions by ranting and raving there. And of course, any family member who interfered or who questioned them would be treated with hostility.

There was quite a range to these outbursts and they varied from family to family, parent to parent. Sometimes a parent would come home angry and upset and simply go around shouting at the injustice and the indignity of his or her lot. At other times the anger would take a more passive form. This was Helen's experience:

> "My mother used to come home from the shop and the moment she walked in I could tell it had been one of those days. She would be tight, cold, formal. You couldn't touch her or talk to her or anything. You just had to leave her alone and she'd go to her room and lie down for the rest of the day. She would say she had a migraine. Trouble was it happened nearly all the time."

Jennifer had much the same experience:

> "When my father came home he would be so uptight, physically, that we all knew he was terribly upset but we daren't say so. We had to treat him with kid gloves because if you didn't he would explode and go to his room, slamming the door and we wouldn't see him again all night. Sometimes he'd sulk for days. 'Everyone's against me,' he used to say. It was best to let him be upset in his own way, to slurp his soup, break a glass, knock over something — but it was awful. Everything he did

seemed to wound him more and more. I felt so sorry for him, he seemed so broken and defeated. And the worst thing was you never really knew what caused it — obviously something terrible. And this would happen every few days. All the time. There were other times though when he'd come home in a terrific mood and then he was so different — he'd hug you and talk to you and be fun to be with — whereas the other times, you just couldn't touch him at all. He was so moody.''

The interaction between parents also formed an important part of these families' lives. Often, one or another of the children would be drawn into managing the home if both parents happened to be 'down' at the same time, or if they happened to be fighting with each other. Jennifer gives a clear picture:

"I often had to take over from my mother. She'd come home and go to sleep with a headache — as usual —mostly I think she just wanted to be alone. Then I would have to get supper ready. Not my brother, note, who was older than me. I had to do it because I was the girl. Sometimes I felt nice doing things for my father but other times it was quite traumatic because he is so particular over food and if you don't do it just right, he won't eat it. Sometimes I think my mother got me to do supper because she couldn't handle his moods. If he was in a bad mood and his eggs weren't just right, it would be another of those little defeats that the world had set up for him.''

In other households with, for example, all-girl siblings, inevitably the girl who later became anorexic was the one who had had to take over the running of the household. Frequently such a girl would be the eldest. Gayle was from a family like this:

"I was the big girl, the responsible one. I used to feel sorry for my parents, life was obviously very unkind to them. They had to work very hard and were very busy. It was the least I could do. I always used to go out of my way to help them. If I could see that my mother was 'down' and my father was in a bad temper and that she couldn't cope with him, I would offer to cook. I also used to protect my father when she was hostile to him — we'd be cooking together in the kitchen and I'd nag her not to let the custard burn or whatever. Sometimes I'd have to see to it myself because she'd get bloody-minded — it was as if she just wanted to make things worse for him. This used to upset me and I never really understood why she could be so neglectful. They were supposed to love each other.''

These quotes give some idea of how the parents dominated their families' lives and turned their children into acolytes in order to provide them with the very consistency and protection they should have been giving to the children. Under such circumstances, children grow up over-focused on home-life, which, in their minds, may collapse at any moment without their constant efforts and presence. There is no time for anything else.

A child believes what she or he is told. If that child is told that 'things out there are tough', that 'people are against us' and so on, then she or he will believe this. It is even more believable for the child when he or she sees his parents in a state of upset or distress; the child panics and becomes desperately afraid lest her parents collapse. Further, when that child is deprived of attention for her own needs, she needs no other evidence to believe that the world is a frightening place: she feels it with every one of her senses. A young child of six or seven or eight does not see material success or the comforts of the home as a contradiction, as evidence of another truth, that in fact mummy and daddy are doing all right after all. All the child senses is that the home, the family and all their possessions are under threat, that they could lose everything on the whim of fate or, more correctly, on account of the doings of someone or something 'out there' beyond the family.

What does this all mean? All this is understandable in the sense that it happens to so many people; we are all familiar with internal family dissension and stress. Most of us can identify with the anorexic's hassles — which adolescent has not had them? And which adolescent is not greatly influenced by her parents? Whose parents do not come home moaning about life? And everyone uses home as a place to let off steam, to be a little selfish every now and then, and we all at some time or other feel threatened by the outside world.

Yes, indeed; but consider the context of the lives of most normal people. People do worry about things, but then again, a lot of the time, they do not worry. They get on with life and take pleasure in it, knowing that there are as many good things as there are bad. In the average family, if mum or dad come home moaning about things, sometimes the kids listen, other times they tease their parents, or get angry with them. Normal parents do the same to each other, openly. Children of such homes know what the real situation is, for instance, father may have a bee in his bonnet about something, mother may be sensitive about this or that, or the boss at work may be a difficult character. Above all, a child in such a home would not have to worry — he or she would just accept that his or her parents do have problems but can look after themselves. Normal children get on with their own lives.

The key words are 'get on with their own lives'. In normal families, growing children are permitted to have their own lives, their own worlds. In early years, normal parents protect their children from the stresses and fears of the outside world until they are old enough and confident enough to see these in perspective. They are protected so that they can be self-centred, be children, and be the most important thing in the whole world for a time. They get proper individual attention and affection. This allows them to take their parents for granted, to trust them and their ability to cope in the world, and to lead their own childish and growing lives. They do not have to focus prematurely upon adult issues.

As a normal child grows, he or she comes increasingly into contact with reality, both through seeing how other people live, act, cope, think and feel, and through having to deal with his or her own problems: other children, school, homework, teachers, and so on. It is in this key matrix of growing that the healthy child learns to think, feel and act as an individual, learns to blend the parents' view of the world and reality, and their dictates on how to behave, with his or her own experience and the experiences of others. When you are eight or nine or ten, going to play at someone's house, for example, is a valuable experience: you see how other parents live. Similarly, seeing your own parents with friends, you see how *they* are treated and you get a sense of who they are. One of the biggest shocks of growing up — in your teens or earlier — is to see your parents as other people see them: the contrast between your (submissive) childlike view and the view of other adults or friends helps you to gain a perspective of your parents and, by implication, of yourself. By the age of 10 or 11, you should be aware of how complex a person you are; the fact that you are one thing with your friends, for example, and another with your parents. A central part of growing up is to develop other 'selves', other parts of you, especially outside the family: it is the only way to equip yourself to deal with the world and with other people.[1]

In other words, an absolutely vital part of growing up properly is the contact you have with the outside world, the chances you get to face reality, yourself, to learn about life, living and getting on with other people through direct and free interaction. So vital is this contact that few people are aware of it and we take it for granted. It is so much an accepted part of living, and so many normal parents automatically do it that it is hard to think of not doing it. At 12, 13 or 14, most adolescents trust their best friends more than their parents. At 16, 17 onwards, most adolescents are just raring to go and are busy leading their own lives to the hilt.

However, if you are anorexic and reading this, the chances are that you will not really know what I am getting at. You will say: "Yes, my friends are important and I have had contact with the outside world, I went to school, had to get on with teachers and had friends and so on, all quite normally."

But this is the crunch! You may believe this but in a very fundamental sense it is not actually true. You may not know this but it is over this point that we found the upbringing of anorexics to differ from that of normal children.

We found, without exception, that anorexics do not have proper contact with the outside world as do other children. They do not form friendships as other children do, and they do not develop their own way in the world. We found that the

1 You can imagine how much of this the anorexic misses. The contact that most anorexics have with adults is limited to relatives; a kind of experiential interbreeding of the worst kind.

parents of anorexics systematically and deliberately cut their children off from the world, and that it is this single but central act that lays most of the grounding for anorexia and other pathological conditions (in siblings) to develop. This is the parental *iron fist* that does all the damage.

Imagine for a moment (if you do not have anorexia) how it would be if you had had to grow up without proper contact with the outside world, in isolation, locked in your parents' world, or rather, the world that they make for you and which differs quite extensively from their own world. Imagine you had never really been naughty, never criticized your parents (or their values and ideas) to your friends, never gone behind their backs, and had never been disloyal. Imagine you had never got into things with other people, such as pop music, modern dancing, clothes, heroes and so on; never dared to do it openly at any rate. Imagine instead that you never had time for these things, never fitted in, never 'got into' it, never found your friends more fun, or more satisfying than mum or dad, never fought with your parents or lost your temper with them, never left home in a huff, never in fact ever done anything that they *really* disapproved of. Imagine too, that most of your time is taken up with them and by them, worrying about them, being with them, helping them, caring for them, doing well at school for them, looking nice when you go out for them; not rebelling for their sake and never going with 'bad' people for their sake.

If you can imagine all this, you have a pretty good idea of what life is like for the average anorexic.

Apart from its boringness, its deathliness, the anxiety and focusing on parents instead of self; apart from its neglect of you and 'self', apart from the sheer strain of living like this, such a life creates a massive deficit in the personality of the anorexic, in her thinking and her emotions. As we noted earlier, in order to survive the rigours of adulthood, to be normal, to have normal anxieties, to be lighthearted about life, to see parental grousing for what it is and to see things in perspective, you must have had your own experiences to build up your own identity, personality and understanding. Without experience of your own, nothing is normal, nothing is straightforward, and everything is distorted. You cannot hope to cope with life. It is far more than just body-image distortion — this is just the final, obvious distortion. It is personality distortion.

THE MECHANICS OF PARENTAL COERCION

We need to organize some of this material now, to try and systematize what actually happens in anorexic families, so that you can understand the context in which you (the anorexic) were reared and how it works. There are a number of key points.

Firstly, you are materially and physically protected by your parents, in fact overprotected. If, as a growing child, you really had become destitute or desperately poor, the condition would at least have broken into your life and you would have seen it. You would have felt reality (poverty, collapse) and you would have had a chance to deal with it; you would have been able to link what your parents said with reality. But anorexics seldom experience this kind of reality. Instead they hear talk about impending doom — continual talk — and what it is going to be like. The grounds of massive anxiety are laid; the worst kind of anxiety. You cannot see impending doom — but you know it is there; your parents are constantly telling you. So your child mind builds this into a monster, and monster it remains — unseen and untested.

Secondly, you hear from an early age how difficult it is 'out there'. You hear how hard it is for your parents and how you must not trust people. It is always people 'out there' who let you down and you are encouraged to trust only parents and family. Often too in the families of anorexics, there is a tremendous emphasis on the superiority of your family in one way or another over all others. You learn very early on that other people are the cause of all your family's troubles because they never recognize your family's true worth and superiority. Other people thus become firmly attached to the outside-world monster picture that you already possess.

Thirdly, and most crucial: you are thus thrown into a massive and abnormally intense dependency on your parents which has three far-reaching effects:

1. You are made to feel that all that stands between you and the outside-world monster is your parents. While this in reality

may be true for a time, children should never be aware of it; anorexics are both acutely aware of it from a very young age and continue to feel it for most of their lives. Imagine the chronic sense of inadequacy this generates, the feelings of inferiority (everyone else seems to be OK) and the perennial sense of panic. How can you ever feel safe enough to explore yourself and the world with this hanging over you, with your having to watch your parents all the time?

2. Because of this dependency, you focus exclusively and obsessively on your parents. Apart from the fact that they force you anyway to focus on them and their problems, your fears of being 'crushed' by the outside-world are only alleviated by their presence. Anorexics worry about their parents abnormally because apart from natural concern, there is the deeper fear that in the absence of their parents they will be swamped. The health, happiness and well-being of parents thus becomes of obsessive concern to the child. This is why the child learns quickly to deeply minimize her own needs even to the extent of denying their existence. To be ill, or weak or needy, is to risk being wiped out; to add an intolerable anxiety to the already pervasive twin anxieties of fear of the outside-world and fear for the parent's well-being. In time, this denial of self-problems generalizes into an obsession with being perfect, for the parents' sake: mentally, emotionally, and physically. This was Andrea's experience:

> "In the years before I became anorexic, I felt I was letting my parents down terribly (and of course myself, I now realize — but at the time, I just sensed it was for them). I knew I was good at school and I tried hard but I sensed they were disappointed in me for a lot of reasons. I was a nuisance, I whined, I cried (sometimes), I was clumsy. I felt I embarrassed them, I was overweight, I was ugly. Oh they didn't say it in so many words but I knew. I knew if I looked better they'd be happier, prouder of me; it would make life easier for them. I wanted to be perfect. I felt my parents were terribly critical of me: if I did well, it was always tentative — 'Well, that's good but you *might* let us down, you *might* get in with a bad crowd or marry badly...' It was as if they were never sure of me, never trusted me entirely."

For Andrea, she had been made to feel from a young age that she was not good enough, a recurring complaint from most anorexics.

3. Given such a focusing for security, it follows that for anorexics, the ideas and beliefs of their parents about everything become abnormally dominant. Because they are the only source of protection, and the outside-world is not to be trusted, their ways of behaving and thinking become absolute, accepted unquestioningly forever and without modification by the anorexic.

THE IRON FIST

Many parental opinions and doctrines flounder and become exposed as authoritarian and out-of-date, silly, pretentious or unreal if the children have normal contact and interaction with other people. All indoctrination programmes are vulnerable to even minor contact with alternative opinions or ideas — and especially in the face of reality that can be manipulated by the child and clearly seen to be much less frightening than it is made out to be. To achieve a complete hold, a complete indoctrination, nearly every anorexic parent operates on a kind of iron-fist in a velvet-glove basis; they ensure in one way or another that their child's contact with reality is kept to a minimum and along lines of which they approve.

Many anorexics report that in their early youth they did have periods when they made ordinary contact with the outside world. This was Maureen's experience:

"I remember until I was seven or eight, I got on with other people, with my friends at school. I was naughty and, I think, normal; it was a lot of fun. I remember thinking how fuddy-duddy and silly my parents seemed. And lonely and sad — I always had more friends than they did. Then my brother left home. Up till then, he'd had the worst of it, he was their 'pet' and he got all the fussing. Then he went to boarding school and *wham*, suddenly I got all the attention. Up till then, they'd just sort of mildly disapproved of me — or sneered at how 'gullible' I was to be 'taken in' and to trust and play with my friends. But then suddenly they weighed in, especially my mother: Don't play with x, she's not from a good home etc. Slowly, over time, my life changed, I lost my friends — my mother disapproved and wouldn't let me have them at home and if they did come it was no fun — all formal and terribly important. You couldn't play and mess around. Also my parents began to take more notice of me, made me do my homework, work harder, sent me to ballet and so on — all of which left me no time for *my* life. At the time I didn't notice it so much or mind, because I was being made a fuss of.''

Many of the anorexics I studied were deprived of even this minimal contact with reality. All of them though were eventually subjected to severe restrictions on their interactional freedom, most of them crippling.

The fact of the matter is that contact with reality is a great restorer and equalizer, even to a child. Many anorexics as children, in my opinion, if allowed to would have formed a better contact with reality than their parents had. This was often evident early on in their lives, as Maureen reports. I also think that there is sufficient evidence to show that bulimarexics as children had greater freedom or more experience with other children at one time or another in their lives, than did people who became classically anorexic. Where I was able to get case data from anorexics who nearly died, they tended to show an even greater degree of isolation than others.

What happens in anorexic homes is that to pre-empt the child from developing better systems of coping or, more practically, exposing the parental system as fake or wrong, anorexic parents act systematically to prevent this interaction from taking place. This is in addition to over-involvement in a superficial way with their child's life.[1] There is one very central way that the anorexic is conditioned to avoid other people. I call it 'The Supreme Sneer'.

---

1 Anorexic parents tend to force their children to do a lot of prestigious things, such as working hard, and taking extra lessons, but they seldom help the child with these things nor do they take note of the strain involved.

THE SUPREME SNEER

It sounds like something invented by Monty Python, but in reality, anorexic parents as a whole do seem to have built up a particularly virulent form of putting other people or 'outsiders' down. Basically the sneer is the anorexic's parents' ultimate weapon: an organized way of looking at 'other people'; it is applied continually to everyone and everything as a matter of course. It is how anorexic parents communicate with one another and of course, with their children. And more importantly, it is the iron fist, the executive or punishing arm whereby the parents control their children, make them do what they want and restrict their contact with other people.

Many of the anorexics I saw when I first began to do research were quite unaware of the peculiarity of their parents' sneering behaviour; in fact, they thought it was normal to focus nearly all of the time on discrediting other people; they thought that was how all families were, that it was the topic of most family discussions.

When you meet anorexic parents as I did to investigate this phenomenon, you see very little of this side of their lives; on the surface everything is good, kind and understanding. If you were to ask, "Do you sneer at other people?" you would get a horrified denial. A kind of martyred look as if to say "Would I do such a thing?" However, if you probe this point, not by asking more questions but by recording how the same parents behaved after they have left the office, you get a completely different picture. For example, this is what Janet's mother said after a completely amiable and apparently frank discussion with me:

> "I don't want to upset you my child, (Janet was with her and carrying the tape in her bag, unknown to her mother) and of course, you must have faith in your doctors, but I don't think this man is going to be able to help you."
>
> *Janet*: "Why not?"
>
> *Mother*: "He asks the wrong sort of questions. You know, he wanted to know if Daddy and I ever argued or had fights, implying that *we* might have upset you in some way. God forbid that we should be the cause of something

so awful to our child. You know we'd never ever do anything to hurt you, don't you?"
Janet: "Yes. But what's wrong with asking that?"
Mother: "Because, my dear, it's not *us* that's got the problem, it's *you*. Don't you see? He's not a very *intelligent* man, is he?"
Janet: "How do you work that out?" (Getting angry)
Mother: "Don't get upset sweetheart, I don't mean it unkindly, it's just...oh, I don't know, he tries very hard... and I'm sure he does his best. But he — well, let's just say — he isn't right for you."

Janet let the tape run whenever she was with her parents during the rest of that day and it became clear that the reason I was not right was because I had upset Janet's mother by daring to ask if there were any personal problems in her marriage. This became the topic of suppertime conversation for the next three days, by the end of which time I had been called many names. At the next interview I had with Janet's mother, on the fourth day, not one word of this was raised or even alluded to: Janet's mother was charm personified, she told me how impressed she had been with me on the first interview, how intelligent she thought I was, how sure she was that I really was going to help her daughter and so on, *ad nauseam*.[1] I recorded all interviews in my clinic quite openly and when she had gone, and with her permission, I played the tape back for Janet to hear the interview with her mother. She smiled throughout.

"That's what always happens. Now you know what it's like living with them. They will run someone down for ages — and really viciously too — and then, face-to-face with that person, they change. It's as if nothing was ever said. Smooth, charming — it's all a lie. She really hates you, believe me."

This little episode helped Janet a lot: she had always known that her parents were 'phoney' as she put it — one thing to the

---

1 This was no joke. It was very difficult to sit and listen to all that after hearing the other side on Janet's tapes. Just keeping my anger in check gave me a headache and also gave me a valuable insight into how anorexics must feel.

world at large and another at home. This ability to lie so effectively, incidentally, will concern us more later; anorexics are known to lie to themselves and to others endlessly. Thanks to Janet and others we now know where the ability comes from; they are taught it at home.[1]

The important point here though is the way in which Janet's mother reacted to me; the disapproval was subtle but penetrating. Subtle disapproval can be more effective than open hostility and naturally this forms an important part of the 'supreme sneer'. Any aspect of behaviour, however mildly out of the ordinary it was, was seized upon and ridiculed by these parents. A parent, for example, would come home and recount how so-and-so had made a fool of himself, had been silly or got something wrong and so on, all the time putting forward the idea of their superiority.

The sense of personal security in these parents was so minimal that they focused obsessively on behaviour at variance from the norm as if it were a sin. One major corollary of this was that not only did their children pick this up and behave in the same way, but they became terrified of failing in the simple immediate sense of doing something silly or wrong. Failure in any sense would immediately result in their being sneered at and being seen as part of the outside-world.

Under this kind of pressure, little trial-and-error learning can take place. There is instead an obsession with appearances, with appeasing the parents, with not doing anything new or wrong. It is this that effectively cuts the child off from contact with reality. She is cut off not only by her parents, but worse, she cuts herself off from the normal childhood learning processes because such learning involves play, imperfection, trial-and-error, silliness, and failure; all the things sneered at by the parents. It is these very elements that are the reality she should be experiencing, not only for her own personal development but also to allow her to make contact with her peers. A

1 All of us put on a social front in mild ways but do not mistake this for what happens in the homes of anorexics. Most of us would like to be more open, sometimes are and often will be if pressed. The families of anorexics deny that they feel anything other than 'nice'. Moreover, they seldom, if ever, let their masks slip — with them it's like a religion.

peer security is essential. In time it grows larger and lays the foundation for trust in the outside world, in people outside the family and ultimately allows the child to leave home safely. The anorexic girl avoids this, establishing instead a fatal over-dependence on her parents and on their pathological way of dealing with the world.

SUMMING UP

To add then to the growing anorexic's fears, we now have this additional anxiety and perhaps the most fundamental one: if she does not please her parents, she will be sneered and jeered at. She fears this (justly) and cannot take it lightly because she knows that this is how they treat the outside-world. So in her child mind she associates these episodes of displeasing her parents with being rejected by the family, pushed away. It is the ultimate threat, the ultimate punishment held over the child and keeps her locked into her parents' world: "Do it our way; please us or we shall treat you as an outsider. And if you dare to persist in getting things wrong, we shall turn all our hostility on you — the hostility with which we treat outsiders; and worse, if you ever rebel or question us, we really will reject you." Now few anorexics ever get to this last stage of rebellion because they dare not. They know what will happen.

In fact, we have found that anorexics' parents are in reality as dangerous to the anorexic as she fears they are. Not only do they selectively neglect their children — over-attending to them only in specific performance-orientated areas — but they really do reject their rebellious children emotionally. Siblings who rebel are cut off in a very fundamental way and often act as examples to the anorexic of the consequences she will face if she should do the same. We found that many siblings escaped the family through marriage — or through deep emotional contact with an 'outsider' — simply because they could not survive on their own as people without the approval of their parents, and also because their parents' reaction to their rebellion was so vicious and total.

We also found that when anorexics tried to go it alone, independent of their parents, they found their parents to be very belittling, hostile, cold and disinterested. The parents were interested in their children only as long as they could have control. They seldom troubled themselves by visiting offspring who no longer lived in the home; the children would have to go home to see the parents. Neither did the parents bother much with the living conditions of offspring outside the home. So for the children of such parents, to leave home, unless it was fulfilling something the parents expressly wanted, such as going to university or getting married, meant in a very real sense to be rejected. To be blunt, we found that the parents of anorexics were capable of a high degree of cruelty and disinterest.

What is worse for the anorexic, is that while this is going on (and she senses it) her parents are saying all the right things socially, such as: "We miss you, darling, come home, we think of you all the time." But they seldom, if ever, do anything to substantiate what they profess, to show genuine caring.

To an anorexic reading this, these findings should not come as a surprise. They should simply confirm what she had sensed for herself. They reveal that the ability of anorexics' parents to neglect their offspring — not to notice, for example, the bony skeleton until someone points it out to them — is a deep and penetrating part of anorexic family life, the tip of the iceberg of neglect.

The ultimate fear, the nightmare of each anorexic, is that if she does not conform to please her parents, she will be thrown out and that without her parents' protection, she would be at the mercy of the 'terrible outside'.

The final result of all this is that as the anorexic approaches adolescence and adulthood, she is already an emotional cripple, increasingly more aware that she is unable to cope with the real world, deeply terrified of remaining so helplessly in the bosom of her family, yet with nowhere else to go. Depressed and frightened, she has to escape from her nightmare. She examines herself and focuses on (as she has been taught) what she thinks is wrong with her, or on what her parents currently hold up as a cliché or set of clichés as to what is wrong with her. In true anorexic fashion, she makes one more effort, as she always has, to get on, to please, to be accepted.

Chapter 5

How does it all start?

How does a child react to growing up in the kind of world described in the last chapter? What are such children like? How do they think, feel, act? We can get some idea of how such a child exists by looking at the central structure of her world. By 'structure' I mean simply how that world is organized.

We have seen that it focuses excessively on the parents and their needs. We have seen too, that it minimizes the child's own 'childish' needs in favour of behaviour that fits into parental modes. From this central structure, everything else follows. It is the organizing principle of the anorexic's life. Let me explain briefly how this works.

The child is discouraged from making significant outside contact apart from attending school and engaging in other parentally-approved activities. The purpose of this is to keep her at all times to help them, materially and emotionally, and to prevent these outside contacts taking up family emotional time and attention. The child is discouraged from behaving childishly because it distresses or disturbs parents, and, above all, demands time and attention that — for whatever reason — they are unable to give. The reason, incidentally, we will go into later. The child is expected to succeed superficially at all she does in order to avoid distressing her parents' fragile stability, to keep up the family tradition and to keep up the family myths of superiority. And of course, to avoid the parents having to spend time and effort in coping with failure or inadequacy.

What does all this mean practically? The previous points are understandable as generalizations but what specifically do they refer to? Specifically, these statements relate to a number of crucial ways of existing that are worth examining closely because they will help us to understand and explain the thought processes of the anorexic as she approaches that significant attempt to lose weight.

THE PRE-ANOREXIC'S MENTAL FRAMEWORK

Normal children have what is best described as a broad experimental framework. That is, by and large, their worlds very much reflect their own levels of childish functioning. They have their homes and school and they have their friends. There are few boundaries to hinder their attempts to explore and to match up what they feel with what they do and what they receive from the world. A child at home can run to mummy or daddy if afraid; he or she can do the same at school with a teacher and the same with friends. The people who can provide the fulfilment of their needs, who can see to it that they are suitably protected, cared for and above all, pushed into doing the things they should be (or want to be) doing, are everywhere: attention, affection and time is there for the taking from teachers, parents, friends and anyone who is prepared to give such care. Normal children do not see their parents solely as their world and they do not focus exclusively on them.

Moreover, the things that interest, excite or frighten a normal child are of a broad nature. In playing with friends, exploring and doing things, the child feels part of what everyone else is being and doing.

The anorexic's world, in contrast, is a shrunken one. Her parents are almost completely dominant, the only source of feedback, comfort, security, excitement and stimulation. They tend to be the only people in the anorexic's world, and the things that they do are the only activities the anorexic has to examine and to explore. Further, only adults — authority figures — have status. Children are of no importance. In fact, other children, by definition, are the lowest of the low. Outsiders, you will remember, are inferior and to be sneered at.

Adult outsiders are bad enough, but child outsiders have no status at all. This is a crucial point and one that we will go into in great detail later; the anorexic is systematically cut off, in reality and in terms of her own conditioning from other children; she is taught to think she does not need other children let alone be like them. And by definition, she is isolated from the shared learning and growth children go through.[1]

What then is the nature of this shrunken world? Consider first the actual time these children spend with both their parents. That is, when school, homework and extra lessons like ballet, piano and speech training are out of the way. Assuming that neither parent is upset or distressed, or busy doing something, locked away in the study or in the bedroom, the average anorexic child has very little time with them, most of it is limited to meal times, preparing meals or clearing meals away. Contact with one parent, the mother or the father, may be greater, but in many of the samples I studied, even this contact was cut down by the parent's overt problems: many mothers had depression, some had agoraphobia, many could not drive and so on. Several of the fathers had pet obsessions for which they demanded help, sometimes with their clothes, their food or their animals; activities that their wives could not or would not help with. The reasons for this are discussed in a later chapter.

The overall result is that the time spent with both parents in a full sense is minimal for the anorexic child. Even the time spent serving a direct parental need is minimal, though more substantial. What would you live for in such a world? You would have individual contact only if you helped one parent or the other; your individuality and your worth as a person would lie solely in your role as helper. If you were not prepared to help, you would not get the contact. Your *individual* world would become restricted to that contact and your *general* world would become focused and restricted to shared family activity, a major one of which would be meal times. Given the nature of your parents' life, meal times would be, along with other contact points, the only time you received an insight into what

---

1 This is the real reason that anorexics feel they do not belong — they really do not in the sense that they have been isolated too early from proper peer contact.

was going on in your world: at meal times, for example, you would find out what was happening between your parents, what was happening to them in the outside world, to your relatives, your siblings and so on. Meal times would be the 'television' of your world. Just as most of us learn about the state of our reality through the medium of television, so the anorexic learns about the state of her world through watching and listening at meal times.

You might think I am exaggerating here but most anorexics will confirm the validity of these statements. What happens in these households is that these different, equally minimal ways of spending time, define the framework in which the anorexic lives. The models for dealing with the world, for growing, for becoming people in the full sense of the word, are learnt here. Not only are they encouraged to imitate their parents and to behave as the parents wish, but their only significant one-to-one contact with people is the time spent at home with each parent. Where there are siblings, the situation is intensified: they vie with one another to please the parents and thus to have more time with them. Again, in such circumstances, mealtimes (or other shared family time) become the arena in which the learning and the security built up with each parent (and against each sibling) is tested. Instead of the child testing constructs and ideas and behaviours in the real world outside the family, the pre-anorexic child focuses obsessively (as do the siblings in most cases) on mealtimes. Here is a report illustrating this from the brother of one of my anorexic patients:

> "I've given a lot of thought to the reasons why T... became anorexic. When I was at home, I learnt from an early age not to get involved in my family's politics and this meant a very specific set of things. I couldn't stand what happened when we were all together. If we went for a drive, there would be competition for who got to sit in front with dad. I usually did because I was the boy. But if dad wanted to punish me, T... got the seat. At mealtimes, it was like a war game — to see who got the best cuts of meat, the most food etc... If mum was pleased with you you got a bit extra and so on. If she was cross with dad,

the food was burnt or there wasn't enough. The only way I felt I could survive — like, have any sanity — was to withdraw. Not to take part. Not to need or want what they had to offer. So I always sat at the back. So I always ate little; if I wanted more, I got it later in the privacy of the kitchen — away from them. And by 'them', I include T... She was more into it than me — she seemed to need them more.

Watching her made me determined not to get involved. She changed with the wind: she had no guts, no individuality. She was so easily 'bought'; if she had been out with dad, she'd come back glowing and you'd know that for the next day or two, she'd be on his side. And then it would start. Mum would get uptight because she'd sense a sort of conspiracy between them and she'd try and prise T... away from dad. 'Come and help me,' she'd say, or she'd make something nice for her to eat to kind of bribe her into coming back into her camp. It was so childish. Did it really matter? I often felt that it was us who were the parents and our parents were the kids.''

Something similar to these interactions do occur in normal homes but rarely as the sole context of the child's world, and rarely with so little attention being given to the child's needs.

What are the rewards in these homes? What are the comforts and the securities? Since the way in which we are comforted and rewarded are major shapers of our behaviour and our personalities, how these operate, and what they are in the anorexics' home and family, is of considerable importance.

In normal families, physical contact acts as both a comfort and a reward. Being held, touched, kissed are key non-verbal ways in which a deep and physical sense of personal worth and well-being are engendered in a child. They are at the base of the normal family and everything else that gives security — the presence of parents, material well-being, routine, being fed and clothed and so on — are simply the structure on which the basic sense of love and being cared for is hung. In anorexic families, affectionate touching is very soon restricted as the child grows up. It falls under the category of 'childish behaviour'. It demands too much time and too much effort.

Again, a little thought shows why.

To love a child means that you have to watch that child and its behaviour. You have to be delighted in the child for itself, for its intrinsic value and its individuality. Free children cannot perform in set times and set places. They behave spontaneously and they demand love, affection, attention and comfort at odd times, seldom conveniently. This is an absorbing task for a parent, catering for all these random needs; a growing child's behaviour has to be gradually channelled to fit into the adult's life and the adult has to change too, to accept the child's right to be a nuisance or to be demanding every now and then, and to accept that this right fluctuates over time. As a child grows up, he or she should become a person to be related to, not a convenience to be used. Sadly, this aspect of bringing up children is missed in the homes of anorexic children.

In place then of this largely non-verbal base, anorexics have to accept as comfort and security the bare bones of such a structure; the forms on which love should be hung. Thus, being with a parent, helping that parent, the presence of parents at home, having a routine, having meals, being given clothes or other material comforts — all these things, having them or having them denied or taken away, form the base of the anorexic's security instead of that deeper physical comfort base. Without this base, the superficial trimmings of home life become focused upon obsessively and possession of them becomes literally a matter of emotional life and death.

One of the corollaries of this is that the child continually feels an inner emptiness. When you are loved properly, you feel confident; you feel you can take things on in the world outside. When you are not loved properly, you feel empty, neglected, lonely. You feel you have to grab at anything around you, anything you are offered. You feel that because you are only given the trimmings you never have enough in life, that whatever you do have can be taken away from you at anytime. Because you never get anything for *you*, you have to grab what you can, every little bit of attention, affection or whatever.

This, in essence, creates the basis for the *frenzy* mentioned earlier. If you deprive a child of proper love and attention, you leave this emptiness unattended and offer instead superficialities which no matter how abundant, never quite fulfill. This kind of thing also happens in homes of non-anorexics and you find such children seeking love and attention outside the home. In the homes of anorexics, this avenue is blocked and only the parents — the very people depriving the child of those strong needs — are allowed to be considered as suppliers.

PRE-ANOREXIC EMOTIONAL PATTERNS

Now that we understand something of the way the anorexic's life at home is structured, we can look at the way she actually behaves. What must be born in mind is that she is trapped in the world imposed on her by her parents and these parents, as people, are essentially insecure and unstable. They are generally moody and inconsistent and their self-esteem and self-confidence are liable to fluctuate at any time, which is one of the reasons why they do not attend to their children properly; they are too needy themselves. These moods create the ebb and flow of the family's emotional life and they serve to direct the energies of the children. The children try, by pleasing the parents, to stabilize their world. This is one level of activity. There is however another.

Each child feels his or her own real needs. What marks anorexics off from people who become psychotic, or from people who develop such psychosomatic conditions as migraine and who come from very similar family contexts, is the fact that they do not lose an awareness of what is wrong 'inside'; they are at least aware of the emptiness. This arises because from time to time, and in some ways, the parents of anorexics do treat their children properly.

Most of my anorexic patients were aware and had been for years of precisely what was going on in their homes; they knew they were neglected and they knew why. They knew their parents' weaknesses and failings. They simply had never been given the opportunity to talk about it openly, nor were they allowed the outside contact necessary to give their insights proper 'truth' status; that is, the right to act on such insight.

Nevertheless, I found that the way in which anorexics actually behaved was an amalgam of their own needs within the framework set up for them by their parents. Thus while a child tried to do what the parents wanted, she also tried to get more extra time and extra attention by demanding through whining, petulance and stubborness. The child's world developed in turn an ebb and flow between helping the parents and seeking more for herself: more time, more food, more clothes, more attention.

This is an important point. This battle for proper (but unacknowledged) attention — expressed in ways that irritate the parents — serves in turn as a perfect justification or explanation for the parents' behaviour. The child whines or clings; this irritates the parents, it is used against the child: "I am not going to take you to town with me," or: "I am not going to buy you anything because you are a nuisance. I am not going to pick you up or hug you because you whine. I won't love you because you are selfish. You are mean and greedy and grabbing." The blame is put back onto the child. What is worse is that she now feels very guilty because she already felt bad for demanding time and attention in the first place. She is afraid of offending mummy and daddy and losing her security with them. It becomes a vicious inner circle: a part of her refuses to stop demanding; another part wants to stop, to conform and so be more secure with her parents.

This pattern, I believe, is established long before anorexia begins. I think it starts more or less after babyhood when the child is first taught to stop being childish. I also think the 'babyness' inside the anorexic (the part that knows she should be getting more) is not entirely crushed owing to the fact that the parents of the anorexic do not form an entire front against it: one or the other parent tends to give in and spoil the child, not solely for the child's sake but in part as a way of competing with the other parent.[1]

What sets up the child for anorexia, as opposed to other forms of pathology, seems to me to depend on how these subtle games are played and how the child is spoilt (that is,

1 One example is the case where the parents will both punish a child for some reason but one parent will later sneak up to the child behind the other's back to gain special favour by being 'the good guy' or the 'pal'.

given the *wrong kind* of attention). Most of my anorexic patients, for instance, tended to be given food as compensation, often by mothers, but sometimes by fathers. I found the same kinds of pathology in the siblings of anorexics but it showed itself in different directions: male siblings, for instance, would be given special status (as sometimes would the eldest child) as males or as the 'responsible' ones and their pathology would manifest itself in the way they reacted to their special status. The way in which they reacted, while being essentially the same as their anorexic sisters, was significantly different in respect of being able to hide their pathology better (more on this in a later chapter). Either way, the tendency in these families appears to be to use the roles and special status to 'divide and rule' in order to control the children.

The net result of all this is to create a context in which the pre-anorexic's world is dominated solely by both her parents and by the individual ways in which each parent reacts with the child and with each other. Thus, as Helen puts it:

> "I used to whine a lot if I was out shopping with my mother. She would get more and more irritable and eventually shout at me but then later she'd feel guilty and buy me a cake or something to make up for it. My father would see this and then sneer at us, at my mother for being weak and giving in to me. But he used to do exactly the same, instead of giving me food, he'd buy me a dress, but tell me not to tell my mum, to say it was a present from someone at work or something..."

Life, in short, is a battle ground with the child struggling to keep herself happy, to cope with her parents' insecurity and to cope with their internicine conflicts with one another acted out in the way in which they reward their children.

When I try to explain all this to 'normal' people, or to people with mental problems but with little insight into them, they have great difficulty in believing that family life can indeed be like this. Especially when one considers the appearance of such families; how they come across to the unwary outsider appears on the surface to contradict these findings. Therefore, I want to digress here briefly to talk a little about family life.

A BRIEF ASIDE ON FAMILY LIFE

In many ways and in many families, children see a side to their parents that nobody else sees and sometimes it is worse than that which anyone else sees. We tend to think that most children are protected by their families from the worst that the world has to offer; that family life, the home, is there to protect them until they grow up. However, in many ways, children are exposed to levels of anxiety and terror seldom experienced in the outside world on a day-to-day basis. And I am not talking about physical abuse.

Take an adult man or woman. Imagine he or she has a deep sense of inferiority and a fear of the world. He or she goes to work and is intimidated by the boss, or bullied, never daring to fight back. He or she goes home after work and it is only there that the roles are reversed, that he or she has power and authority. Now, give people like this children, and nine times out of ten, they will over-dominate them and over-control them. The children, who have no rights, no power to answer back (and anyway, would face all that pent-up anger if they did), are put through emotional regimes that the parents themselves cannot get away with outside the home. Parents are more irritable with their children (and also more loving) than they are with most adults, more demanding, more authoritative and so on. Some of this is very necessary for the healthy rearing of a child but it has to be continually adjusted and watched: a healthy parent will treat his children with balance. Inferior or inadequate parents, in contrast, tend too often to use their children to get their own back on a world that treats them harshly.

Look at it like this. If a person is insecure and lacking in confidence, she will usually feel on the defensive. Insecurity, lack of confidence and inadequacy are always felt in some *context*. You feel insecure in a particular situation and by the same token, you feel safe outside or away from that situation. Grossly insecure people tend only to feel safe away from society and away from anything or anyone, even a part of anyone, that makes them feel insecure. As a consequence, such people only love or like those things about people that make them feel secure. People often say that they 'love' something or someone, when in fact all they are really doing is loving little bits of them, the bits that support them. To really love someone, you have to feel safe yourself, so that you are free to explore, respect and love those things about the world and about other people that make you feel insecure as well as those things that make you feel safe. Despite popular opinion, healthy people don't in fact feel totally secure all the time but they are able to confront, explore and learn to understand those aspects of life that make them feel insecure. The meat of a full life is learning to live with the things you are insecure about. Insecure people run away from their insecurities and try to create worlds around them populated by things that don't threaten them — and these are usually populated by compliant or easily 'shaped' objects such as children, animals, secretaries, underlings and so on. I am not talking solely about inadequate or unfortunate human beings who cannot say boo to a goose. Insecure people abound everywhere often with overtly confident, superior, even brash, fronts. They are in the professions, the arts, business, show business, everywhere. Often, very successful people have deep feelings of inadequacy and try to build secure worlds to stop themselves feeling insecure.

Do not think for a minute that I am talking solely about sweet old nobodies who protect themselves by a kind of passive apathy. There is in fact, a whole breed of people —anorexic parents among their number — who insure their own security by an as-yet little understood form of violence: not physical violence, but a kind of psychological violence perpetrated by comfortably-off, educated, respectable people who compensate for their own inadequacies by using their children as tools to gain social approval, and to insulate them from facing up to their insecurities. Because such people can cover their insecure drives by using slogans that are popular among the educated middle classes — improving learning skills, improving performance, the ethic of the 'gifted' child, early learning and so on — they ensure that they never have to spend time being challenged by their children. Moreover their childrens' childhoods are converted into a life of misery and overwork with regimes that would make the normal adult trade unionist explode: extra art classes, speech lessons, violin, ballet, piano, French classes and so on. There is no time for anything, let alone random unco-ordinated, messy childish play, so frowned-upon by those who want to see 'creative' children. In adopting this attitude, they also ensure that no one will ever be able to point a finger at them for failing as parents.

Similarly, by using socially acceptable motivational slogans, such as building a career, doing a good job, working for charities, campaigning, being an intellectual, an artist and so on, these people ensure that they avoid having to spend time alone with themselves — thinking about themselves, their lives and relationships. They are too busy. They make themselves busy and in so doing, achieve isolation from the world and from their families. It is a strange form of violence but it is nevertheless very prominent in our modern societies and its effects, such as anorexia, depression, insomnia, and other psychosomatic conditions, are there for us all to see if we choose to examine the links closely.

I was once approached for help by a young woman whose father had effectively destroyed her psychological life by his obsession that she should reach the top in her field. He was a well-known and well-liked member of the community but of all the people he came into contact with, he treated his daughter the harshest. For her, there had been no rest literally since she had been able to walk. In his determination to gain glory through her, he dragged her through a series of mental hospitals and doctors, all in the interests of keeping her fragile personality sufficiently under control to achieve *his* goals. No one questioned his actions because he was being a good father, he was caring for his daughter, giving up his time for her, spending all his money on her, and giving her the best. Anorexia had been one of her problems. When, late in life, he himself achieved fame — and a fame considerably greater than that of his daughter's — he did an abrupt about-face and literally left her to live out the rest of her life on her own. It was a tragic example of how society frequently supports this process because it has no room for digging beneath the surface of its own value system.

To return to our understanding of pre-anorexic behaviour, in effect, what this family life does is to set up two value systems: the one is the social, superficial one involving role

playing, appearances and so on; the other is the
personal-need system of the parents. Anorexics are taught
social slogans about their home life and behaviour; but they
understand these slogans to have a meaning very different
from that normally accorded to them.

To conclude this section, let me quote from the report of
one of my researchers who investigated such a family.[1]
She visited the home on several occasions as a friend of the
daughter, my patient:

> "When I went there the first time, with Joanne, there was
> just the four of us — Joanne, me and her folks. It was like
> a pantomime. Immediately we got there, her folks vied
> with each other to show Joanne how pleased they were to
> see her. Then they focused on me and ignored Joanne
> entirely (I also noticed that they quickly ran out of things to
> say — something which Joanne confirms always hap-
> pens). Joanne's father tried to patronize me, then her
> mother, feeling pretty miffed, and obviously neglected,
> 'ganged up' quite openly with Joanne against him. Poor
> Joanne — she looked so confused and naïve. When her
> father went to the toilet, her mother used the opportunity
> to befriend me, promptly dropping Joanne. There was no
> subtlety about all this, Joanne just ceased to exist; she
> wasn't drawn into the conversation or anything. In fact,
> her mother became snappy and cold with her and got her
> out of the way by telling her to clear the table. As soon as
> she heard the toilet flushing, she insisted — mid-meal —
> on showing me how well she could play the piano. We left
> the room. Her husband, so Joanne told me later, was
> angry, wanting to know where we were; when we came
> back to the table — would you believe it — he sulked with
> *me*. Perhaps for not waiting for him. Or for not being
> loyal to him.

> "What was important was that Joanne's parents wanted
> attention paid to them all the time. They fought with each
> other for it and literally kicked the children aside if they
> got in the way.

> "It was like a blind fixation — they had no sensitivity

1 With approval by the patient, and only after months of work when the two
of them really felt at ease with each other and had in fact become good friends.

about it. Another time I went there with Joanne, her brother was home on holiday and things were totally different. I was ignored and dismissed because I now counted as 'just a friend of Joanne's' and therefore, just another 'child': I was 25, Joanne was 28. In the same way as Joanne, I ceased to exist and was expected to help with the dishes and so on. There was time only for her brother. After a while he became embarrassed and deliberately talked to us, whereupon mother and father, after glowering at us hostilely for five minutes, insisted on taking the brother out to see the town (which he'd seen all his life) and we were openly discouraged from going along with them.''

Most of these pressures were there all the time in the house, reported my researcher, but at mealtimes they seemed to intensify — an ongoing battle with every mouthful, every gesture a minor skirmish between the parents for power, authority or attention. My analysis is that the conflicts were intensified by the physical closeness of mealtimes, and by the fact that in a way, eating a meal was a little like being in prison: you cannot escape from it till your time is up. This is a convenient point at which to turn, at last, to eating and mealtimes.

THE ROLE OF MEALS AND OTHER JOINT FAMILY ACTIVITIES

Every one of my researchers who spent time in anorexic households had the same complaint: they hated it when the whole family got together. Individually, parents could be managed if they were given undivided attention and if the researcher-guests did not 'make waves'. In fact, several reports state that many parents appeared "quite pathetic and needy, like little children wanting to show off, to show you what they could do''.

At joint family times, and especially over mealtimes, the basic emptiness in the family and in the parents and their relationships to one another quickly became apparent. Conversations rapidly dropped to the level of "making jokes about your behaviour or reading character into every little nuance''. In Joanne's home, for example, her mother has classified the family, and anyone else who visited, into firm and sloppy eaters. She could tell, apparently, by the way a person would hold his or her fork. Her classifications did not stop at eating mannerisms; with little else to talk about, Joanne's parents would begin commenting on the way a person sat; "How you walked, talked — everything." This was always done with favourable comments in the presence of an outsider such as my researcher, but our anorexic patients reported that their parents immediately re-assessed their opinions unfavourably, against the outsider, as soon as that person was absent. In short, devoid of proper contact with the outside world, the anorexic's family become obsessed with irrelevant minutiae onto which all varieties of social and personal traits are laid.

Naturally enough, the family's tendency to sneer and deprecate outsiders is also practised on the 'inside', with the difference that criticism no longer has to be hidden. Within the closeness of the family, there is no need to pretend, the truth can come out. It is one of the unfortunate traits of insecure adults with little insight, that one of the main ways in which they protect themselves from self-analysis and criticism is continually to have someone else to criticize or attack. In the parents of anorexics, I found that this tendency was a very dominating and obsessive one. These parents were unable, in fact, to function without someone to talk about and put down. Not surprisingly, the children in the family easily adapted to this pattern.

By studying the families of anorexics with more than one sibling, it became apparent to me that the anorexic child was the one most often used as a target, acting as the family scapegoat. The reason for this seemed to lie in the fact that anorexic (or pre-anorexic) children (unlike their siblings who did not become anorexic) were inevitably unable to cover up or control their childish behaviour, as their siblings could. The siblings seemed able to escape being family scapegoats either by withdrawing from family life or by seeming to be more as the parents wanted them to be. The anorexic was inevitably the one who both needed her parents more and was more aware of the conflicts and neglects being propagated. In short, *they were more like normal children*. The other siblings in the family survived better superficially (in the sense that they did not become anorexic) but at a very high price. Anorexic children seemed to be vulnerable, compliant and showed less guile than others in the same family — ideal targets for insecure parents.

Anorexic children seemed to take criticisms and 'put-downs' by their siblings and parents very seriously. All my anorexics with siblings complained of being ganged up against by the rest of the family. Their parents and siblings would mock their childishness, (whining, grabbing for more food and so on) and continously point to other people, in the family or relatives, as being more suitable because they were more mature and less childish. Such comparisons, mockings and sneers would form the discussion points at many family meetings, such as meal-times.

To make matters worse, the anorexic would not consistently be the scapegoat. If you are *always* the scapegoat, it is at least a stable role, something to identify with, to fight against. However, in the families of anorexics, the role of being scapegoat depended upon who was present. In the absence of a favourite sibling, or at times of parental conflict, the whole pattern would change temporarily and the scapegoat would become the favoured one, the praised one. It was this combination of vulnerability and inconsistent 'scapegoating' that served as the crucible which, when the new and pressing problems of adolescence were added, pushed the child over into anorexia.

This pattern of family activity goes on throughout the pre-teens years of the anorexic. In this time, she makes continual attempts to transcend or overcome what she feels is her basic problem: her 'emptiness' because she 'is not good enough' and is childish. She fights herself, to control her childishness and to become more like the person her parents want. In her mind she seldom succeeds because she lacks the discipline. In reality, she does not succeed because, firstly, a child of 9, 10 or 11 should not have to succeed like this and cannot, and secondly, her parents' inconsistencies never allow her to. Her life, as a consequence, becomes peppered with failed attempts at all levels to succeed:

> *Helen*: "My parents used to make a lot of fuss over my brother who was away at boarding school. I tried to

replace him in their lives, to be like him. It never really worked though. I'd try to act like he did — but I just got laughed at because I would break things and he didn't.''

Maureen: "I tried to be like my elder sister. She became a great dancer. So I tried. No good. I looked like a Christmas pudding in a tutu and everyone mocked me."

Gayle: "I just didn't seem to be really good at anything. I did OK at school but I wasn't a genius. I was just ordinary really. I didn't stand out in any way. The ugly duckling in the family. What I felt was that everyone else at least had something or someone. My brother was the clever one. My younger sister was really pretty. My mum lectured and was really good at it. My father was a business genius. My brother had a terrific-looking girlfriend whom everyone liked. My sister had hundreds of boyfriends who were always calling and taking her out. My mum and dad had each other...I failed with guys. I was too easy (I now see) and no one stayed. Also I clung and it put them off. Even if I didn't cling, they left anyway. It was terrible. I had nothing. My life was over at 15. I was in a panic, a kind of dread that I would never be good enough for anything. I would have to stay at home forever."

Sometimes the attempt to gain status, to override the emptiness inside and the feeling of being the scapegoat ('the fool-on-the-hill status,' as Gayle put it) in the family succeeded in part. A good account is given here by Sheila who, like Maureen, had a very successful older sister who danced:

"First came dancing and then came dieting. Thinking back, I clung to anything which gave me attention or to anybody who made a fuss of me. At school, I was automatically the teacher's pet — even though I didn't like the teacher — and it was nice but it wasn't enough.

When I was about 11, I started dancing lessons (encouraged by my sister) and after a year or so, we had a new teacher who one day casually said that I had some talent. From then on, I loved her. I adored her. I threw everything into my dancing — I ate it, slept it, and my parents began to hassle. I think my mother was jealous. Anyway, this went on for ages but it too wasn't enough.

I was impatient. I wanted to be a child prodigy. I hated it if the dancing teacher gave anyone else attention — I would sulk and be in a depression for days. I would stop eating —no appetite. I wanted to die, heartbroken. Then, at the next class, if it was all right again, I'd feel on top of the world.

Eventually my father made me cut down on my dancing because he said it was interfering with my school work. And shortly after that, the teacher left. And I was in limbo. It was back to the old round of sitting in the bosom of the family, hearing about how well my sister was doing or how many boyfriends my cousin had; I only had one and he wasn't even good-looking.

You see, dancing had saved me. Someone had really cared and I became a person. I loved Elizabeth (the dancing teacher) and had fantasies of her being my 'real life' mother. Dancing felt like the only place where I'd ever mattered. At home I was a nobody, the 'dumbo'.

Six months after giving up dancing, I was going mad. Supper time was the worst and at the table I felt trapped. To get up and leave would have insulted my mother's cooking and gone against my dad's authority. So I announced I was going on a diet, so I could look like Rochelle my sister. Better even. So on a diet I went and of course I failed and everyone laughed. But it gave me something to fight for. It was as if there was a little beast inside me saying, 'Fuck you, I'll do it and show you all.' It began to obsess me until after a while it worked. I dieted and got thin and I looked good and everyone was really surprised. I felt so fucking fantastic, you've no idea.''

I have let Sheila's quote run on a bit because it all followed so clearly for her: she dieted in anger and frustration. Not everyone does this in quite this way but the motivation arises out of a similar crucible. Before looking at some of the different patterns, let us pause for a moment and be clear about one or two points.

Firstly, it is important to see that dieting is one of *many* actions tried by the anorexic to escape the pressures on her. Technically, any one of these actions could have pre-empted the later development of anorexia. If Sheila had been allowed to continue dancing, for example, she might never have become anorexic, or the process might simply have been delayed. In fact, I believe the siblings in the families of anorexics avoid anorexia only because they are involved in another obsession which gives them a special status the anorexic does not have. However, while these siblings may not suffer anorexia, I believe the underlying family pathology guarantees that they will hit problems elsewhere.

The second point to bear in mind is that the first diets do not always succeed, so we have to examine what makes one diet successful and not another. Sometimes sheer despair is the key to success; other times the child is helped by the parents. What really matters is that for the person involved, most other avenues for success are closed and disciplining their eating (dieting) is all that is left.

Thirdly, remember that the same try-and-fail pattern used on everything in the anorexic's life is usually well developed long before she became anorexic. The onset of adolescence and all that it involves may therefore just be the significant factor in the development of anorexia. But not in the way in which we usually understand it, so let us look at this briefly.

ADOLESCENT PRESSURES IN THE HOMES OF ANOREXICS

Adolescence has been made, by us and our societies, into a major event in our lives. However, there is no reason why this time of life should not be as straightforward as any other time. Adolescence does not just happen from one day to the next: it comes on slowly over time, just like any other phase of growth. We never stand still in growth; there is always movement of one kind or another.

However, adolescence can be characterised as *the* time of life and it can be, and is, used by people — parents, authorities, society — to impose certain categories of behaviour on their charges. In the families of anorexics (or anorexics-to-be) the coming of adolescence is seen as the change-over time: time to grow up, time to stop all that whining, all that childishness, time to go out and face the real world, to go out with boys, to think of the future, of marriage, a career, kids of your own. Parents who put pressure on their children in this way have a lot of back-up in our society. Schools start changing the emphasis; so does the media. Everything seems to intensify. To an insecure girl struggling to keep body and soul together in an insecure family, adolescence is like the Apocalypse. It is terrifying. What should be an exciting merging into the mainstream of society, becomes a nightmare to the anorexic girl. Not just because she has to work harder, do things more independently, start going out with boys and make relationships, and be an adult (all of which she *can* do superficially because she has been trained for appearances), but because it means she has run out of time. She has been fighting a rearguard action for years to get what is hers by right — proper love — and she has in the process been delaying growing up. Now her last support and hope (namely the outside world) steps in to back up her parents, to fill her time and her mind with the same kind of expectations and demands her parents have been making all along. She is caught on two fronts. There is nowhere to go any longer; she has to give in and grow up. She must crush the child within her. She must stop herself from feeling empty. She must crush her anger and insight into what is really happening to her. She must crush her rights, her normality.

This is what adolescence means for the anorexic. Do not underestimate it. Far too many people (parents, authorities, doctors) simply do not appreciate what has been going on in the anorexic's life, and fail to grasp the significance of adolescence for her. Further, it is far too easy in our society to be glib about adolescence. It is not the same for everyone and it is not necessarily any tougher a time of life than any other. It is who you are and how you approach it that counts. I am labouring this point because it is a very vital one in our understanding of how anorexia develops.

VARIANTS OF THE ANOREXIC SOLUTION

All the anorexics quoted here wanted attention and interest: love, in short. See how Sheila 'loved' her teachers, 'loved' dancing. The internal needs of the anorexic are massive —they have been neglected for a long time — and so they latch onto anything that gives them even the least bit more comfort and attention than provided in the past by parents.

The key therefore to understanding why an anorexic sticks to her diet lies in the kind of attention, interest or fuss that is made of her for doing so and the fact that there is no other source of attention as intense. So who or what gives the anorexic this attention, the kind that makes her stick at being thin? What changes her life? What happens in her life to make her hold onto the appearance of thinness at any cost?

It took me a long time to work this one out because there are already many clichéd answers currently available: ''Being thin gives the girl special attention, more boyfriends;'' ''Being thin means the girl is accepted into the family. Like a tribal initiation ritual, being thin is being a 'good' person is being 'mature', 'grown-up' and so on.''

When a person is neglected, any attention at all, any port in a storm, will suffice to add a little comfort, a little direction to that person's life and behaviour. This bit of attention, this identification with something — anything — can take many forms. We have already heard what it was that finally pushed Sheila into anorexia; let us have a look at a broader selection of cases now so that you can get a fuller picture.

One of my patients was Clare. Her family was an exceedingly empty and depressing one, lacking even the vitality of the conflict found in the parents of most anorexics. Clare didn't so much set out to diet but simply over the months slipped into a dissociated world in which eating ceased to matter.

Some people, when they are lonely and emotionally or spiritually neglected, try to create a world to replace the one that offers so little. To do this, they take things they've seen or read, people they may have met in books, who seem warm and caring, and they think about them, searching for clues as to *how and why* it all happened. They are looking for a solution, a way out, and to do this, search for someone like themselves whose experiences help in a sense to 'explain' what is happening. Inevitably they blend family fictions about themselves (''You are special, talented and so on'') with fictional identifications (people they read about and whose qualities they admire) into an ideal fantasy world.

Clare was a great reader and saw herself very firmly as a kind of dying Shelley character; she found comfort in the great sad heroes and heroines of literature (and in authors too). The more she read, the more she identified with the role and the 'explanations' contained therein. Following the life of a chosen heroine gradually assumed an exaggerated role in Clare's life because it offered her, strangely, the only contact with the world outside her family that she'd ever had. For people like Clare, contact like this is the only way in which they 'meet' other people (in the form of characters in books) who have feelings and sufferings like their own. Because such feelings touch their own experience, so unexpressed and unformulated within them, all their caring and affection and devotion goes to these fictional people. For Clare, her characters were the only people in the whole world who 'understood' her. She could love them and know them, quite sure that they would love her and know her with as much devotion and caring.

Gradually Clare identified more and more with her heroines and heroes, and time spent reading (that is, 'being with them') became more and more important, more stimulating than time spent with her family and its pressures. Lost in this literary world, she was able to cut off from the unpleasantness and emptiness of her real world. The need to read replaced Clare's need to eat or get succour from her family. When she stopped taking her meals with her parents, she felt as if she had triumphed over her bodily self and was at last free from needing anything. Clare had had very little real love in her life. Her literary world was all she had and was all she ever was to have. By the time she was seen in hospital she was near death. She died after a week's struggle to save her.

This is an extreme example but there are many other cases which come close to this. In some cases that I have treated, I have felt the *relief* with which the girls fell into anorexia — it removed them from needing anything from their parents. Beyond a certain point, it is extremely difficult to help such cases. In one hospitalized case I was called in to see, by sheer coincidence I happened to have a copy of a music book by Stockhausen with me, belonging to the patient in question. The girl had much the same fixation as Clare, only with music, and Stockhausen was her god. Without that book and my nascent awareness of how fragile and difficult to reach these cases could be, I feel sure she would have suffered the same fate as Clare. Luckily, however, she saw the book and I saw her interest. Through this, I entered her world just long enough to help her abort her death drive.

The initial impetus, then, into anorexia, is given by the new-found identification or contact with another world. Often it is literate but it may be anything that vaguely touches on the anorexic's world or has meaning for her. One person I treated identified with a long-dead sister, the only surviving photograph of whom showed a waif-like mystical girl with long hair. Other identity figures have been relatives (usually distant and seldom seen). "You're just like your aunt Jessie" is the sort of favourite family utterance referring to a family black sheep who had 'character' or some other fascination for the family. It may be a film star or a fashion model. The girl identified with Mick Jagger of the Rolling Stones and read hidden meanings into songs and performances.

Some of the people I treated managed to delay a breakdown into anorexia long into adulthood because their fantasy world took on elements of reality. This is what Janet had to say:

> "I was at boarding school and got very into George Eliot. One of the teachers, a young woman who was very thin, reacted to this and we got very friendly and it went on for years — we both admired Eliot and wished we could have been like her. I lived my life through this teacher. Holidays were spent together and of course, my family liked her. She 'saved' me, if you like. But eventually she met a guy and got married. I couldn't handle their intimacy. I couldn't share her so we slowly drifted apart. I was very depressed; I realised I had nothing and there I was, in my twenties. I just sort of slowly collapsed and lost interest in everything, stopped eating and became anorexic."

Elaine had a different experience:

> "I was a pretty girl but very unhappy. I just spent my days day-dreaming about a wealthy older man who'd come and rescue me from all this misery. One did. A business

associate of my father's. I'd just begun to lose weight and I think I would have become anorexic at 17 when he proposed to me. I was horrified but it was my fantasy; it was also what my parents wanted and so I went along with it. It stopped my being anorexic and for the next few years, I thought I was happy. We had two children, servants, a lovely life. But a year after the birth of my youngest child, I was so miserable. My life felt so empty and I gradually drifted back into the spiral. After the excitement was over, being married was just like being at home. I became anorexic.''

What happens here is quite clear: the family situation leads the girl-woman into seeking some other form of succour or attention (literature, music, marriage) which in time leads to the neglect of ordinary needs and ordinary relationships and anorexia nervosa is the result. In cases I have seen where older women develop anorexia (sometimes over the age of 60), it is possible to see the reason quite easily: they have inevitably led sheltered lives since their teens — straight from home, like Elaine, into marriage, pregnancy and motherhood. It is only later, at menopause for example or when the children have left home or a husband has died or left, that the underlying pathology becomes apparent. There is then nothing else around to use as a support, no alternate life-style to the old demands of home. Believe it or not, in the few cases like this I've seen, these people had mothers or fathers still alive and still treating them in the same old ways.

By far the most common pattern though is that which has concerned us throughout: the teenage girl going into drastic weight-reducing diet in order to *be* something in the family at last, and thus control her 'childishness' and her child status. Almost inevitably, what pushes the girl into dieting are two simple facts: Firstly, nothing else has ever worked to change her status in the family; secondly, she has nothing else to try; everything else has failed. When all is said and done, the tight control exerted by the families of anorexics, the lack of contact with the outside world, the abnormal dominance and dependency lead only to one area of personal independence and freedom: how she performs her private functions — eating, sleeping, evacuating. In her eyes, she is a mess; she has tried to be disciplined in every other area and feels that if she can't even control her eating, can't lose weight and 'grow-up' and look like she should (in her parents' eyes), then she is really utterly worthless. It is her last chance, she feels, to join the human race.

SUMMING UP

One of the most important consequences for an anorexic of choosing to limit what she eats is that she chooses to cut herself off from one of the major sources of enjoyment in her life. In the anorexic's world, eating is Mount Everest — mainly because there is so little else to enjoy. She feels empty. Her parents' lives are empty and she is cut off from much of everything else in life. Moreover, in the families of anorexics, eating is one of the few reliably consistent actions the family engages in. Further, food is one of the major expressions of reward or affection or caring. It is one of the few avenues of communication: a parent wanting to regain the interest of a sulky child uses food to do so instead of either talking about it (forbidden, the family *never* argues) or physically making it up (equally forbidden: the parent must not seem to be in the 'wrong' or 'childish'). It is a vital avenue along which the anorexic's family's subtext is acted out.

The anorexic trying to diet does not, of course, cognitively acknowledge all this. To her, she is really trying to please her parents: to show maturity and discipline and to look good; and to control what she feels is the childish animal inside her. She thinks — as do many adolescents and as is encouraged by social and religious clichés — that the best way to achieve discipline is to deny herself pleasure. She has tried to change by doing other things, by denying other lesser pleasures, and now, with failure staring her in the face, she feels she must make a bigger sacrifice — a really big sacrifice: control her appetite.

I don't know whether many people are aware just how important eating is to an adolescent. Adolescents tend to have huge appetites. I certainly did. And, largely, this is because you need something immediate and quick to make your churning, awkward insides settle down for the next onslaught. If someone had tried to stop me eating as an adolescent I don't know what I would have done; it was like a drug. And I was by no means overweight. When adolescents begin to gain in confidence and actually start solving some of their problems, appetites begin to diminish and other 'goodies' replace eating as a source of enjoyment. For an adolescent, therefore, to decide to stop eating is an immense sacrifice, a decision not to be taken lightly.

The parents of anorexics, however, don't see it as this. To them the situation is very different and each parent reacts to it in a different way, according to the uses to which they are putting their daughter. How an anorexic's parents react at this time gives the definitive shape to the way in which the girl's anorexia will develop: whether it be of the starvation kind or the gorging-vomiting kind. In the next chapter, we shall see how this happens.

Chapter 6

How simple dieting turns into
anorexia nervosa or bulimarexia

As I said earlier, when you diet, your family diets with you. In this chapter, we will examine what happens during the course of the anorexic's successful attempt to reduce her weight through dieting. We will see, too, how the direction taken by each individual anorexic — be it to anorexia nervosa or bulimarexia — is conditioned largely by the reaction of parents and other family members in the first few months after the diet has begun.

THE EFFECT OF THE DIET ON THE FAMILY

While it is not possible to detail how every individual parent or every individual family behaves once *the* diet has begun, it is possible to identify the central patterns that create the various forms of anorexia we have defined. Bear in mind, therefore, that the patterns that follow are general and that they may and do vary from case to case.

Pattern 1: classical anorexia nervosa

In cases of severe anorexia nervosa, where there is eventually a risk to life, I found that the diet made very little difference to the family dynamics. In other words, parents of women with this resultant pattern seemed to notice very little about their daughter's lives, seldom commented on their actions and in short seemed disinterested. In some cases, patients remarked that they felt vaguely that their parents were annoyed in some way about the diet but only in the way they were annoyed about any change in household routine. Neither parent seemed to respond in any significant way. In a number of less severe cases of anorexia nervosa, I found that both parents commented on their daughter's lack of appetite or said that they were worried about it — but never in any convincing way.

Pattern 2: ordinary anorexia nervosa

In most of the cases of ordinary anorexia nervosa I saw there was a mixed pattern of reaction, with one parent — usually the mother — reacting to the diet by trying to get her daughter to eat, and the other — usually the father — either not noticing or mildly siding with the girl. What seemed to happen here was that the mother would feel resentful of her daughter's success at dieting, at her ability to resist food. Fathers, in contrast, seemed not to care one way or another but picked up their wives' disturbed feelings and resented them for one of two reasons: either because the concern of the wives took interest or attention away from the fathers' own eating habits (*father* is the one who is usually fussed over and fed); or, because the clash between mother and daughter disturbed father's peace and equilibrium. Let us take a look at all these reactions.

Mothers

Often, mothers of girls who became ordinarily anorexic had suggested and encouraged the diet in the first place. Sometimes this was because they themselves had problems with eating, and dieted from time to time. In short, they offered the cliché: "Diet and you will be saved". Sometimes the anorexic's mother would eat very small meals in public and the daughter, wanting to emulate her, would follow suit. Either way, once the diet succeeded, this encouragement disappeared because it threatened the mother's status and stability within the family's eating pattern.

Some mothers, it was clear, used feeding their families as a means of atoning for any accumulated guilt (bad temper, neglect and so on) from the day. If the girl refuses food in such a context, it may seem as a rejection of this atonement; the mother reacts with fear, anger and guilt, and angrily demands that the girl eat.[1]

Some mothers are unable to control their need for role stability and, while openly encouraging their daughter's diet, continually try to undermine it. When it comes to a matter of psychological survival in the family, they (the mothers) come first.

Other mothers resent their daughters' self-control. This may be because the mothers themselves cannot manage a proper diet, and cheat in secret. But often it is simply because the mother enjoys the power she has over her child and does not like the idea of any change in her authority, especially in the context of her relationship with her husband and other family members. Mothers of this kind tend to let their daughter's diet run on for a while and then order it to stop.

Now, while these consequences may seem more likely to crush the diet than encourage it, we must be careful to interpret them in the light of the context described in the last chapter. Then we will see that in fact these actions, of trying to force the girl to eat, represent a change in the girl's life. *They show that the girl has had an effect.* From a position of having little or no effect prior to dieting, the anorexic is now receiving the attention of her mother: unpleasant and anxiety-provoking perhaps, but nevertheless attention. Whether she eats or does not eat takes on a meaning; and meaning was previously missing from her life. It gives her, in miniature, some will of her own, some power of her own within the framework of her mother's domination.

In fact, this kind of minor power-game frequently occurs before the anorexia-inducing diet begins, but then the mother still has the power to crush the daughter's will and the status quo remains.[2]

---

1 Just as the anorexic's focusing on food hides an obsessive frenzy, so too does the mother's focusing on feeding her family. The daughter is simply copying her mother's pattern.

2 There is a history behind these earlier bouts, which are best understood in terms of the mother's psychology: we will come to that in Chapter 10.

There are two factors that help the anorexic girl finally to win out against her mother. First, as we've said earlier, in adolescence, children become much more aware of the world outside their families, in particular the world of ideas and fashion and other social phenomena. These offer a wide range of possible 'reasons' — good excuses — to help the girl to stick to her diet. We saw earlier how literature helped Clare. This was an extreme case, however. For most anorexics in adolescence, the popular female concerns with being thin, glamorous or food-conscious help them to resist the covert hostility of their mothers. They use the commonplace world presented by fashion and the media to back up their actions.

However, on their own, such images as are provided by fashion are seldom enough. In the extreme cases I have seen, fashion and being thin formed only a small part of the girl's fantasy world. People like Clare needed far more than just an image in a magazine; they needed the lives and actions of people they could only find in books or movies to replace the empty lives they led in their families. In ordinary anorexia nervosa, the images of fashion provide the superficial gloss on their rebellion. Nine times out of ten, I found, the real impetus to defy mother came from another source — a male figure. In most cases this was the father, but it could be a brother, an uncle, even a doctor. Whoever it was, I found that it was this male person's reaction to the girl's struggles against her mother that provided the real push into anorexia or bulimarexia. On one or two occasions, I have come across families in which elder sisters or female teachers served the same function, but always it was by playing the male role.

Fathers

Fathers tended to behave with disinterest or mild irritation to the earlier diets of their daughters. As I have said, there would be irritation because of the disturbance or because of a lessening of the attention he was used to. However, beyond a certain point — usually if the daughter was able to resist her mother's pressure (and her own) to eat — the father seemed to take a different interest.

For a start, he became interested in the possibility of having the daughter as an ally in an area that had previously been the domain of his wife. In the sort of families we are discussing, as was pointed out earlier, a great deal of covert conflict is expressed in eating between the parents — as much as between the children and them. Many anorexics' fathers use eating (their fussiness, etc) as a means of gaining attention, and much anger and conflict over domination-versus-submission is acted out and interpreted by each parent at meal times. When the daughter, in her father's eyes, begins to be fussy about her food, just as he is, he at first tries to crush her behaviour (as we all do in ways when we see others doing things we do but which we feel bad or guilty about); but then, when he sees her succeed in part, he starts to back up her behaviour, usually by agreeing with the girl's arguments, accepting her reasons and applauding what he sees as the deeper issues — discipline, self-denial, self-control and so on.

Now, how much support the father actually gives seems to be *the key factor* in determining whether what develops is ordinary anorexia or bulimarexia. However, the matter is quite complicated.

In ordinary anorexia nervosa, I found that the support given to the girl by her father did not last long and was essentially covert. In contrast, I found that the support given by thd fathers of girls who went on to become bulimarexic was far more substantial. It all depended on the intensity of the relationship between mother and father. For instance, in the families of daughters who developed ordinary anorexia nervosa, fathers would support their daughters up to a point. While in the families of both bulimarexics and ordinary anorexics the ebb and flow of security and possessiveness was inconsistent and unreliable; in the families of bulimarexics, the vying for the daughter's support formed a much more substantial avenue of conflict between mother and father. That is, unpleasant though it was, it was nevertheless more stable in its unpleasantness than in the families of ordinary anorexics. In the ordinary anorexics' families, the fathers tended to withdraw their support if the conflict between mother and daughter became too open or too rough. Further, they tended to challenge their wives by supporting their daughters only very occasionally. The conflict between these parents tended to be much more covert and passive. In short, ordinary anorexics tended to find themselves much more out on a limb, or on their own, than did bulimarexics in those crucial few months after the diet began.

For the ordinary anorexic, though, even this passive and unreliable support is sufficient to help her cling to her diet-ideology and to her appetite control. It is the combination of being a teenager, being keyed to a weight-loss-equals-happiness cliché, and being the subject of her mother's antagonism and her father's (albeit erratic) support that ensures that *this* diet actually works.

Now, once the diet is in progress, given the emptiness of the family, the diet's *success* has a very important effect on family members. It changes the structure of the family hierarchy and changes the focus, while, at the same time, it begins to chip away at the 'scapegoat' status of the anorexic girl. Under such circumstances, the previous pattern of conflict between the parents comes under much more stress. It can, and often does, encourage the father of the ordinary anorexic to be more consistent, more open in his support of his daughter. And this alters the previous balance and can in turn lead to the anorexic girl becoming bulimarexic. So let us take a look now at this third pattern.

Pattern 3: bulimarexia

On occasion, right from the start, a father will back up his daughter's rebellion against her mother. More often, however, the support comes only after a while. It need not always come directly from the father but it comes inevitably from a dominant male figure.

This is how Heather saw it:

> "I went on a diet. I could feel some approval from my father but not a lot. My brother was more open and more pleased. He come home from university and saw I'd lost weight, and he 'took me in hand', delighted that I had got over being fat and 'being a kid'. I loved it of course and adored him for it. My father saw how my brother was

closer to me (and he always believed every word my brother said) and he too began to take an interest. My mother just got lost. We wiped her out. I just knew I'd never eat like a pig again. I had it made.''

In a number of previously hospitalized cases I saw, the special attention came from a doctor. Jane told me this:

"I lost weight and went into hospital, went through several doctors until one in particular just seemed to like me. Later he said he'd been determined to rescue me, which of course he did. I think he found me attractive. I don't know. But he treated me as a person, as an individual; told me I was pretty and must just put on a little weight. I did (through eating and vomiting) just to please him.''

You may wonder why a dominant female figure, such as a female doctor, does not usually have the same kind of effect. Occasionally a dominant female doctor can get through to an anorexic, but more often the anorexic has unfortunately been keyed by her experiences at home in two ways to see her salvation in male hands. Firstly, she is indoctrinated into believing in the primacy of males; and secondly, she is mistrustful of females. Her only experiences are with her mother and it is the mother from whom she is trying to break away and it is against her mother's disapproval that she is persisting in her diet.

The important point is that the onset of the diet, the weight loss (remember, many anorexics, prior to their diet, needed to lose weight anyway and, as a consequence, look better) the age of the girl (13 plus) and her needs create the crucible into which any available male figure of authority will fall if he reacts appropriately: that is, take over the power previously held by the mother. Since it takes a great deal of insight not to fall into such a relationship or to manage it in the girl's best interests, you can see that it is highly unlikely that the anorexic's father will be able to interpret accurately what is happening to his daughter. What may surprise you are the numbers of doctors and male nurses who fall into precisely the same crucible as the anorexic's father for precisely the same reasons: their own needs and lack of insight prevent them from either seeing or tackling the problem properly. I have come across emotional contexts in hospital wards which exactly duplicate the anorexic's family pattern and which sometimes complete the job left undone by the parents. I have seen male doctors coerce anorexics to eat with subtle (and sometimes not-so-subtle) attention and affection in order to triumph over their female colleagues who were unable to get them to do so —thus taking on exactly the same role as the father. I have seen a hospital staff convert an ordinary anorexic into a bulimarexic because the conflict between (say) a female nurse and a male nurse, to gain the ward's and the doctor's approval, set the scene whereby the girl ate to please the staff in order to get out of hospital, but stayed thin by vomiting. The girl sensed the conflict and solved it her own way. Hospital wards, doctors and nurses can form contexts that are in some ways just like the home. So bear in mind that what I have to say next is not limited solely to families. You can enter a hospital with one form of anorexia — caused by your family context — and leave with another — caused by the hospital staff.

A note on dominant males

I want to recap a little here. As we have seen, the anorexic girl who goes on a diet is trying to better her state, to get more out of life, her family and so on. She is trying to do so usually in the face of her mother's opposition. Up to this point, she has been very much tied to her mother for most of her ideology about life and her role in it. Dimly inside her she senses that it has been less than perfect and that her mother's ways might be wrong. So far so good. Now for the dominant male, her father, her brother, a nurse or a doctor perhaps. Let us assume that it is her father.

For reasons that we will go into later, it appears that many of the fathers of bulimarexics have a set image of women and generally search for a relationship with women that differs from their relationship with their wives. This idealized relationship is not primarily a sexual one: they want to be a dominant and superior figure of vitality, wisdom and intelligence. They also want to be looked after in return for being this figure. Early on in their marriages, they may have had some of this role fulfilled, but by the time their daughters move into adolescence, they have become isolated and lonely: isolated from the outside world and from their wives.[1]

Most fathers of anorexics, by the time their daughters enter their own crisis, have intense needs for affection and attention. They are approaching middle-age having done little in life emotionally and some fathers may have even had affairs in the hope of capturing what they have never had. Most are very deeply female-orientated, seeking an idealised female figure, perfect in every way. Inside, they live in hope that one day their needs will be fulfilled.[2]

Into this comes the anorexic girl. Now at first glance it would seem unlikely that the average anorexic would meet these massive requirements — but hold on. In many significant ways the anorexic girl taps feelings and fantasies within her father which few other women do, or ever will do.

For one thing, most adult women frighten these men, the fathers of anorexics. They feel safe only in a submissive childlike way, or when they are in complete control. Normal women, including their wives, are a threat because they make normal adult demands: they are sometimes selfish, sometimes demanding, they seek equality, they think, argue and exist as individuals. That is, they want to be partners. What these fathers want, however, is a role, a fantasy, someone to be, to do, to exist purely for them. At the beginning of their marriage, most of them try to force their wives into this role by using social stereotypes ('obey your husband', 'let him be in charge', 'let him run everything' and so on) but these soon fail — very often because the fathers are ill-equipped to play their

1 As we will see in Chapter 10, anorexics' mothers, and especially the mothers of bulimarexics, tend to rebel against their maternal and female roles early on in their married lives and busy themselves outside, partly to cope with the overwhelming guilt they feel for not conforming to social standards and partly to feel a sense of personal achievement.

2 Do not assume that these men seek women like their mothers — that is, in appearance — or even that they seek maternal figures. They want something of what their mothers gave them certainly; but as they grow older, this becomes fantasized and mythicized, creating a fantasy woman with every conceivable quality: their mother plus sex, looks, social grace, sensitivity and so on.

part of the role: they have no experience, no training and often they tend to muddle through family or home tasks. In fact, a lot of the frustration felt by their wives towards them occurs because of this muddling through, and their refusal to let the wives help. Eventually the wives have to break out simply in order to get things done, but do this while paying lip service to the stereotypes their husbands insist upon and which they themselves have absorbed from society. They cook their husbands special food, fuss and engage in silly role-playing clichés, while in reality often themselves carry out their husbands role in the family and the world outside.

Such a man attempts to make himself secure in the face of this by adhering obsessively to roles, and by drawing his children round to boost him and protect him. He expects his children, especially his female children, to give him the support he does not get from his wife. Further, such a man tends to be wary and removed from his sons: as males they reflect his own problems. So by the time his daughter starts dieting in her teens, he is in most respects very much keyed to forming a dependency on her or someone like her.

Suddenly a plumpish child loses weight and begins to look like a woman, challenging her mother, upsetting the equilibrium of the family. Father sits up and takes notice. In addition, the child-woman needs affection, attention and interest. Father plays a double game: his regular adult and father stereotype and his little-boy-seeking-fantasy-woman stereotype. While appearing to support his wife on the one hand, he is secretly supporting his daughter on the other, subtly encouraging her to conform to the image he desires, the role he is seeking for her.

Think of how this affects the anorexic girl. She is fighting for her emotional life and after a long dependency on her mother, she begins to challenge her, to fear and mistrust her. Her father then notices her and is warmer, kinder, providing a valuable direction for her thinking and behaviour. She is grateful. Her father seems to understand her special needs. The anorexic girl, remember, has no awareness of the deeper issues and fixates on the overt issues which she thinks motivate her. She wants to be thin and attractive and both of these are important parts of her father's fantasy woman.

Her dieting, her neediness, her femininity, her helpfulness (she has been keyed to serving by her mother) and her gratitude blend very neatly with what he has been seeking. This cross-matching of needs ensures that the diet remains and that the anorexic girl makes a firm bonding with her father against her mother.

In nearly all the cases I saw of anorexics who later developed bulimarexia, most of the fathers welcomed the change in weight and eating habits of their daughters. Most of them thought their daughters looked better than before, were prouder of them and soon took pleasure in showing them off. They felt companionable with their daughters and took more notice of them, took them out and in fact sometimes preferred their company to that of their wives. This is what Maryanne had to say about her father:

> "Shortly after my anorexia began, I found my father began to want me to go out shopping with him. This was really incredible for me. He took me and showed me off to his friends and of course, I loved it. He used to want me to take his arm —which my mother never did — and then he began to buy clothes for me. He would take me into boutiques to try on clothes — you know, model for him. I think I was looking so much more sophisticated then, being thin and it fitted with what he considered a sophisticated woman should be. It swept me off my feet! Sometimes I felt more like his mistress than his daughter and you know, I think he really liked that."

This new development satisfied many of these fathers' needs, especially the need for companionship. It also gave them a power they had not previously enjoyed in the family — and a new relationship. The girl, well-trained as an acolyte, transfers her dependence from mother to father. He delights in this because he has, for the first time, perhaps, someone who adores him, does what he wants, listens to him and needs him and is socially presentable (often more so than his wife). His response is to permit his daughter a status, trust and intimacy with him that no one else has.

For the girl, all this attention and intimacy has tragic consequences and side-tracks her from her real problems. For a start, it reinforces her anorexia: in her mind, she believes that all this is consequent purely on her losing weight and staying thin — looking feminine. As an overprotected and needy person, the dieting anorexic is quite unable to see the new relationship for what it is, as a more experienced woman might. Moreover, she trusts her father and does not expect him to misuse her emotionally.

Moreover, it introduces her to a new dependency that is immediately more satisfying than her first, with her mother, but that, in the long run, is as hard to break as the first. She enters as it were, a new world: her father's world, a world of men. But she enters it at far too young an age and in a privileged way, with no experience whatsoever.

The male world is very different from the one she has been used to with her mother. The anorexic girl trusts her father and, by inference, men at large: they give her more than her mother did. They focus on looks and appearances which they reward with attention and something that the anorexic has always wanted — physicality. It is this physicality that seals the link between dieting and attention in the girl's mind.

The male world, as I have said, is a different one. Males relate very little to one another on the physical level. Unlike women, they show one another very little physical affection, focusing it instead nearly always on women. Encouraged by her contact with her father and her new looks, the anorexic girl throws herself into the world of men, inexperienced and unsuspecting; because of her untapped and unattended-to needs and her trust of her father, she seeks out men and complies gratefully with what men have to offer and with what they demand.

As a consequence, as soon as the anorexic girl goes out with men, she gets in one bound all the physical comfort she has long been denied at home — but she gets it in a sexual form. She cannot relate — talk, argue, discuss — but she can be an acolyte and she can give her body.

The anorexic girl is a child, wanting child comforts. She is passive, conforming and obedient, quite unable to play boy-girl games or to manipulate relationships properly. She gives the man what he wants and what, initially, she thinks she wants — physical contact. Most of my anorexics who became bulimarexic reported long series of relationships with men (or boys) in which physical contact often formed the only basis for the relationship because they were unable to relate properly and were unable to experience sex as simply sex. They wanted a child's physical contact and, getting sex instead, the relationships rapidly disintegrated.

Many anorexics have scores of bad relationships in which nothing seems to work, nothing is satisfying; they drift from one to the other, do as they are told, hoping that the next one will be 'it' — will solve all the problems. After all, that is what the girl has been told by her mother and it is what she believes because of her trust in her father.

Some girls do actually 'make it' with a man. There are as many disturbed men around as there are women: men who want a fast physical way out of personal involvement. The only result is to delay the inevitable and side-step the deeper issues, by now really deeply buried away. Other girls become involved with careers or with special relationships with men — bosses, married men, even therapists — that fulfill them in similar ways for a time.

The real difficulty is that all this camouflages the underlying pathology and in some cases makes it impossible for the anorexic ever to straighten herself out. For one thing, it is so easy to convince yourself that you are doing all right; for another, there is very definite and clear happiness or satisfaction to be gained in some of these relationships and achievements. All of this makes it very difficult for the girl to see that the symbiosis with men in general is both pathological and almost inescapable. A bad relationship with a man is simply rationalized: "It was just that one—wait till I meet Mr Right." It is a familiar attitude and one which society helps you to believe in. Very few people seem able to see that 'having a man' can sometimes be as unhealthy as being stuck without one.

Of course, these developments take time. You do not just start a diet, find your father responding favourably, go out with men, have sex, all in the space of a few weeks. These things can take months, sometimes a couple of years. Sometimes the anorexic is hospitalized in between, or gets married, or wins a beauty contest, or a scholarship or whatever, but the important fact remains that, over time, the kind of process described above takes place and in the manner and for the reasons I have described.

The needs of the father and how he resolves them places the girl in a fix and the men she later meets make the fix inescapable. The magic that locks the girl into her obsession with staying thin is the *attention* from father and the physical contact that he and other men give her. Once this attention becomes a central part of the anorexic's life it is only a matter of time before bulimarexia develops.

HOW GORGING AND VOMITING START

It is important to realize that all the above is laid, as it were, on top of the already well-established patterns of both existing family behaviour and the individual anorexic's habitual behaviour. That is, these new developments do not emerge as a new and powerful event in the anorexic's life, much as she may see them as such. They possess the same ebb and flow, the same instability and insecurity as the well-established patterns laid down earlier. That is, when the father begins to give his daughter attention he does so sporadically, often covertly. Much the same applies to boyfriends and doctors: in the eyes of the anorexic, while their attentions are welcome, they are seldom enough or all-encompassing. Remember, she is trying to kill that empty child-space inside her; she wants someone who will take over her mother's role and more — look after her completely, as if she really were a child. In reality, no one person can meet these demands.

The consequence of this is that often, the anorexic, after some experience with men, literally has to go back to mother. If a father or a boyfriend can replace mother, as can sometimes happen in an early marriage or in a divorce where the father has custody of the girl, it is unlikely that either bulimarexia or anorexia nervosa will occur for a time. However, it is more often the case that male interest in the girl, be it from father or boyfriend, has to co-exist with the established mother-daughter relationship. What happens, then, is that after an initial 'honeymoon' period with father and/or boyfriend, a depression sets in when the girl realizes that the hoped-for Utopia is not going to materialize. She stays on the diet but begins to find her appetite harder and harder to control. If the onset of her father's or her boyfriend's attentions is not in itself reward enough, the girl's control begins to wilt. She is afraid of defying her mother for too long and afraid of giving up for too long one of her few solid pleasures and securities — eating. So she is caught between two extremes: her mother and her system of behaving, thinking and being, and her father and his system. The girl feels this as a battle between her new adult self (or rather, the specific direction or meaning of 'adultness' she has received from her father) and the child-self within her that she soon learns to identify with her mother and her system. To eat is to be the child again. Not to eat is to be the adult woman. Both lead nowhere. Both are empty and unfulfilling. But both are necessary because both parents exist and have given these shape and direction. She knows no other life.

What happens in the practical sense is that there is, after a time, a relapse in which the girl breaks her diet. She gives in to her appetite or to her mother's cajoling to eat. When a diet is first broken, there is a tendency to over-eat — to cram in all that has been missed, straightaway. It is like crying after a long period of stress: you break down in floods of tears. The anorexic girl gorges. Then she is faced with a full, extended stomach. She may also feel nauseous from all the food and anxious at what she has done. She has not only broken all her resolutions and shown herself to be weak and ill-disciplined, but she may put on weight, she may get fat. In her terrified state, she thinks that this will mean the end of her relationship with her father and with men. Ergo, she must vomit. Physically she wants to vomit anyway. So she vomits and, hey presto, everything is back to normal; she will not get fat.

Naturally for a while she feels upset, ashamed of herself and what she has done and she vows not to do it again. Certainly she is not going to let anyone know what she has done. However, pretty soon, things on the outside upset her again and she is greatly tempted to eat again. She fights it, but then thinks, "Oh well, I can eat, I'll feel nice, then I'll bring it all up." It strikes her that the idea leaves her the best of both worlds — her mother's security and her father's attention. Slowly she falls into the pattern of gorging and vomiting. She eats and she stays thin. She pleases her mother and she pleases her father. Moreover, in a deeper sense she has won a major victory for herself: she is free of total dependence on one parent, she gets more out of life and above all, she is in control at last. She can cheat and survive. She can be both a baby and an adult in a way that is under her control and which no one can take away from her. This is the condition we call bulimarexia.

ACTIVITY CYCLES IN ANOREXIA AND BULIMAREXIA

In a significant sense, bulimarexia is a cyclic activity: you eat and then you vomit. It is rather like encapsulating the whole of the anorexia nervosa conflict (having an appetite versus controlling it) into one ritual. There is first a period of massive eating and then a period of deprivation (vomiting). It replaces, or condenses, the pre-anorexic's cycle of trying to diet and failing and then having to return to her previous pattern of eating.

In ordinary anorexia nervosa that does not end in either starvation or bulimarexia, a similar cycle develops over time. That is, the anorexic girl alternates between periods when she eats normally and periods when she is anorexic, when she does not eat and approaches starvation.

So, to sum up, we can identify four outcomes to the anorexic crisis:

1. Return to normal (temporary anorexia).
2. Anorexia nervosa continued until death (classical anorexia nervosa).
3. Periods of anorexia nervosa alternating with periods of normal eating (ordinary anorexia nervosa).
4. Cycles of gorging and vomiting (bulimarexia).

It is, of course, possible to have variants of all four as well as cycles within cycles: that is, for example, periods of bulimarexia alternating with periods of normal eating. In my experience, however, a period of ordinary anorexia nervosa and even classical anorexia nervosa must precede bulimarexia. It is very rare for bulimarexia to lead into anorexia nervosa.

Chapter 7

Taking stock

In most cases of typical anorexia and bulimarexia, the patterns described in the last chapter form the basis of adolescent and adult development. That is, once a serious eating-dieting or vomiting-gorging cycle has been established, the consequent life-style of the girl or woman revolves almost entirely around these cycles. The adolescent girl grows up, completes school, starts a job or goes to university, has affairs, gets married, rears a family — just like anyone else. But underneath it all lies a deception. The real core of her personality and her proper development as a person, making proper contact with other people, ceases once she becomes anorexic or bulimarexic. It is easy in our society to survive in appearance but very difficult to survive emotionally. Open up an anorexic's life and achievements and look behind the façades and a very different, often tragic story emerges. What then are the consequences of becoming anorexic or bulimarexic?

The formal consequences of becoming anorexic or bulimarexic are by now fairly well-known. Death through starvation is clearly the most serious, but there are many others: malnutrition, loss of periods, constipation, circulatory problems, hypothermia, blood pressure disorders, to mention a few. And each gives rise in turn to other disorders. Constipation, for example, due to the change in diet and eating habits, often gives rise to laxative abuse, which in turn can lead to such things as chronic diarrhoea, abdominal pain and other problems of the colon. Similarly, poor circulation can lead to skin problems. The dried-out, rough skin cracks and becomes a source of irritation that is easily turned into a major skin disease by scratching. Frequent vomiting leads to massive and fast-working dental decay necessitating major dental work. This in turn is almost immediately undone by further vomiting. Epileptic fits and even some deaths have been reported during or after vomiting bouts.[1]

Not surprisingly, each of these effects helps to absorb the anorexic's time and energy so that simply dieting or simply gorging and vomiting becomes — with their side-effects — a full-time occupation. Eating, preparing or avoiding food, trying new diets, going to the dentist, to the physician, buying pills from the chemist, taking laxatives, seeing dermatologists, keeping warm, hiding a skinny frame, hiding vomiting — all this ensures that any private time for reflection or self-analysis is quickly swallowed up by being an anorexic or a bulimarexic. All this helps to build walls around the victim which, when taken together with the family's régime and the limited contact with the outside world, ensure that the anorexic never sees beyond her private rituals and the social rituals she engages in. The child inside her, the real casualty of all this, is silently and systematically buried under the weight of problems compounded by other problems.

To my mind, the formal consequences, are only the superficial manifestations of the deeper, more widespread damage that is really done to that once-growing child inside. We tend unfortunately in our society today, to focus far too much on appearances and not enough on the depths beyond them. When it comes to understanding anorexia in the case of society and parents, or in the case of doctors and anorexics themselves, to explaining and treating it, anorexia and bulimarexia are seen in terms of their symptoms and their appearances, rather than the deeper damage to personality existing within the victim.

I have heard doctors arguing that if an anorexic's weight is normal, she is normal. I have heard more sophisticated doctors arguing that if only the vomiting and gorging in their bulimarexics would stop, they would be normal. I have heard

---

1 A full discussion of these consequences can be found in P. Dally and J. Gomez, *Anorexia Nervosa* (Heinemann, London, 1979).

parents say, "But she goes out with men, she's done well at university — she's a qualified doctor or architect or whatever, she's normal, she doesn't behave strangely in public." I have heard anorexics defend themselves and their rituals with, "But it doesn't harm anyone, least of all me. I don't beat up old ladies or take drugs, I don't even look neurotic." All of these statements are only partly true. The better socially adjusted the anorexic or bulimarexic, the harder it is for them, or anyone else, to see what is really wrong. Anorexics and bulimarexics who belong to the professions, such as doctors, architects, lawyers and accountants, find it easier to ignore the real issues because socially they get by, hiding behind the protection from life that these labels provide. Married anorexics and bulimarexics with children and with a profession to boot, are very difficult to convince that they may have a major flaw in their personalities.

The point is that anorexics and bulimarexics can do things in life and appear to be normal without ever really getting the benefit of a deep or proper involvement. What I am saying is that anorexia and bulimarexia are illnesses of involvement both in life itself and in personal relationships. The anorexic is there in the flesh only — her mind and her existence are elsewhere, locked away. Once committed to using anorexia or bulimarexia, the anorexic is committed to a shady and hollow contact with life where only the forms of living are engaged in. The real world and all its challenges, enjoyments and fears is vaguely felt 'out there' but the moment it encroaches, the moment a challenge or a real anxiety appears, waiting to be solved or tackled, the anorexic retreats into ritual to cocoon herself — safe from normality. So long as things appear to go smoothly, seem to be controlled, so long as the anorexic feels on top, then there is a calmness. But the moment inadequacies are exposed or intimacies become demanding, the anorexic runs. If the pressures become too great, she will shut off, change jobs, change partners, all to avoid facing up to herself, and all the while using her ritual to support her — to give herself comfort in the only way she knows how.

Dieting or gorging and vomiting are child-like methods of producing self-comfort. In adolescence, anorexics discover other methods of producing self-indulgent comforts: masturbation, for example, bathing, buying clothes, presents, little goodies for herself. All are used to create things to look forward to, such as eating, to block off the anxiety, fear, depression and loneliness. Most people, especially teenagers, use these things for a time in the same way, but for the anorexic, life becomes a frenzied round of working, dieting, gorging, vomiting, buying, and worrying.[1] When normal teenagers are learning about being with a boyfriend, for example, and going through the agonies of learning to trust and feel safe with a man, anorexics or bulimarexics are hanging onto their rituals and focusing on what they must appear to be in order to keep their man happy, or rather, just to keep him there, a security. Their rituals remain their focal point.

I have laboured these points because in the rest of the book, we are going to look at what can be *done* about anorexia or bulimarexia, and it is vital that you see clearly what the key issues are. It is very easy to over-simplify the problems involved and especially easy to focus on the wrong ways of going about treatment, or self-help. It is not just a matter of putting on weight or stopping anorexia or stopping gorging and vomiting. It is also not a matter of learning a new vocabulary about yourself or 'understanding' what has gone wrong. Real change, real recovery means to *be* normal. That means not that you must look normal or sound normal or do normal things, it means you must go through the same growth processes that a normal person goes through, meet the same challenges, cope with the same crises, even if it means going back to being an adolescent, or being 'immature' to do it. To be normal is something you have to earn not something you just get or simply grow up to become. And let me explain straight away that I believe very few people are ever really 'normal' naturally — that is, few people manage to grow up properly without a struggle. Most people — and I include myself — grow up trying to run away from ordinary challenges, ordinary living. It takes a lot of courage and discipline to be normal; precisely what that involves we will go into soon.

When an anorexic decides to get better, or is encouraged to

1 Most anorexics are insomniac because they go over, endlessly, their performances and find they cannot get off to sleep. See my book, *Insomnia and Other Sleep Disorders* (Sphere, London, 1982).

do so, there are a lot of choices open to her as to how to go about it. What I shall do in the next chapter is to examine some of these avenues of treatment and self-help and guide your thinking about what constitutes actual recovery (which I will go into), but these are specific goals; how each individual achieves them is up to her. Whatever an individual does, however, has a shaping influence on his or her behaviour and since this is a survival guide, I am going to tell you what the various options for treatment are and where, in my opinion, they help and where they fail.

I am including this information because anorexics or bulimarexics will have already tried various forms of therapy before bothering to buy this book. It is important, I think, to know about the values and limitations of the therapies available, firstly because they can shape your behaviour and secondly because if you choose to do standard psychotherapy — such as psychoanalysis or behaviour therapy — it is as well to know something about them. Indeed, in some of the stages of achieving proper recovery, you need help from someone and it is as likely to be a doctor or a self-help group leader as anyone. Contrary to popular belief, some doctors will listen to their patients' demands and if you are forearmed with the appropriate knowledge, you can often encourage your doctor to help you better than he or she might otherwise be able to do. As I will argue later, *relationships* are the key to new learning and recovery in all forms of mental illness, and your doctor is as liable to form a useful relationship with you as anyone is. It is up to you and your doctor to ensure that it really is a useful one.

Chapter 8

Standard forms of help

Some people (few, I think, and mainly teenagers) recover from anorexia with very little trouble, often without even needing help or a book of this kind. Sometimes a kind word in the right place, a helpful friend explaining things, parents coming to their senses and seeing the stress their children are under, an older brother or sister providing the right support — any of these things can push the anorexic into joining 'the gang', the mainstream of adolescence. Sometimes parents, through upset of their own take stock and improve their relations with their children. Sometimes a few chats with a doctor, a psychiatrist or with someone with experience can help a parent or an anorexic child unload a whole set of emotions and anxieties which helps to alleviate the crisis. Some treatment methods are based entirely on this, holding that anorexia is a reaction to the kind of unexpressed emotions that occur, for example, the death of a relative or after some unpleasant shock. Once the person has released the pent-up feelings by crying, breaking down, mourning or whatever, the anorexia subsides.

These recoveries — though undoubtedly genuine — represent a small number of cases. For most anorexics, the problems run much deeper and Lady Luck is less favourably inclined. Recovery for these people takes a lot longer and is less easily achieved.

When I first began treating anorexia, like most doctors, I focused on the main symptoms of the illness — the anorexia or the bulimarexia itself — and tried to encourage the patient to give up the ritual and return to normal. I used two basic approaches in current use: first I started to give reasons why the patient should drop the ritual and encouraged her to give it up of her own free will — that is, I tried to get my patient to have *insight* into her condition and then to do the right thing. If that did not work, I applied pressure through one of several behavioural techniques whereby I used positive reinforcement (approval, attention, kindness) if she stopped vomiting or dieting and negative reinforcement (disapproval, lack of attention, coldness) if she did not. These techniques are really the mainstays of conventional approaches to anorexia and bulimarexia and most methods fall into one or another of these categories. Sometimes only one is offered, sometimes both are used together. Medical treatment in the form of drugs, shock therapy or other techniques comes into the picture in important but marginal ways, usually as an accompaniment to either the 'insight' or 'behaviour change' methods. Medical help is vital in severe cases.

MEDICAL CARE

When starvation has gone too far and your medical health is threatened, when you face doing serious harm to your organs, risking death itself through starvation or the risk of infection, then you — or those around you — have no choice: you must be hospitalized. In hospital your life can be saved. This involves various medical treatments — force feeding, saline drips — that will be given to you in an attempt to save you. Once you are out of danger, it is usual for the physician to call in the psychiatric department of the hospital to help you.

BASIC PSYCHIATRIC TECHNIQUES

In general, the psychiatric department of a hospital offers drug therapy in the first instance. That is, you will be put on to a tranquillizer in order to help you cope with your upset (if you have been a serious medical case). Some hospitals issue drugs of one form or another for even mild (non-medical) cases of anorexia on the grounds that once calmed and anxiety-free, you are in a better position to examine your life. Other hospital units do not issue drugs as a matter of course and wait to assess your particular case to see whether or not you will need them. It is general practice to give support and guidance in addition to other treatments but sometimes, especially in busy units, this is very brief and of little depth.

The drugs used to calm you are largely of the minor tranquillizer variety with few side effects, and they generally work well in the sense of making you feel pleasant. In some hospitals, stronger drugs are used and here the main effects and side effects are more severe. Major tranquillizers and certain of the anti-depressant drugs really knock you out and you feel as if you are floating on air; you are calm but feel very removed, very lethargic and out-of-touch. The side effects need watching; amongst other things, they can cause constipation (a problem if you are also over-using laxatives) and can make you dizzy and disorientated. I think you will appreciate that these side-effects and the feeling of loss of control over yourself and your body can be very frightening, especially to the anorexic who puts a premium on stability and self-control. This fact, together with the fairly well-proven fact that drugs do not change personality, makes their use, in my opinion, of dubious value. When you stop taking them and leave hospital, you are back in the same *milieu* with the same problems.

Most psychiatrists and psychologists recognize the limitations of psychotropic drugs and they use them only in the beginning to help you over the stress on a temporary basis. As soon as possible, you are seen either by a psychologist or a psychiatrist, (sometimes both[1]) who give you some

---

1 A psychiatrist is a medical doctor who specializes in psychiatry; a psychologist has at least a master's degree and has completed a two year hospital course in clinical psychology.

idea of how to restructure your life to help you overcome anorexia.

The kind of help you get varies. Sometimes it is little more than a friendly chat with advice about not starving yourself again or that you must stop vomiting or else. Many outpatients get 'supportive psychotherapy', but again the quality and value of this varies. In essence, the doctor tries to keep you going by encouraging you, giving advice and so on, but in some hospital departments this is limited to about ten minutes a week if you are lucky (after a wait of two hours).

Some hospital units offer much more, however. In addition, it is possible, by going to a private doctor, to be referred to a private psychiatrist or a psychologist who may also offer more substantial help.

INSIGHT PSYCHOTHERAPY

Much of modern psychotherapy stems from the work of a few very prominent people such as Sigmund Freud, C.G. Jung, Carl Rogers and Erik Erikson. What they separately believe is that the 'causes' of mental illness vary but their methods are all essentially the same. That is, the therapist talks to the patient, explains what is going on, and generally encourages the person to see how or why her illness (in this case anorexia) developed. The patient is encouraged to think things out for herself and then to change her behaviour accordingly.

An essential part of psychotherapy is the relationship you form with your doctor. Different orientations give this major or minor status depending on the role they believe the therapist should take. Psychoanalysts, for example, followers of Freud and his earlier disciples, believe the therapist is there to help you work through the problems you have with your own parents. So he or she allows you to be angry with the therapist, to love, hate or need him or her and so on — the idea being that as you show the emotions, the therapist will explain where they come from and what they mean. You are then expected to use this insight to understand your personality processes more clearly.

Other psychotherapies tend to minimize this 'interpretative-transference' role and more or less give you support, encouraging you to think things out, try them out and so on. They support you in the hope that you will see the error of your ways.

While these techniques sound good (and undoubtedly make sense) there are many problems attached to their practice. For a start, they have been generalized, I think, far beyond their original focus. Freud and Jung for example, wrote about fairly specific conditions and developed their ideas empirically — that is, by trying to create a framework and a method that helped the specific people they saw. Once their ideas had become movements, however, doctors who had trained in Freudian and Jungian ideas tended, in fact, to practise in quite the opposite direction; that is, they tried to fit every problem into the framework that they had been trained in, rather than fit the framework to the problem.

I, for one, value the ideas of Jung and Freud immensely; philosophically and theoretically they were extremely perceptive observers of the human condition. But I would hesitate to use their ideas out of context — to try to twist a new problem (and anorexia is a new problem in many aspects) into an old framework.

As it happens, I think abstract and standard insight therapy has very little use in the treatment of anorexia mainly because it has no specific theory or method for anorexia. Nearly all the anorexics or bulimarexics I have seen that have been treated by insight approaches (including some of my early cases) have one thing and one thing only in common over non-treated anorexics: they are all able to talk much more fluently about their illness. They know the jargon, they know all about anorexia and what causes it or how to treat it, or rather what their doctors think causes it. But they remain anorexic because their therapy has consisted almost entirely of discussion alone.

One of the biggest problems faced in any form of psychotherapy is that it relies enormously on the ability of the patient to transfer the insights and ideas or language learned with the therapist to the outside world. Many patients cannot do this. They make good patients in the sense that they do and say what the therapist wants, but only within the confines of his or her office. Psychotherapy of the 'insight' kind only challenges a person's verbal world, and there are many classes of mental disorder that do not respond to it. Anorexics are highly verbal people, highly articulate, intelligent and pleasing. But most of their lives have been built on being able to do only this — to please. They respond to any discussion in the appropriate way — but that is all. They agree to things one moment, knowing they will never do them. It is a pattern they have been used to in their families all their lives. They know no other. Standard insight therapy, I believe, simply compounds this tendency, encouraging a false complacency about being in therapy. Anorexics learn a psycho-jargon — not how to get well.

There are psychotherapists, however, whose personalities allow them to be more empirical, more flexible in the way they perform their jobs. Sometimes you may be able to see one of these people and make some headway. Here the relationship will count and you as a person will matter, not the particular theory of therapy involved. It is also as well to warn you that some therapists make excellent livings out of doing long-term therapy without actually doing much for you. You cannot blame them; they are in business like many people. But it is as well to be aware that doctors are human beings and it is very tempting — in the words of one of my colleagues — "to sit back, let them chat away while the money piles up".

BEHAVIOUR THERAPY

This second of the major techniques once again arose out of the work of a handful of prominent people, some of whom you may have heard of: I. Pavlov, J. B. Watson, Joseph Wolpe, B. F. Skinner, H. J. Eysenck and Arnold Lazarus. Its main base lies in learning theory, which in turn is derived from animal experiments designed to find out what makes animals behave the way they do. Classical conditioning (as with Pavlov's dogs), operant conditioning, reinforcement, rewards and punishment, token economies, these are all terms from learning theory used to explain how and why we do things. For example, we stop at traffic lights because we are *conditioned* to do so. We eat because the feeling of food going down *rewards* us and reduces our drive for hunger.

Behaviour therapy started off in South Africa where a psychiatrist named Joseph Wolpe began to try to cure patients of phobias and anxieties using a method he had perfected on animals. Called *reciprocal inhibition*, the practice involved first thinking about the feared object (say, a rat) linking it to a good or pleasant response (relaxing) and then touching the feared object. The idea is that you can relearn your way out of old fears.

Since then, of course, behaviour therapy has exploded into hundreds of directions with people controlling, or treating, virtually every known mental disorder by varying conditioning reinforcements, by rewarding, punishing and so on. Let me tell you how you are likely to meet behaviour therapy.

Most behaviour therapy is conducted in hospitals, either in wards or on an outpatient basis. In anorexia nervosa, one approach in particular has gained favour with many doctors, and that is the selective rewards system. You, the patient, are encouraged to eat (in order to put on weight) by the use of certain deprivations or rewards. Thus you are liable to find yourself locked in a ward without a television, visitors, books and so on unless you eat; you get a reward (a book, say) for every significant bit of weight you put on, until, hey presto, you achieve normal bodyweight. It is a very effective method in that few anorexics fail to achieve the criterion — putting on weight in that hospital. However, it has massive drawbacks. For one thing, it is often temporary in its efficacy; research in the United States has established that numbers of hospitalized anorexics conform simply to get out of hospital. For another thing, it often may be the very impetus an anorexic needs to push her into bulimarexia. Lastly, it often involves quite marked hostility and personality conflict between the patient and the staff which, along with the shock of hospitalization and the discipline of the régime, distresses the patient.

The point is that where all else fails and there is risk to life, then clearly such techniques have their place — but only for a certain length of time; then they should be superseded by deeper and more individual work.

There are other more pleasant ways of meeting with behaviour therapy. One form, for example, attempts to teach you new assertive skills and encourages you to try them out at home and on the outside world. Other forms concentrate on conditioning the starvation, the anorexic's phobia to food, by using much the same methods as Wolpe initiated, gradually getting you used to the touch and feel of food and so on.

Often you get a thorough mixture of behaviour techniques being applied: assertive training, personal support, deconditioning, reinforcement and the like. There is a lot of good in behaviour therapy: I used it (and continue to use it) extensively, not in the formal senses that I have described here, but in the same way that I have used psychoanalytic techniques or other insight therapies: to help me achieve what seemed necessary in the empirical reality described to me by my patients. I found re-learning, conditioning, reinforcement and so on very powerful tools if used for each individual, specific to them and not in a generalized way.

What troubles me is that behaviour theory has led to a sense of simplicity amongst many behaviour therapists; I find they think about mental illness very shallowly and that they grossly overestimate their techniques and their ability. Behaviour therapy journals are marred, in my opinion, by countless research reports and experiments, in which sometimes quite shoddy and piffling techniques are claimed to cure every known mental illness. I know because I have contributed to these journals and have had fights in them over just such issues.

What worries me is the ease with which degradations are sometimes heaped upon patients in the name of science and behaviour therapy. Here are a couple of these treatment régimes reported by patients. The first is the experience of a 15-year old patient:

> "I was given the following ritual to perform if I vomited (I was an outpatient at a hospital, living at home): first I had to vomit in a plastic bag which I had to keep in my room for three days afterwards, opening it every day to smell it (punishment). Second I had to burn a £1 note (punishment). Third, I had to fill out a questionnaire on how I

felt. Fourth, I had to write a three-page essay on what I'd done wrong.''

If she did not do these things, her doctor threatened to discharge her from his care. The second report is by a 19-year old hospital patient:

> "I was locked in this room (at the hospital) and given three meals a day under constant supervision day and night. The light was never turned off. If I vomited up my food, I was made to eat it."

You can picture the circumstances under which these admittedly extreme régimes are imposed: desperate to get the patient 'better', angry and frustrated when the textbook approaches do not work, it is so easy to lose track of the fact that the model might be wrong or wrongly applied. So the doctor simply steps up the punishment. I have seen the same thing happen in mental hospitals where I have sat and heard doctors justify massive doses of drugs, hundreds of shock treatments, simply because their patients have not responded to the standard levels. It is so tempting just to turn up the electric voltage when giving shock to a difficult person. Who is going to complain? Who has the right to complain? Certainly not the patient, who often has no legal means of making his complaint heard. Others are discouraged by convention the rest of the time.

Try to be aware of this tendency — that is, the tendency to push one method too far — in most of the professionals you may come across. There are some terrific practitioners, but there are also a lot of mediocre people who seem more willing to sit back and see you suffer than they are to get off their backsides and reassess you, their methods and their own personalities. Be warned. If a person is decent, he or she will be decent irrespective of whether they are a psychiatrist, a psychologist, behaviourist, psychoanalyst or whatever. Do not throw away your judgement just because you are expected to trust a professional. Some cannot be trusted to help you. There have been instances known of behaviour therapists who have been more intent on getting cases published and thus earning a name for experimentation, than they are with helping you. Others are determined simply to get through masses of cases per week.

OTHER FORMS OF HELP

There are, today, many ways of getting organized help from non-medical sources. You can try, for example, hypnosis, yoga, meditation and so on. None of the various groups who practise these have, to my knowledge, organized programmes specifically for anorexia or related eating problems but there are individual practitioners who work well with anorexics, and I know of some anorexics who have had some help from transcendental meditation groups, yogis and hypnotists. However, it is hard to evaluate these specific groups because there is no general theory to examine, nor set ways of doing whatever it is that each group does. My own feelings are that any effect will be due to the quality of the contact made by the individuals involved, and the degree to which a person can translate the ideology involved into real change in his or her behaviour. Since there is no specific programme, it seems likely that achieving real change would be a very difficult task. Unfortunately, I have found in patients who have joined such groups that the beneficial effects tend to disappear after the patient stops attending. Hypnosis in particular is vulnerable to this since its power lies in suggestibility and the personality of the hypnotist; if you make contact, well and good — but if not, nothing happens for you. There is also something else. Real change comes about through constructive individual relearning. Change brought about through someone else's power of suggestion tends to diminish the role of the patient. When *you*, as an individual, have worked at something and done it for yourself, consciously, you are more likely to be able to exist without the people who helped you. Hypnosis, psychotherapy, psychoanalysis, all work through a relationship, but not always thoroughly enough. The true mark of recovery is that you can keep going with your new learning after you have stopped your consultations. What worries me about things like hypnosis, yoga and transcendental meditation as they apply to anorexia (and only in this regard) is that to know anorexia properly, you must have researched it specifically, specialized in it, treated many cases, and so on. In short, you have to be thoroughly familiar with the whole field. Few medical practitioners, psychiatrists and psychologists are fully competent in this respect and I think with non-medical practitioners, this is even more the case.

SELF-HELP ORGANIZATIONS

Quite separate from the above are the various movements which have appeared in recent years specifically for anorexia. These tend to be well-informed and up-to-date in the information, advice and guidance they offer; and, of course, they draw on the experiences of people with anorexia. Here is a list of those I am aware of:

> *Society for the Advancement of Research into Anorexia* (S.A.R.A.)
> 'Stanthorpe', New Pound, Wisborough Green, Billingshurst, West Sussex.
> This organization concentrates on providing information about anorexia and research into treatment and prevention.
> *Anorexia Aid*
> The Priory Centre, 11 Priory Road, High Wycombe, Buckinghamshire.
> This group focuses on giving advice and support to anorexics, their families and friends, with the aim of helping to overcome the anorexic's isolation.
> *The Women's Therapy Centre*
> 6 Manor Gardens, London N.7.
> This centre runs discussion groups for women in general and offers short-term theme-centred groups on anorexia and a range of related conditions.
> *The Spare Tyre Theatre Company*
> 86 Holmleigh Road, London N.16.
> This company works closely with The Women's Therapy Centre and focuses on compulsive eating.
> *The Anorexic Counselling Service*
> 3 Woodbine Terrace, Leeds 6, Yorkshire.

Where these groups help best, I think, is in the encouragement they give to the individual anorexic to help herself. Some of them offer discussions, grouped or otherwise, and counselling. For someone wanting to work for herself they can be a valuable support during times of crisis and the early stages of trying to get better. Do not, however, expect them to cure you or to do everything for you. What I like about them is the fact that at the moment, they are the only organized form of the kind of co-operative effort that I believe should be happening in anorexia — namely, that in which doctors and patients get together to pool their wisdom and information.

There may be other forms of help that I have left out but the ones mentioned here are those you are most likely to come into contact with.[1] Again, if you do use any of them, do so with your eyes open and with some determination to help yourself as much as possible.

---

1. I have not gone into family therapy here because it is not much practised in the U.K. MacLeod (1981) provides a good, critical review if you are interested.

Chapter 9

The logic of self-help

Standard therapies sometimes work and sometimes do not. Sometimes, as I have tried to show, they complicate matters. This alone is sufficient reason to believe that an individual must be well-informed, must try to help herself. There are also other reasons.

First, modern psychology and psychiatry still have a long way to go: not only in the sense of getting the research done that will really open up our understanding of what goes on in families and in individuals' minds, but also in the sense of accepting that society, families and individuals are much more tightly interwoven and interdependent than they are seen to be at present. A psychotherapist who really wants to help must take note of all three and try to work at all three. Thus, if I, as a doctor, can see what any given individual is doing to create problems for him or herself, and I can see how the family contributes to maintaining his or her behaviour, and I am also able to see where society is to blame (through its conventions or institutions or political practices), then to be truly scientific I should have the right as a scientist to investigate each and to try to change each where necessary. As things stand at the moment, psychiatrists and psychologists are only really able to concentrate on one aspect of the full matrix which creates the 'mental problem' — the individual. And even then, the doctor is limited in how much he or she can do. Societies are not only slow to change and inevitably require mass movements to do so, but they also do not like being investigated too closely. It is all very well to study society formally and make criticisms of its formal structure but the heart of real social behaviour lies behind the scenes — the informal, person-to-person contact that enables each social institution to run — be it political, business orientated, educational or financial. These networks are almost impossible to penetrate yet it is through their structures that ideas, attitudes, moral standards and standards of behaviour (the framework in which individuals grow up) emerge.

We all know how we heave a sigh of relief when we read about the 'bad old days' in history books, about slavery, child labour, imperial wars, atrocious working conditions and so on; we are relieved that times have changed and that these previously socially tolerated ideas have passed on. But in 50 years from now, people are going to say the same about the present. Even today, we are critical of the mid-1900s. Imagine how much more useful it would be if we could actually research our societies properly *now* and make the changes *now*. Think of the many individuals who might be helped if they did not have to fight social mores or prejudice as well as their families and their own pathological selves. At another level, families are still able to hide behind half-truths simply because they are embedded in unexamined social conventions and rituals.

Psychiatrists and psychologists have only marginal rights to try and change individuals' behaviour; they have almost no recognized rights to work properly on families or communities. Not just in the legal sense but in the sense of having cultural approval for it. We have only recently recognized the right of individuals to have mental problems and to have psychological treatment for them without being considered insane and thrown into mental homes or socially ostracized. There is still a stigma attached to mental illness.

When I had been in practice for four years, I realized that the only way my patients were really going to be helped was by my building an environment for them in which they could work together and go through the correct learning necessary to recover. I had tried to work with families, tried to work within ordinary social frameworks, but they were never enough; far too much is involved in mental problems. I did not create a community, or a hospital or a 'freak-out' joint, but rather a way of doing therapy and a place in which each individual could go through whatever was necessary while working and living normally outside, being part of a community or family and so on. It was essentially individual and self-help orientated, teaching a person how to survive 'out there' and how to focus on their own problems and their own therapies without being distracted or side-tracked by families or social issues. What I write about in the next chapters comes from my work in this way with anorexics and bulimarexics. I did not find answers but I found the roads to be taken that may of course, in time, reveal answers.

There is a second reason why you should consider self-help. At a fundamental level, the anorexic's problems and her reactions are about surviving as a personality in the face of massive indifference and neglect. Her actions, in a way, constitute a search for truth or reality while caught in the web of lies and contradictions she sees in her family, in the society around her and in herself; her ritual and her anorexia are the only ways she has of doing something for herself. To purge and vomit or to be thin are the only truths in the anorexic's life that are under her control and that give her satisfaction, albeit marginal, in any form. She is cut off and isolated from any other forms of reality or modes of action. She is not free to be herself, to be a person; she is constrained by her family, conditioned to behave in very narrow, stereotyped ways, to live in fear of the 'outside' and to fear deviating from her parents' values and dictates. As a result, she is totally dependent on them for what little security she has. The only way she can be someone is through her rituals. She knows that if she gives those up, her life as a person, as an individual, ends. So she clings to them, lives in and through them, emerging only to do the necessary to get by outside. They become her life-raft, the centre point of her existence.

In this, paradoxically, she is right. She really does know best. Yes, she is damaging herself; yes, she could die or do herself irreparable harm. But the alternative for her is to give in and be nothing. It should be clear by now that the heart of the anorexic's problem, the tragedy of her life, is that she has been exposed to her parents' pathology in the worst possible way. It is one thing exposing the full weight of an adult's inconsistencies and contradictions to another adult; an adult has at least some power, he or she can fight against it, laugh at it sometimes, tease, even undermine — simply because he or she is needed (as a wife or husband) and can manipulate that need. To expose the same demands to a child is to commit emotional murder on that child; a child has no rights, has no real power to manipulate or coerce and worse, is totally dependent, totally helpless against the weight of viciousness and anger that is turned on her if she disobeys. As I have said, children often do get exposed to the very worst of all human emotion. Their rights as individuals need protection and care. In anorexic households, this does not occur; the child is traumatized beyond belief and used and exposed to the pathology of both parents. Only when she becomes anorexic is this terrible experience halted or modified in any way. For her, to give up the ritual is to return to that childhood state of terror and anguish and humiliation. Unlike psychotics, who are usually only vaguely aware of the abyss beneath them, the anorexic girl knows and has always known. Jane's report shows this clearly:

> "I knew all along, from eight or nine, that it was all wrong. I knew my parents cheated. I knew they were phoney. But if they were, so was I. I had to help them, to do what they wanted, to bolster them. I was terrified of what could happen if the world ever found out we cheated and lied and found out how weak my parents were (and how weak I really was). After years of this I had to break out, I couldn't pretend any longer. But there was nowhere to go so I got thin and then I got my ritual. I saved myself. All along I was humiliated. I was disgusted with myself for how they were and how I was. But I could never ever do anything real about it."

For the anorexic person there can be no turning back, nor any going forward.

The important thing here is that in choosing to be anorexic in the first place, the girl is doing something to *help* herself. Later if the purging ritual begins, the anorexic girl is again trying to help herself. This time, often against both her parents' and society's (doctors and hospitals) attempts to coerce her into submission. Survival means, for the anorexic or bulimarexic girl, to help herself. Eventually she trusts only herself after trying desperately to trust her parents, their ideas and those of society.

The point is this: think of the little teenage girl who becomes anorexic. Think of the energy and power she pours into helping herself in the only way she believes (and has been taught) will help her and her family. She really tries to become a person as she understands it. And yet, what do the families do? What do some hospitals, doctors and members of society do? They *act* to help; it is true that they recognize the distress, they write and otherwise publicize information about the problem, but what they focus on is *stopping* the girl from being anorexic or bulimarexic. They do not focus on the background nor the context; they expect the girl to stop her actions, and then, with a pat on the back, to rejoin her world and simply carry on. In short, albeit for the best of reasons, they try to crush the girl's own attempts to help herself. They try to crush the only part of her life that she considers her own, her only individuality. They take her life-jacket away.

I include myself in these criticisms. I too tried to take away the 'bad' things in anorexic women in the same way that one operates to remove a cancerous growth. I did not mean harm but it was only when I knew more that I was able to see that it was the wrong way to approach the problem. And, incidentally, it is the reason why so many anorexics or bulimarexics go 'secret', leave hospitals supposedly cured or fool their therapists and so on, precisely because, just as they resisted the efforts of parents, so they can learn to resist the efforts of doctors.

Where I turned things around for myself and my patients was by realizing that if you make self-help the key and you build on it and with it, you change the whole pattern. Instead of the therapist being someone to be manipulated (like a parent) or fought against, he becomes someone from whom information and guidance is sought. But more: if, as a doctor, I stopped fighting the anorexic's desire to binge or vomit, I would then be able to make use of that massive energy, that pent-up creativity and drive, originally focussed on food and eating, and use it to push my anorexics into the kind of growth and learning experiences that they should have gone through as teenagers.

This may sound easy but it was not and is not. It was not just a case of saying to my anorexics: "You have a right to your pathology, it is your individuality — go ahead and eat or do not eat, as you choose". This misses the point somewhat.[1] The rituals are the keys to the anorexic's or to the bulimarexic's personality and growth and I believe that unless the person is in a medically serious condition, they must not be stopped initially, as such. They have to be opened up and explored, to expose the child underneath. Then the child and the child's needs have to be worked with and the rituals deepened and broadened so that the personality inside can grow and become part of the full adult person the anorexic is. And this, in time, means that the ritual must fall away and be replaced by other better interpersonal rituals (as opposed to isolated anorexic rituals) just as happens in normal people.

I hope you understand the logic here. Self-help is vital. Most anorexics know this and actually try to help themselves but they do so from a bad position. All the anorexic girl knows in the real world is how to form a symbiotic and acolyte-type dependency on whoever takes notice of her. She knows no other way of behaving. Outside of her ritual, therefore, her attempts to save herself are not only restricted, but damaging. As we saw earlier, the anorexic can only shift dependencies, first from her mother, then to her father and then generally to men outside the family. Each new person in the anorexic's life is seen by her as a potential saviour and latched onto. Each new man (particularly in the case of bulimarexics) is seen as a marriage hope and grabbed at. When these shifts bring no change and the real person (the child) is still locked away in the ritual, a further shift is taken towards anyone who seems even remotely able to show caring. Thus you get an anorexic who tries marriage in the hope of solving her problems. It works for a time but because the ritual is never unlocked or changed, the basic depression, the feelings of ugliness, uselessness and inferiority, persist and gradually erode the relationship. Many

---

1 This kind of philosophy is, alas, one of the features of 'pop' psychology found in the United States and in Britain.

of the older bulimarexics I treated had sought their salvation in men first, then had given men up in disgust and formed relationships with women and then in turn had given them up for men again in an endless cycle of seeking someone to help them.

Each such relationship fills in time and helps to hide what is really going on: namely that the anorexic is only doing what is always done — accepting conformity and the role of helper to make her feel important but never getting anything purely for herself.[1]

It is clear, therefore, that while anorexics need help and do try to help themselves, most of their contacts with the outside world offer little help; they may even compound their problems and make them even more dependent on their rituals, and as time goes on, more determined to simply carry on as they have before.

How, then, can anorexics be helped? Or more appropriately, how can they be helped to help themselves? And, more relevant here, how can a book of all things hope to provide a survival guide?

As you can imagine, I gave this serious thought before setting out to write this book. What I have been able to do for anorexics has been done through intensive, long-term therapy in which the closeness of the relationship between me and my patients helped more than anything to repair the damage. How can this relationship possibly be transferred to a book?

The answer is simple and practical: I have not set out here to duplicate in a book what I do in therapy. Instead I have tried to lay down a full appraisal of what you have to do to your life, to change it, and to focus on the real problems in order to truly help yourself. Further, since many anorexics and bulimarexics do not seek psychotherapy and do try to help themselves, it occurred to me that I should really say "Good luck" to you; give you an idea of what to do and some advice and guide lines to help you on your way.

Since I believe that relationships are the key to most human

---

1 Interestingly enough, nearly a quarter of the people I saw with anorexia or bulimarexia were in the 'helping' professions. Many were doctors, psychiatrists, psychologists, social workers and charity workers.

learning anyway, be they with a mother, a father, a doctor or a lover, and since there are thousands of apparently normal people around who live through relationships with almost as much pathology as do anorexics, it also follows that if you knew what to look for in a relationship and what should be happening to best help you, then you would be able to direct your relationship better and get somewhere on your own. Maybe you could even get further than so-called normal people.

So, where to begin? Well, one very crucial way to begin is to try to get a perspective of what anorexia is and how it comes about. This, I hope, you will have done by now. Reading through the previous chapters should hopefully have opened your eyes a little. The second part of that perspective, however, is to try to understand far more about the world around you, first your immediate world and by that, I mean your family and your siblings, and secondly, about the big, real world beyond that. You need an insight into what was being covered up, what was really going on between your parents and your siblings. I will tell you why. Inside you, you know or sense the mess your parents were in and perhaps your brothers and sisters too, but you do not know for certain. As long as they can cover up their real pathology, you will continue to mistrust your instincts about them. If you are uncertain about them and do not know whether or not to believe your senses or their clichés-cum-lies, you will treat yourself with the same uncertainty. If you find out that your parents really are inadequate or afraid of the world, you may be unpleasantly surprised but at least it is a base on which you can fight and build. If, however, you sense that they feel inadequate while they pretend to be terrific people, coping well, you will feel confused and trapped. Worse, you will feel much more inadequate because you fail in life and you think that they do not. Knowing that they really do struggle but just cover it up at least gives you the satisfaction of knowing that part of the reason you fail is because you have been taught incorrectly by them. That knowledge *frees* you to go out and try it a different way — to use your own instincts and ideas for a change instead of theirs.

So a lot depends on you learning about your world, learning to trust your instincts and being brave enough to get out there and find out how to live for yourself.

This leads us to the next step. You need to know something about what constitutes normal development, what life is really like, what normal adolescence is all about. So in the next chapter, we will first look at your parents and siblings and see what it is they were covering up (and how society helped them to do it). Then in the following chapter, we will look at what you have to go through to be normal.

These are essential steps to be taken *before* you try to stop your rituals. You must be more aware of what is going on to begin with, otherwise you will make mistakes. Once your eyes are opened, however, you can begin to look at yourself more deeply and especially at what lies behind your rituals (within yourself) and what to do about them. In the last few chapters, we will explore them and talk about the way to use relationships to fill your needs and how, eventually, your rituals can be stopped.

"But," you will want to know, "what is all this based on? What are your theories, your methods?" Good questions. So here is an overview of how I did therapy and how I understood anorexia. It will help to explain, I think, the next few chapters and show why it is that I stress *not* trying to stop the anorexia and bulimarexia immediately and why I focus so much on relationships as a means of survival.

MY OWN WORK

In my clinic I blended a number of techniques in order to achieve a single end — to ensure that the anorexic could be put through the right learning so that all the childhood and adolescent experiences omitted in her upbringing could be completed. I used the power of the intimate and deep relationship between doctor and patient — as described in psychoanalysis and psychotherapy and as minimized by behaviour therapists — to give my patients the kind of context (symbiotic and secure) in which they could feel safe to be little, to be childish and adolescent, no matter what age they were. Then I used the power of behaviour techniques (environmental control, structured relearning, rewards and punishment) to build the necessary emotional and social environment in which their learning could take place. In short, instead of using the psychoanalytic relationship (of transference and dependency) to develop insight, I used it as a means of making my patients feel safe and as a way of coercing them into going through the terror of their new learning — of keeping going, sticking to their tasks, keeping on the road. I became, for a time, their parents, ensuring all the things that should have taken place. Once the new learning had actually been done, the building up of individuality and independence (based on the new learning) were allowed to occur naturally. Insight was encouraged in relation to all the new things that were happening.[1]

There were a number of important steps in this programme that characterized the various aspects of relearning that had to be done. I will give only a brief overview here because each step is dealt with in a later chapter. I had one golden rule: do not stop the rituals. It was the one sure way of losing the patient, of ensuring that her individuality died or was pushed down. So for a long time, early on in psychotherapy, my patients' rituals were sacrosanct. The following explains why.

Rituals are the only way that an anorexic and a bulimarexic have of behaving that are absolutely in accord with their internal realities. The anorexic's rituals are a reaction to her life circumstances. They are all that is real to her and so they should be to whoever helps her. For a therapist or helper, they are all she or he has to build on. Imagine you are towing a doomed ship in a stormy sea. If you cut the tow rope, you have lost it. It is the same with the anorexics' rituals.

The rituals are all that is left of the anorexic's childhood. They must be preserved, broadened and deepened rather than reduced. Inside every anorexic is a beaten child, almost crushed out of existence. The anorexic has been taught to hide that part of her, to see it as ugly, dangerous, threatening, demanding. It is the part of her that is separate from her family

---

1 Initially, psychotherapy meetings were solely on a one-to-one basis. When key stages had been reached, group and fellow patient contact was added in to provide support and opportunities for social testing-out of what had been learnt in individual psychotherapy. Later still, working outside — with parents, friends, jobs — was introduced and carefully structured as tests to ensure a smooth transition of the 'new' person into her full life.

— her only form of privacy. It is the part that cries, whines, grabs and eats and vomits, masturbates and scratches; it makes a noise, pities, sees tragedy, loves, shows need — all the things it has been forbidden to show. Above all, buried in the rituals is the residue of all the true feeling and thinking of the anorexic.

The rituals are disturbing symptoms of mental illness, but their meaning must be seen in the context of the person experiencing them. As such, we need to look at what is inside (or underneath) them; not, as is current practice, what the symptoms mean to people who are not experiencing them. The symptoms are harmful and socially distasteful, but to remove them in order to ease the discomfort of those around the anorexic (the family, doctors) does nothing for her, inside.

Every anorexic is looking for someone to *care* for her. She is like a lost child seeking her mother. To care means to listen to the meaning of the rituals, to attend to the 'baby' inside her. Practically, to care also means not to impose, not to make your demands on the person so that she has to attend or listen to you instead of herself. A large part of early treatment in my practice was to watch, listen and record. No attempt was made to change or to cure, or even to treat for that matter. The very words, "Let's see what we can do to stop your vomiting (or whatever)" are like a knife in the anorexic's heart. Yes, she would love to be cured and please her parents, but inside she shudders. Underneath the frenzy of the rituals are a lot of feelings, thoughts and ideas; by listening you can hear them (feel them) and then you can begin deepening them and later, broadening them.

DEEPENING THE RITUALS

It would be easy to believe after reading the above that the rituals of anorexia are sacrosanct — never to be touched — but this, of course, is not actually the case. The rituals are signs, symbols of things within. Once established as that and listened to, they must be opened up and deepened as the first step to changing them and bringing them into the rest of the personality. In practice, this means a number of things.

Firstly, each part of the ritual has to be probed. Underneath each is a whole set of deeper feelings, half-buried in the anorexic's mind, which in turn have to be exposed; that is, first felt by the anorexic and then experienced and thought about.

This is how I put it to my patients:

"As you go about your normal day, your consciousness — that is, what you think, feel and talk about — is a very much reduced one. There are a whole range of feelings — instincts, moods, ideas — that you ignore. They are there but you do not attend to them because you have never had to — or have never been shown how to. Being keyed to others so much, you think only as you expect they would. The only time you think for yourself (or do anything for yourself) is in your ritual. And there your consciousness is radically different. It is also narrowed, but at the other extreme: you focus on your body — again, another external aspect. In this (very limited) consciousness, you are only aware of acts and feelings, of you as a reacting person. As you starve and eat, or binge and vomit, you are doing something to yourself in a certain way and for certain reasons. There will be obvious current reasons — what it was on a particular day that upset you — and also, old residual reasons. In the ritual — that is, what you do to yourself — you are acting out on yourself the anger, upset and fear you felt during the day, using a pattern you've long used. When I talk of deepening the ritual, I mean learning to dwell on those intermediate feelings and then to build in ways and means of expressing them. Let's say you felt humiliated during the day. Most bulimarexics would simply wait for the first opportunity to perform their ritual — go out, buy food, stuff it into their stomachs then vomit it up. Each of these steps carries out a function for the 'child' inside; deepening the ritual means becoming aware of the functions and their relationship to the things in the environment that caused them. Thus when you are humiliated by someone, you feel hurt and upset, misunderstood and frightened by someone being angry with you or stronger than you. You also feel upset and angry with yourself for being beaten, which usually means not reacting properly. That is, inside you have a whole range of fantasies about what you'd like to have done but were too afraid to do. Your rituals are in part your way of acting out these feelings in a passive safe way.

"Look at them: buying food and clothes are a waste of money and an extravagance — values which you flaunt and in so doing, make yourself feel just a little powerful; you're getting your own back; forcing food down (punishing yourself violently for being weak, for being frightened, humiliated, hurt), eating it lasciviously (mouthing, chewing, swallowing) — all serve the same function. For the bulimarexic, vomiting it all up later is the cleansing part in which with one bound —superman becomes Clark Kent again — you return to normal. That is, you vent your hurt, anger and frustration in private and then, also in private, comfort yourself, apologize and return to the fray.

"If you are anorexic, the same is true of the elation you feel at someone else having to eat while you are supremely indifferent. In therapy, a big part of this phase was for my patients to *share* all this with me. Most anorexics don't admit the links to themselves — that these are the feelings that run parallel to the ritual. It is too frightening to think about them. So they block these thoughts with the actions of the ritual. It is too frightening to think about them, also upsetting and depressing; better simply to *do*. In fact, in a very fundamental way, anorexic rituals survive because they block those upsetting, depressing and humiliating feelings that trigger it all off. You simply can't stand them, you feel you'll explode, go mad, break down. The first part of deepening your ritual involves being aware of this and feeling that volcano within you. The second part involves learning to live with it, bit by bit."

Within their rituals, anorexics are acting out a deeper and broader family ritual which has the following chain of progression:

1. The child experiences upset, caused by someone or something outside the family.
2. The child begins to express upset normally.
3. The parents register this distress; it starts off their own

ever-present distress which they immediately attempt to block by

4. Stopping the child from being upset by

5. Invoking the family stress ritual, which involves retreating from the world, denigrating those responsible, boosting the family's superiority etc. As a last step

6. The child is encouraged to lie down, relax, have something to eat to distract it from being openly upset.

You can see that a normal act of distress — for example, crying — is the thing that seems to cause the trouble. It triggers off the family ritual of coping, with all its trauma, and it triggers off parental distress. The anorexic learns in time to eliminate step 2 (normal crying), and also to try to eliminate step 3 (parental distress); so she jumps straight from step 1 to step 5 and 6, reassuring herself with the family ritual in private so as to upset no-one.

In therapy, my patients had to see that they needed to recreate a trust relationship with someone who could perform the lapsed parental functions of giving comfort and allowing normal emotions to flow. These normal emotions, blocked for years, are the volcano you feel inside you, and in therapy it was usually me who acted as the emotional catalyst to link steps 1, 2 and 3 together.

To go back to the humiliation example we started with, the anorexic had to learn to recognize how upset she was, and to feel the volcano by turning to me to allow herself to feel the emotions as and when they happened. By putting myself in the gap between the time at which she was humiliated — at work or at college — and then rushing out to perform her ritual, my patient would learn to add an extra dimension to the ritual — a deeper one. My patient would have to call me — usually by telephone — to tell me what had upset her and what she felt. Once that was done, she could go ahead and perform the ritual. I found that this simple act forced my patient to begin to feel the volcano within herself. Sometimes there was a tremendous resistance to doing this, to sharing the ritual in even a small way but inevitably, as time went on, I would not only hear a verbal account of the distress but would encourage my patient to *show* the distress — over the telephone if necessary. The telephone, incidentally, in the beginning was a very useful instrument for my patients because it was impersonal — a step from talking about being upset to becoming upset and then having to be upset with someone there (me). It was a longish process; but by lengthening the time spent on the telephone before getting lost in the ritual, the anorexic deepened her consciousness both of what she felt and what she was allowed to do and say to me. By allowing her to perform her rituals as well, the links between the insights and the new learning *and* the ritual were strengthened. I found too that, over time, the act of getting upset with me would occasionally replace the ritual. Once or twice, I tried to push things by suggesting that the anorexic should omit the ritual and just come and be upset with me, but I found it was not a good thing because, as I later learnt, we actually needed the ritual at that stage for a full recovery. People who cut off the ritual too soon, pretty quickly slipped back if left alone and, more important, they lacked a central vital emotionalism.

All this may seem quite simple and straightforward, which in many respects it is. There is little that is mysterious about understanding how to cure mental illness; the problems usually come in actually doing it or getting it done. Everyone understands the links between being overweight and having heart problems or between smoking and lung disease. The solutions are very simple: do not overeat, do not smoke. However, the act of achieving this is massively difficult — very few perfectly normal and intelligent people can actually do it. The reason is that, hidden behind smoking or over-eating are whole chains of habits, whole questions of personality, locked into place or reinforced by circumstances and society. Seen through the eyes of an excessive eater or smoker, the short step to health is like a minefield of torture, a nightmare of deprivation and torment. Similarly, if you are anorexic, taking these short steps may sound simple, but they are really massively difficult. In my clinic I soon learnt to understand what held my patients back, but it was a while before I saw how vital it was to focus on the actual act of taking the necessary steps. That was the really tough part for me and for them.

This is where I used conditioning, withdrawal and reward —all behaviour techniques. I had to coerce my patients to phone me or see me, to *say* what they felt, to be upset, to cry and so on. And I did it by being angry, by refusing to see my patients if they would not do what was necessary and so on. I would be warm and kind if they did do it — cruel to be kind. But it was the only way in which my patients learnt to see how vitally important the steps were. I was real — they often said they saw the links but would not perform them, would not be *real*. I was there to make sure they did.

Clearly my patients were helped by having me to coerce them to do these tasks. Their relationship with me held them together. But there is no reason why someone armed with this book as a guide cannot achieve this for herself — either with the help of the people in her life to whom she feels close, or with the help of a professional of one kind or another.

BROADENING THE RITUAL

Before the rituals can be modified, the insights, feelings and ideas gained in the process of deepening them have to be given a life of their own. Having learnt to recognize the emotional precursors of the rituals, that is, both in the immediate sense of being humiliated, for example, and in the structural sense of how they all came about, you have to go on to do something with them. In the process of deepening the rituals, my patients learnt to be upset, to express distress and be comforted with me, which effectively brought them back to the childhood phase of normality. This, however, was still a secret and private activity, albeit broadened to include me; the rest of life went on as before. In the stage called 'broadening the rituals' my patients had to learn one key thing — to *act* on their new feelings in the safety of their relationship with me; in other words, to broaden the rituals to include a whole range of new behaviours linked very closely to those expressed covertly in the rituals.

Again, straightforward as it may seem, it was tough. Look at the vast range of emotions locked inside the rituals: anger, hurt, viciousness, defeat, power, pathos and depression; anorexics know how to express these only through their rituals. Frequently, I had to teach my patients how to cry, how to be angry properly, how to feel self-pity constructively, how to hate, how to be depressed — everything. All these emotions are vital to the survival of normal people. Depression, humiliation, anger, frustration, tears, these are not simply the prerogative of neurotic or mentally ill people. Far from it. Normal people have to learn how to do these things too, and to do them properly; to be able to cry uncontrollably, for instance, to cry discreetly, to cry with happiness, in anger or sorrow — there are many different ways of crying and each has to be learnt because each is a vital part of being able to form private, personal relationships. It is no use crying uncontrollably with someone whom you cannot trust. It is no use crying in sympathy when it is not what you really feel. Knowing how to cry, and when and with whom are all essential ingredients for healthy living. Not crying at the right time, for example, or crying in the wrong way, can actually do harm.

The same goes for other emotions — anger for instance. Anger is a major emotion, a vital component of your psychological defence system. You must know when to be angry in your own defence, when to move anger from a verbal to a physical level. You must know when to be gently angry, when to use passive ways and when not to and so on. Contrary to popular opinion, depression is another vital component of living. You have to know how to use it, to control it, how to fall into it and what it means and so on. Depression is often necessary under stress to force you to attend to your feelings. In some circumstances, your body forces you to be depressed so that you can rest your mind. This applies as well to anorexics, who tend to avoid depression through all kinds of hyperactivity.

Yes, living is complicated. Anorexics, like many other people, believe that to be normal means to be anxiety-free, to find life smooth and calm. But this is not so. Normality means to cry a lot, to laugh a lot, to be angry a lot and a whole range of other things.

Some of my patients were afraid of the sound of their own voices: they had never shouted, screamed, cried or raised their voices in anger. They were terrified of hearing any form of emotional distress, let alone their own. In broadening their rituals with me, they had to learn to do all these things. The important point is that by doing this with me (or with someone else), these feelings are given a right to exist. When someone accepts these feelings, sees them as normal, you do not feel so alone, so isolated. You begin to feel normal, you begin to discover a whole world existing that you had previously ignored or avoided. I found that some of my anorexic patients began to read books that they had previously shunned because of the emotions involved. They also began to seek out experiences of anger and other emotions by going to movies or joining groups they had avoided in order to watch in fascination how other people do things. The perennial 'put-down' (the 'sneer') begins to lose its edge.

My patients generally learnt about all this in the security of their therapeutic relationship with me; but I had a number of married women anorexics to treat, or single women in deep relationships with other women or men. It was possible to use the security of these relationships, once both partners understood what had to be done, to achieve this broadening behaviour.

Once a strong basis of acting-out some of the emotions ordinarily tied up in the rituals was under way, other aspects of the rituals had to be examined and built up as a preparation for the next step — shifting the rituals. Within the rituals, a range of fantasies and wish fulfillments usually coexist quite apart from the range of feelings previously described. Anorexics daydream a lot about being superior as a solution to their problems; being thin is just one such intermediate fantasy — part of a daydream based on the supposition that "If I am thin and beautiful and intelligent, some fantastic, rich and successful man will come along and marry me": the trouble with these fantasies is that they actually guide the normal activity of the anorexic; nearly every patient I treated was continually on the look out for someone like this and spent wasted hours of waking activity and energy on daydreaming and watching for 'Mr Right', to the extent that all sorts of games are engaged in — trying to arrange an accidental 'bumping into' the chosen man, for instance, or having affairs without recourse to morality or sensitivity. In the words of one patient, "I decided to take my boss away from his wife and I spent two years on it.

I succeeded but I soon got bored and I left. I felt no compassion, nothing. It was me or her. I needed him." She had a long record of doing this.

There is nothing wrong with having fantasies but they should be achievable and be related to personal abilities. Some anorexics unfortunately do get their fantasies fulfilled, and find it actually puts them back because the fantasy is inevitably used as a means of gaining an easy solution to all the inadequacies inherent in their personalities.

Before any attempt can be made to attack the rituals themselves, these fantasies in anorexics have to be disbanded and attached to a whole range of attainable and useful fantasies, linked to the new behaviours they are learning.

Again, this is not a very mysterious process in therapy. Instead of wasting her time on relationships and fantasies of little use to her, the anorexic has to concentrate on the emotions within her rituals and those within her daily life. In therapy, each upsetting situation can give birth to a whole set of specific-situation fantasies which in time can be *realistically* acted upon. It is much more realistic to fantasize about shouting back at your boss, walking out or giving notice, than to imagine that the managing director will marry you, and it is more realistic to fantasize about sexual power games with your boyfriend to punish him for something he might have done to annoy you, than to fantasize about getting Mick Jagger to pick you up. One key tactic I used in the situation of being upset in the office was initially to get the patient to fantasize about crying and breaking down to make someone (the boss) feel sorry and guilty. Making people feel properly sorry and guilty is one thing anorexics are terrified of doing openly — much better, they think, to do it in passive insignificant ways and attract passive and insignificant feedback.

As the anorexic's rituals and emotions deepen, they create a new source of energy (the volcano of emotions). This is acted-out slowly through the anorexic being taught how to express the emotions in simple ways — anger, tears, proper depression and so on. The next step (played with in the safety of psychotherapy) is to link the volcano further to the big outside world. To do this, you need relationships. My patients learnt to be more emotional, to show their feelings — for the first time with me, but then they had to move on to doing much the same thing with other people, not strangers or mere acquaintances, but people in close, personal relationships with them.

BUILDING UP RELATIONSHIPS

Briefly, the tasks involved in building up relationships are geared to making the anorexic *be* what she is. The danger, relative to other people, is that anorexics try to hide what they really are both from others and from themselves. Thus to a boyfriend, they will be what he wants — sweet, responsive, sexy or whatever; to her boss the anorexic will be a doormat and so on. When anyone sets out to build proper relationships, whoever they are, they need to have people around who will see them and accept them as they are and give back something of what they need. You need a boyfriend who sees you as you really are — that is, if you are anorexic, as a growing child or teenager and very raw. You need someone who will grow with you, who will take and respond to your emotions, who will play with you; someone who will let you hit him (or her), cry with him or her, who will wrestle with you, shout at you, and with you, and so on, all without turning each situation necessarily into lovemaking or into 'laying a trip'. You need people around you who will compromise with who you are and will help you and let you help them.

Learning to cry at the time someone upsets you, learning to be what you are (a terrified little girl) and to show your feelings — all this opens up whole new dimensions for you: you become more normal and of course, more 'human'. By being upset more openly, for example, you elicit a different reaction from people and you begin to see people in a different light too. This is normal adolescence.

You will be growing tired of simply tossing off these huge tasks. Yes, they *sound* simple — but here is one I believe really *is* simple. One problem with the current myths about living and relationships is that many people pretend to be a lot healthier emotionally than they are. When I was a teenager I really thought that most people were 'together', happy and neurosis-free — unlike me who was moody, disgruntled and so on. In time, I discovered that people pretend, and that many many people are only too glad to drop the cover and reveal the pressures inside: to be 'little', to go back to childhood and learn to be comforted, to explore, experiment with life and people and so on. They do not, of course, want to do this in public; they want to do it in private — which is why I place such emphasis on private relationships. There are many men and women today — especially amongst the younger generation — who want to explore relationships more fully, who want to look beyond the sex and grown-up stuff to deeper issues, to proper emotionality, proper adulthood and proper growth. The tragedy of our era is that far to much time is spent publicly on directing our attention away from the search for proper intimacy. As a clinician, I was constantly surprised and gratified by the number of people who wanted better relationships with their partners and were prepared to go further than the stereotypes with which they had grown up. What was important for my anorexic patients was for them to see that, beneath the stereotypes put out by people, there is a level of intimacy to be reached that makes possible the links between their child needs, and the child needs of others.

REMOVING THE RITUALS

This is the last step. In my practice, how this worked was fairly straightforward; once I was sure that my patient had successfully learnt to deepen and broaden her rituals, and was acting out her emotions both with me and in the security of her relationships outside in the 'big' world, then it was time to drop the rituals. Sometimes this happened spontaneously; more often than not it needed a little push from me to force the issue and get the girl to shift her dependence from the rituals to the new behaviours. Frequently, it required more than a little push and firm control. This is a sensitive time; there is regression and fear of the future. Anorexics feel lost without their rituals, without having something to fall back on. Often my bulimarexics took up smoking or chewing gum obsessively in the first months: ''I just had to have something in my mouth —

something immediate to replace the food or the thought of it''.

Once the rituals stop there are, as you can imagine, a whole lot of new problems to deal with and these have to be dealt with over time. Therapy does not just stop because the anorexia or bulimarexia stops. For one thing, anorexics tend to put on weight and this upsets them. Also, no matter how supportive they find their relationships, they continue to be distressing for a while. Anorexics have to get used to a new body shape and they also have to come to terms with their new personalities, which are usually a lot less socially respectful than their old ones. Anorexics have to deal with their parents and have to come to terms with all that has happened to them. Although this is all normal in that we all have to go through these things, it is that much harder to do when you start late.

SUMMING UP

This then briefly is the programme of 'normalizing' that I found worked with my patients. It may seem daunting and you may have been a little upset by it or made wary by some of the things I have said you have to do, but bear in mind that while the alternative — to carry on as you are — may be a lot more familiar and seem safer or more secure to you, it leads nowhere. You can be certain of that, especially if your rituals are deeply embedded.

Just remember this: there are two problems in anorexia, two things to change: the rituals and then the underdeveloped child inside. If you want to do the job thoroughly, you have to do both. Becoming anorexic or bulimarexic stops your emotional development. What is clear is that not only is it possible to overcome anorexia, but in so doing, you will rejoin the human race. Sounds tempting, doesn't it?

Chapter 10

The world about you and how it may help to cover up reality

Before you can start work on yourself, you need to improve your insight into what is going on around you. You need to do this not only so that you can begin to assess your life better, but also as an exercise in making your intellect work for you as opposed to working for other people — mainly your parents. What follows in this chapter is information about what we found to be operating behind the scenes, as it were, in your world. We will look here at what your parents, your partners, your siblings and your society are covering up and why they do so. This should give you a suitable framework to build on.

The emphasis in our discussion to date has been focused very much on the family and it is clear that how parents behave and the kind of people they are determines whether or not you become anorexic and, to some extent, the form your illness takes. It would be a mistake though to simply place the blame on 'bad' parents and to leave it at that. For one thing it is an approach adopted by too many people today. Doctors are sometimes too quick to blame the parents — usually mothers — without thinking about the whole situation. Patients blame parents and use it as a kind of excuse to avoid ever changing — "I can't help it, it was my mum's fault."

In a sense, parents too are victims of forces that they themselves do not fully understand. Quite apart from their own upbringings and their parents' pathology, they have been exposed to social pressures and ways of thinking that in turn may have bad results. For example, most parents raised between the 1920s and 1940s had to contend with massive social and political upheavals, the likes of which people raised from the 1950s onwards have not seen. Under such stresses — depressions, strikes, war — people tend to cling to social fabrics and roles far more rigorously than at other times. This has helped to create a kind of rigidity in family life that is only now beginning to disappear. Therefore, in assessing the role of parents in the development of anorexia, we must also consider in which way society contributes to both family or parental pathology and to maintaining the 'fog' in which the anorexic girl grows up.

We can thus identify four key actions whereby the anorexic girl is kept from being informed about the way things really are in her life and in her family: firstly, her parents minimize her contact with the outside world and also present a false picture of their own problems, relationships and adjustments to the world. Secondly, siblings within the family frequently subscribe to the sets of myths and fabrications developed by parents and cover up their own experiences. Thirdly, if the anorexic is married or living in a relationship, her partner can cover up and obscure reality by continuing the patterns originally laid down in the anorexic's family. Fourthly, certain social trends and ideas, not the 'thinness' ethic, help to perpetuate the family's myths and so further confine the anorexic. We will examine each of these 'cover-ups' in turn to see how they work and what lies behind them.

PARENTAL COVER-UPS

Parents cover up for a lot of reasons and all parents do so to some degree, not just the parents of anorexics. One reason is to preserve an image in the eyes of their children. As I mentioned in an earlier chapter, for many parents, having children is the only experience in life in which they are in control, on top — supreme. To some parents, the years during which they have this image are terribly precious; it gives them a feeling of confidence and security and when the time comes for them to give it up, they resist it with all their might. Some parents hide behind their roles as father or mother, having an authority over and getting an obedience from their children they would never get anywhere else or in any other way. Because of this, some children never really get to know their parents as people.

What marks off the parents of anorexics from most other kinds of parents is the way in which they mask themselves and the way in which they keep their children away from the outside world. Not only do they give their children a set of false myths about themselves, but they cut them off from finding out whether the myths are true or not. Why? What are they hiding?

Not unexpectedly, when I first asked these questions I did so in a spirit of mild anger. As a person working with anorexics and researching the causes of their behaviour, I had become increasingly more disturbed at the depth of the damage done to them and the subtlety of it. It seemed to me as if society, parents and some doctors even had conspired through ignorance and unwillingness not to probe too deeply, lest they rock the boat. Too many researchers had, I thought, tried to find the causes of anorexia anywhere but with the parents of the girl.[1] I felt that the neglect of the physical and emotional health of these girls was under-attended to, even ignored. I also found many anorexics' parents to be hostile to any suggestion that they may have had failings as parents. I also found them capable of great deception.

However, in time I came to understand better what had happened to anorexics' parents to make them behave as they had. Viewing them objectively, I found these parents to be, themselves, deeply distressed people with their own quite tragic histories.

Parental backgrounds

One reason for one person neglecting another is that he or she is unaware of doing so. Here is an excerpt from a very early interview with Karl, Maureen's father. I had asked him if he had ever been emotionally neglected as a child:

1 Parents often foot the bill for their daughters' treatment, are legally responsible for them and can create the most fuss if threatened or upset; so some doctors choose not to upset or offend them.

Karl: "I suppose it never occurred to us to think about it. We just didn't see things like that. When I was a child we didn't think about neglect as an emotional thing — it was physical: I still can't see what Maureen's complaining about — or you: she had everything, more than I ever did."

Me: "What do you mean?"

Karl: "Well, we struggled to live. It was during the war. If you got food, that mattered. There was no time to worry about other things. My parents never concerned themselves with us 'emotionally' and we never bothered. You just did as you were told."

Me: "In other words, you were very much a *child* in your parents' home; your role was to respond, to do whatever you were told?"

Karl: "Absolutely. And this went on even when I was quite old you know, in my twenties. I never was part of the family like we have allowed our kids to become. I mean, we discuss things in our home, family discussions and so on, and we do whatever the children want; everything we do is for the kids. It wasn't like that in my home. We just did what our parents said. I would never have dared question my father or talk back to him. When Jo (Maureen's elder brother) started rebelling I found it very ugly. We didn't do things like that."

Me: "You said, 'Everything we do is for our kids' with a lot of feeling. Did your parents have the same attitude towards you."

Karl: "Yes, I suppose so. I've never thought about it. No — wait a minute — I see what you're getting at. No, in fact, it upsets me. I'm doing everything for my kids and I know why — because we really came second in my family. Not that my folks didn't do their best for us but we didn't count, not like my kids do."

Karl was very reluctant to go into his own childhood. He found it painful and he disliked even thinking about it too much. However, he persisted and provided us with a lot of valuable material to guide our later research efforts. He had barely known his own father, for example:

Karl: "Oh he was there all right, in the house — but we never saw much of him. He came and went and when he was there we just sort of kept out of his way."
Me: "Were you scared of him?"
Karl: "Oh yes, we all were. He had a temper and could hit hard. I was one of the youngest and I felt it a lot, a kind of feeling that he didn't have much time for us and that I was so small that he barely noticed me anyway."
Me: "And what about your mother?"
Karl: "Well, I think she felt sorry for me and tried to make it up. But don't get me wrong. I loved my father and he loved me. We were a very close family and I never wanted for anything. I just would have liked to have been, well, to have known my father better, that's all."

Karl could not understand what I was getting at. He thought he had had a normal childhood just like anyone else, but it was clear that he had been lonely and neglected by his father while being over-protected and spoilt by his mother. Karl would spontaneously remember something about his father, for example, how he had once taken him to town and it stuck out like a beacon in his mind. But when I suggested that his father perhaps could have done this more often Karl immediately rushed to his father's defence and protested: "Oh no, he was a good man — he was too busy. You can't expect a man to work all day and then come home and play with the kids. That's not his job. It's his wife's or the maids'. Especially as a boy, you can't expect a man to hug and kiss his sons — it's not done."

I had not introduced the phrase, 'hug and kiss'; Karl had slipped it in. So I asked him if his father used to hug him much. "Oh God no! Heaven forbid! We didn't go in for that kind of thing in our family. Only my mother did that." He was not even aware of the implications of what he was saying. He had needed to be hugged more, to have more contact with his father, he had felt left out and — we subsequently found out from a relative — he had been teased by his father for being a 'sissy' because he always ran to his mother to be hugged and kissed. Karl's conversation was full of male and female stereotypes that he used to explain and excuse things. All this helped him to obscure to himself the essential neglect he had felt from his father.

Basically, what we found in interviews such as this was that most of our anorexics' parents had created whole sets of quite erroneous and misleading myths about their childhood. In common with a lot of people who 'get by' in life with a struggle and never seek help, they *feel* things very differently from the way they think about them. In a way, this in itself is a measure of their neglect. When you begin to ask penetrating questions, you unearth a whole mess of emotions, often starting a trail of distress and insight that in time develops a momentum of its own. Karl would tell us what he thought about his life but he could say nothing of his feelings. He could not put them into words and had never been encouraged to do so or to think about them. After his first interview with me he went away feeling extremely depressed and could not understand why. It was only later that he was able to link his feeling of depression (and vague feeling of anger with me for upsetting him) with thinking about his past. In fact, as we shall see, like many anorexics' parents, he had had a very tough time emotionally.

In time, you too will have to deal with your parents and you will need to understand why some parents react with a lot of hostility if you even raise certain questions about their lives. They will snap at you and say they were fine and "Why couldn't you be a little more like I was" and so on. Also, more pertinent to your own problems, a lot of their negative or hostile reactions to you and your needs arise precisely because underneath their bland exteriors they are troubled by much the same things as you are.

Perhaps the most crucial thing we found about anorexics' parents was that in many ways, as individuals, they had had quite major struggles with their own parents, struggles that had clearly flawed their ability to deal with the world at large and more particularly, to relate to people in general. We found too, that while the parents of anorexics came from very similar family backgrounds, fathers had somewhat different upbringings from the mothers and that these differences formed a vital part of the way these parents reacted to each other later in marriage and how they reacted to their children.

The fathers of anorexics

Very broadly speaking, fathers of anorexic girls who manifested the classic thinness type of reaction, tended to be more
insecure and colder, almost pathologically so, than fathers of
bulimarexic girls. The fathers of bulimarexic girls tended to
show at least minimal warmth and concern in their relationships with their daughters. Both sets of fathers appeared to
suffer from chronic personal insecurity.

Fathers of anorexics tended to come from very emotionally
deprived homes; they had received very little attention as
children and had been forced to conform to very narrow
patterns of behaviour in order to gain approval. Most of them
reported a sense of deep frustration and dissatisfaction with
life without really knowing why. Their wives, when interviewed, usually complained that they were never able to make
their husbands happy and that most of all they felt their
husbands had very little interest in living or in enjoying things.
They did what was expected of them and no more. Here is an
excerpt from an interview with Toni's mother and father after
several consultations:

> *Father*: When I was a kid, only one thing mattered: to get
> on with your job and do what was right. And I've done
> that.
> *Mother*: No one's complaining about what you've done
> — it's that you don't seem able to *feel* like everyone
> else — you never cry, you never get upset. You show
> no emotion. All you seem to enjoy in life is, well I don't
> know — all I can think of is that you enjoy eating and
> sleeping. Nothing else.
> *Father*: Oh no, I like a lot of things — I enjoy a good walk.
> *Mother*: You've missed the point again. When things go
> wrong, when things don't work out as they should, you
> don't *do* anything — you just look bewildered, you don't
> *react*.

As you might have gathered, Toni's father and mother were
in the throes of a marital crisis precipitated by Toni's anorexia.
They were later divorced. However, Toni's mother had pin-
pointed an essential feature of the personality of anorexic's

fathers: a massive passivity originating out of a deep sense of insecurity and inadequacy. These fathers felt they did not count, were not anything outside their social roles. They did what they were told, were constantly (or so it seemed) being nagged by someone or other (not always a wife, often a mother or a boss) and seldom reacted. It was as if they behaved or thought or felt only as was expected: everything that did not fit into stereotypes was ignored or neglected.[1]

Do not think though that this implies that the fathers I studied were 'failures', or men in a state of permanent help-lessness. Far from it. Often they were achievers who did well and got things done — but only along lines laid out for them. Toni's father was a highly respected businessman. So were most. They felt they had done all right in life and materially they had. Underneath however, they had almost an obsession with conforming and with doing the right thing. There was a kind of anger in it too, almost a manic spite to do what they were told no matter what; they often used their roles, their conformity, to justify their unresponsiveness and neglect in other areas.

A person who is brought up in a fairly authoritarian way, given little emotional care, tends to dissociate from normal emotional relationships; they tend to 'go blank', pretend not to notice feelings, or do notice but do not attend. They apply the same principle to everyone else. If, for example, you are not allowed to cry when you feel upset as a child, if you are punished for crying, either physically or through withdrawal and disapproval, then to avoid the punishment you cut off, dissociate from your real natural feelings. You use whatever slogans have been used on you, such as 'Don't cry, be a man', and you discipline yourself with them — you justify your dissociation. Later, you apply the same approach to others: if someone cries, your child perhaps, you will find it upsetting; it will remind you, probably unconsciously, of your own punish-ment and you will try to stop the crying either through ignoring

---

1 Interestingly enough, as a key indicator of how neglected some of these fathers were as children, a large number of the fathers studied had very bad personal habits. They did not brush their teeth or follow other habits of personal cleanliness simply because they had never been taught to do so regularly — no one had ever checked them on this.

it or through punishing the person, just as happened to you.

Another way to avoid feeling is to busy yourself with something, usually something that is socially approved of. That is, you use some social role — or even a family role — to avoid facing the disturbing feelings for example, hobbies, fussiness about food and so on.

These are powerful devices in the personality and they ensure that all emotional demands are restricted. Living with someone like this, for a child, is very frustrating and demoralizing. The child senses the father's distress and helplessness in the face of proper emotions but is unable to do anything about it. Worse, in the process of demanding normal attention and affection, the child steps on very dangerous ground and meets with anxiety, irritability or hostility — frightening for a fully comprehending adult but even more so for a dependent child.

The fathers of bulimarexics

The fathers of bulimarexics tend to be very similar to the fathers of anorexics, in my study, but they usually had one modifying feature. Most bulimarexics' fathers had been fairly close to their mothers and this had given a different line and impetus to their upbringing. For one thing, it made them less isolated and more able to give and take certain kinds of affection. With a bulimarexics' father you can feel that there is a certain wealth of emotion, of affection and caring hidden in them somewhere, just waiting to come out. In contrast, the fathers of classical anorexics appear to me to be shut off, as if they are emotionally dead.

Bulimarexics' fathers, when faced with the same crippling neglect and harsh, rule-bound reality as anorexics' fathers, appear to have been more protected by their mothers and in subtle and surreptitious ways. This was Karl's experience:

> "My mother was very good to me; always slipped me a little something extra at supper or an extra sandwich to take to school. When no one was looking, she'd give me a big hug or a kiss. She seemed to know that I struggled a bit. She called me a sensitive child because I used to cry more than the others. She had to be careful though — in

case pop saw. If he did, there would be a big row and he
would accuse her of ruining me and she'd get very angry
and upset.''

For Karl and his mother, these little contacts had to be done
in secret; not only was there the danger of his father finding
out but Karl sensed that his mother was also afraid of his
brothers and people outside finding out; in short, these
contacts had to be kept hidden. Karl remembers feeling very
jealous on many occasions when he saw his mother hugging
one of his brothers and he notes that at mealtimes it became
an obsession with the two younger brothers to see who would
get that little extra from mother.

You can see what was happening: Karl's mother lived in a
society that gave her very little status in the home and very few
rights to bring up her children as she wanted. She had to obey
her husband, she had been conditioned to do so unquestioningly as an unbreakable social rule. She did not agree with
the way he wanted things to be done (with regard to the
children) so she did things her own way in secret. This in turn
shaped Karl's own thinking and feeling: he was brought up as
his father wanted, superficially, but he had learnt to live under
the protection of a woman — his mother. When he grew up,
he looked for, and was conditioned to look for, the same thing.
He wanted a woman who would give him the relationship he
was used to: that is, someone who would play up to his male
social needs in public (pay lip service to his masculinity and his
toughness, be socially unaffectionate and discreet, boost him
and give him status as the head of his household etc), while in
private, he wanted to be excused from the usual male
demands, to be spoilt, petted, treated like a child and above
all, he wanted to be understood and excused from the
pressures he was up against.

Such a person in control of a family would be difficult to live
with. Everyone would be involved in playing a double game
and would have to be prepared to accept his being one thing at
home but quite the opposite in public. Further, and most
important, the children would have to cease to exist in their
own right. Deprived and neglected people tend to be very
selfish, grabbing and demanding when they do eventually get

attention and affection. Starved of it for so long, they try to make up for all they missed, as it were. Remember how jealous Karl was of his brother? Well, this is a very typical reaction. When children are deprived of certain things, and have to compete for what little they get, the need may seem to go away but in fact it is still there, inside, frozen, at the very level at which it was stopped. It is only the expression of the need that is stopped. Later, no matter how old the person, the need will come out just as strongly as a child's and in the same way; Karl wanted his wife to be just like his mother; he wanted all her affection and attention just as a child would and he did not want anyone else to share it — just as he had felt with his brothers.[1] Karl's children had to learn to live with his jealousy and hostility towards them as if it were the natural right of a father.

In all the bulimarexics' families that we studied, this pattern was paramount; the father was capable of human needs, but he was also too demanding, too jealous, too possessive. We will look at how these needs evolved in marriage and how they affected the children once we have built up the picture of anorexics' mothers.

The mothers of anorexics

The majority of the mothers we spoke to seemed in most respects to have come from families very similar to those of their husbands. That is, they were neglected emotionally and to some extent, physically as well. No attention was given to minor ailments or to individuality. Maureen's mother, for example, received very little by way of proper medical care; as a result she lost most of her teeth at an early age and was often ill. Affection came in very short supply and was usually through one of two ways: through being ill or through pleasing her father.

Nearly all anorexics' mothers reported feeling that their own

---

1 In a normal family where love is not like money, a currency used for reward, there is plenty of it to go around — so there is no need for a child to fight for it with other siblings or guard what little there is with jealousy. There is always jealousy and competition but not of the Cain and Abel type felt by Karl.

mothers were quite cold, even hard people who were forever complaining and demanding. They felt that their mothers made them conform rigidly to their roles as women and daughters, almost slaves; they felt as if they were being punished for being woman in the first place. In contrast, they adored their fathers. This is what Eileen's mother had to say about her father:

> "My father was a kind man but very stern and strict. We didn't see much of him and he was quite aloof most of the time; he was quite hard on the boys (her brothers) but to me, every now and then, he'd take me on his knee or take me to town with him. I liked that very much. It was special. I also think that as I got older he found me more of a companion, more intelligent than my mother, and, of course, she resented this.

In the same way that Karl adored his mother for giving him what he should have had anyway, the mothers of anorexics adored their fathers for the few crumbs of attention that came their way. As with anorexics' fathers, these bits of attention also shaped their direction of growth. They became over-keyed to receiving special attention from their fathers, authority figures, and too eager to conform to the roles and ideas laid out for them by their fathers. Let us look at this in a little more detail.

Firstly, a typical anorexics' mother was nearly always brought up in a highly conforming household where 'a woman's place is in the home'; she was expected to be a servant in doing the daily work around the house and in accepting the authority of her father. The growing girl's mother applied these expectations with very little affection, no doubt through her own resentment and hostility. The only relief came from the father. Now this created a rather special setting. The growing girl was forced intellectually and socially to accept the role of a woman but her individuality and affection were dependent on her being a close companion to her father at times. And sometimes even in secret. Gayle's mother found that her own father was quite different when he was alone with her and appeared wary of his wife finding out how affectionate he was with his daughter. Such women grew up, therefore, to be a strange mixture — superficially very strongly orientated towards the traditional woman's role but in need of a kind of illicit, dependent/controlling relationship with a man, learnt from her father. Laura's mother demonstrates this quite clearly:

"I found in fact from the age of about 13 or 14 that I was quite important in the house in reality — although it was never admitted openly. I had literally replaced my mother in relation to my father, in all things that really mattered. He never discussed anything with her, it was always with me. He treated me like a son — better in fact; he felt more at ease with me because I was a girl, he felt he could be more open, more confiding. My mother wasn't very bright and I was. So in time, she just sort of faded. I grew up more as a male — in our society anyway. I knew about business and the family finance. I ran the house."

However, when it came to these women leaving home or entering society, problems occurred precisely because of this special relationship with father. This can be seen in another quote from Laura's mother:

"The trouble was that I couldn't leave home. My parents, or rather my father, didn't want me to. He seemed to believe that we could go on forever just as we were; he didn't believe I rated a life of my own. And so he put every spoke into it he could. As my father, he said, he had to approve of whom I married. He felt it best I leave home only to marry and so on. Everything I wanted to do, he wouldn't allow. I even ran away once. I suppose I'd had a taste of power already, if you like, with him; I wanted to form my own business or at least do something exciting in life — travel maybe. But — 'Oh no, not you — you're a girl, you stay at home'."

Anorexics' mothers were doubly confined and pressured: their special relationship with their fathers gave them a very 'unfeminine' (for their time) view of life. By and large, they found life a challenge and exciting — far more so than their mothers who had not been permitted this glimpse into men's affairs; and more so perhaps than many of their contemporaries who were still bound by the social roles of the 1920s, 1930s and 1940s.[1] At the same time, by virtue of their fathers' stereotyped roles and the rules of their communities, they were prevented from acting on their new insights, ideas and talents. Most of the mothers we studied felt forced into strict roles after leaving home, and most ended up with marriage partners chosen for them by their parents. All were unanimous that they had started off married life deeply frustrated and angry, determined to have their own way in time.

Mothers of classical anorexics differed from mothers of bulimarexics as did the fathers, but the differences were less clearly defined. The mothers of classical anorexics seemed less determined to change, more helpless, more accepting of the *status quo*, more withdrawn and less interested in life than the mothers of bulimarexics. One felt a kind of fatalism present in these women as if they would give up the world and collapse at any moment. By and large, they seemed to have had a more removed and less intense relationship with their fathers than had the mothers of bulimarexics. Where they were active in life, it was accompanied by depression and withdrawal neglect of self and the children and a tendency to collapse into illness at the slightest setback.

The effects of marriage

What happens when these two sets of partners get together to 'honour and obey?' Well, there seems to be no single pattern but there are a number of common factors. Fundamental to these is that, by and large, far from marriage being a growth experience, I found that within a few years, both partners had inevitably settled into life with their new family with things pretty much as they had been in their own homes; in short, a kind of stalemate developed with each partner trying to get from the other the same feeling of being special that they had had from their respective mothers and fathers, and using the

---

1 We tend to forget how much society kept women out of dealing with life and reality — and how much it still does. Life is a challenge and it is exciting, but only if you can face it and deal with it, feel your effect on it and its effect on you.

rest of the family as a battleground in which to do it.

Both husbands and wives in these families appear to have in common a problem in dealing with the outside world. Take the anorexic's father: he may cope well with the outside world on the surface but he needs something else, some special thing to make him feel 'safe', more comfortable. This is usually that special relationship he had with his mother — now transferred to his wife and their home. Their home becomes the refuge from the outside world. For both husband and wife the outside world is threatening because it deprives them of any sense of specialness. This is an important point because it is how they experienced life in their own homes: the outside world is seen in very stereotypical ways. There is little sense of excitement about life and an inability to see that the outside world can be challenged and changed. Normal people tend to see life the other way round.

Such husbands and wives then, 'cover up', role-play at being adults on the outside, and then come home and behave like the children they feel they are. At first sight, this may seem fine because in a sense they seem to be well-matched: the anorexic's mother needs a male who gives lip service to male roles but who will in reality let her help and will in fact rely on her, while the anorexic's father needs a woman who will appear to play the feminine role while in reality making things easy for him and allowing him to be molly-coddled.

In time, however, problems emerge, especially when children arrive. The 'little-boy' fathers resent their wives taking note of the new baby and do not want to share. 'Little-girl' mothers struggle with their role as mothers and do not want to lose their special place as head of the family, directing things. They resent the time they have to spend on being mothers. It is to them, denigrating and humiliating, carrying with it remembrances of what life was like at home with their own mothers. All this, of course, happens 'inside', privately; none of it is openly discussed, in fact, the very opposite. On the surface, lip service is paid to how nice it is to have children, how happy they all are. In reality, having children seems just like being at home again with brothers and sisters.

There are even deeper issues. Through neglect, the anorexic's parents do not really know how to relate. They know the social forms but not the private ones. They cannot relate to each other outside of the father-daughter, mother-son roles simply because they have never learnt any other way. So they struggle with each other and with their children.

What the parents of anorexics cover up, therefore, is their own histories and their own problems, their real needs and the trouble and struggle they had had in life and in marriage. By the time the soon-to-be anorexic girl becomes a teenager, if she is the eldest, it is clear that her parents' marriage has developed tragic elements that have been so well masked that no one, least of all the anorexic, recognizes them. The pre-anorexic girl, in short, walks into a lion's den. All her instincts tell her this but owing to the deceptive forms and appearances, she is confused and deceived.

Moreover, the parents of most anorexics tend to be extremely isolated from each other, to be disappointed with their marriages and their lives. They are not only separated and isolated from each other but also from the outside world. Further, each has sunk into his or her own way of coping, just as they did in their own homes. Here are some examples of these very characteristic coping patterns.

Fathers

Laura's father had done well in business and had had many affairs, none of which meant much to him but, in each case, he was seeking someone who 'understood' him — like his mother had. Gayle's father did the same. Maureen's father had bought a racehorse and spent every minute of his time absorbed in it. Margaret's father — a skin specialist — was devoted to his patients for whom he would go out in snowstorms if asked, while his own family were medically neglected. His female patients received extra-special attention. Janet's father had formed a platonic relationship with a woman at the office — thus ensuring that he was protected both at work and at home. All fathers had fastidious eating habits and were choosy about food, reluctant to share their 'little treats' with others, and would often leave work secretly to buy little delicacies for themselves. Each treated his wife 'correctly' and played an exaggeratedly masculine 'husband' role. Most of these men were very inadequate sexually, afraid of physical contact and often insensitive to simple touch and affection — all signs of deep neglect in childhood.

Mothers

While the fathers were busy ensuring their material comforts, most anorexics' mothers were trying to find a way to satisfy their needs to be part of the world from which they had been deprived of contact. Gayle's mother started by giving in, in her marriage; after several attempts to run away from her husband, she seemed to have decided to become the 'perfect' mother. She did this for a few years but rapidly tired of it and the lack of rewards. So she started her own business and did so very successfully, doing everything herself. This helped her to justify her desire to avoid the role of being mother and gave her the contact with reality she wanted. Her guilt, though, was enormous (about breaking her role and neglecting her duties) and she developed agoraphobia very early on which, I think, effectively stopped her from facing up to these issues.[1]

Laura's mother raised four children and then rebelled. She went to university, got a degree and became a lecturer. While Laura was growing up, her mother kept herself busy lecturing and was hardly ever at home.

Summing up

It is difficult not to feel sympathetic towards these parents, especially the women. They were simply trying to correct their own childhood ills, to achieve things for themselves, to break through the web of their own parents' myths and social conformity and rigidity. They felt guilty but they persisted. It is unfortunately true though that in the process of satisfying their own childlike needs, they deprived their own children of a great deal.[2]

1 I found many of my patients' mothers became so desperate that suicide was often contemplated and sometimes attempted — often at the time of their daughter's breakdown.
2 Not surprisingly, I, in common with other researchers, have found many instances of secret anorexia nervosa in mothers and other relatives. For an explanation, see farther on in this chapter.

What struck me as important about anorexics' mothers, was that they themselves were rebelling against society at a time when it was not fashionable to do so, and when, as a consequence, the hostility and pressure on them to conform was intense. I feel sure that their single-mindedness and obsession with doing things outside the home were the only way they could preserve what little individuality and independence they had. I think when such a person has to deal with an adolescent daughter, who is in turn striving for independence and rebelling, it re-opens old wounds and the mother cannot fail but vent her own distress on her daughter. In a sense — but only a dim one — I have had the feeling that anorexics' mothers try to stop their daughters from leading the kind of frozen and distraught lives they themselves led. In trying to 'save' their daughters I think they contribute heavily towards the development of anorexia. If such mothers could see this and try to help themselves by accepting their own rebellion and struggle, I think things would be a lot easier. If you are anorexic show your mother this chapter and discuss it with her.

THE SIBLINGS' COVER-UP

The siblings' cover-up is more a side effect of parental pathology than an actual contributary factor to the development of anorexia. Anorexia can happen to children where there are no siblings. The important thing here though is that someone trying to understand what went on in her family, or what *is* going on, would be helped a great deal if another member of the family would be open about what was happening in their own lives or in their relationship to the family. This is how Laura put it:

> "I would have understood more, at least known that my instincts were based on something real and not just something I'd made up, if my brother or anyone in the family had said something. As it was, I thought it was only me that brought the family into disgrace. It wasn't till I was 30 that I found out what had really gone on with my brother."

What Laura is describing is the kind of family conspiracy present in most anorexics' families: siblings do not really talk to each other, are as isolated from each other as from the outside world. Moreover, I have found that siblings often take cover in the anorexic's breakdown and use it as a way of turning attention away from themselves and their own problems and, within the family hierarchy, boosting their own ability to cope, their own 'perfection'. This not only further isolates the anorexic from her family, it heightens her sense of being a 'mental case' and a failure. This is an extremely crippling feeling, especially when you remember that in reality, it is the anorexic who is behaving in the most realistic fashion within her family — it is she who at least reacts to the insanity, the charade, that everyone else has tolerated for so long.

The point is that it is usually the anorexic girl who is the first to break the family tradition of putting up with extreme levels of insecurity and neglect. As such, she pays a terrific price in incurring the wrath and frustration of family and relatives — and of course, the guilt and doubt that perhaps if she had not developed anorexia, all would have been well. Imagine how much comfort she would feel if someone else chipped in about his or her distress and struggles in the family? But usually she is alone, the rest of the family and most of the family's friends choosing to remain mute.

What are siblings covering up? Basically they mask not only their own distress and suffering but also the extent of their own pathology. This may not concern the anorexic over-much but it certainly concerns researchers and therapists. It helped tremendously, for instance, to know how other family members coped because it helped to pinpoint the kinds of areas in personality function that were common to all siblings. If I found an anorexic and her brother, for example, both had similar problems in forming close relationships, it suggested that the area of forming relationships was flawed for anyone raised in that family; it also suggested that anorexia was not in itself the underlying pathology in my patients but rather a stress reaction to insecurity faced by all siblings. Few relatives, let alone siblings of anorexics, have ever been studied by doctors, which explains in part why so little is known and why so much is focused on the anorexic, the only family member with *obvious* problems.

I was lucky in being able to examine several siblings of anorexics but again this took time and patience and a lot of cross-checking to establish precisely what was going on. If you remember that the families of anorexics have a tradition of fabrication in the face of the outside world you will understand why. In one instance, for example, we had a series of long interviews with the wife of an anorexic's brother. In them, she reassured us that they had no problems and everything was O.K. We could not flaw her arguments and were convinced. Two years later, however, they divorced and she admitted to my researcher that she had lied to us throughout the interviews because her husband had so conditioned her to fabricate, to maintain a social pretence, that she had learnt to do so with ease.

The typical pathology we found in anorexics' siblings was that they lied to themselves about the kinds of existences they led. We found, for example, many of the siblings we studied to be very high achievers (especially in the case of the eldest) who put a tremendous price on appearances and status. Underneath, though, we often found their personal lives were led in a chaotic way, unconnected with their social appearances. We found, for instance, many siblings to have experimented extensively with drugs and with sexuality — not in the sense of 'exploration' and 'growth' but in the sense of a kind of angry frenzy in which anything was tried if it had a kick in it. In short, not surprisingly, we found these people to be manic, dissociated, unable to be honest or act on insight. They were able to justify their actions superficially and glibly but this was often purely a defence used to buy time to get on with the next thing. Their relationships were a mess; husbands complained that their wives were unreachable, obsessive, almost self-destructive; wives complained of their husbands' affairs (with men and women) and their inability to express feelings or be consistent at even the most basic levels of stability. Over and over again, we came up against needy people, many with forms of anorexia themselves, many seriously disturbed, all of them hostile, angry and very superficial. They were inevitably deeply convinced that nothing was wrong with them despite their own evidence to the contrary. Long term follow-ups in a few cases showed a sad pattern: a trail of broken relationships, drug and alcohol abuse, occasional nervous breakdowns and some suicides.

There were of course exceptions. But not enough to seriously bring the rule into question. Anorexics' families are a disturbing environment and everyone in them suffers — usually in their inability to form lasting and proper private relationships. Only the anorexic dares to challenge the family social conventions by breaking down openly.

ANOREXICS' PARTNERS

When I began collecting data on anorexics' partners — husbands, live-in boyfriends and so on — I simply wrote down whatever information I could get on them. I have in front of me now the first data I collected and while it is not entirely representative, it is nevertheless informative.

The first ten anorexics I ever saw were all hospitalized cases. Of these, six were married or had been engaged or became married within a year of my first seeing them. Of the six, four of their husbands or fiancés had hospital diagnoses. I will list them in the order I saw them:

(i) Passive depressive (ii) Psychopath (iii) Schizophrenic breakdown (iv) Drug addict

Fair enough! Hospital psychiatric diagnoses being what they are, they may have missed more than a point or two, but this pattern — namely that anorexics tend to make poor choices of partners — I did find tended to run more or less consistently. The more serious the case of anorexia, the more serious the disturbance present in the partner.

What tended to happen in the cases I saw was that anorexics chose partners on the basis of their upbringing rather than on the basis of sexual, romantic or just plain personal preference. I found that my anorexics and bulimarexics were extremely blinkered in their choices, selecting one aspect of a person and ignoring the 'feel' of the man. They lacked that sixth sense that most people have in determining whether or not the person 'hangs together' as a personality. Thus my patients chose men who filled one or other of the following categories:

1. Were willing to get married very very quickly after first meeting.
2. Looked very prestigious.
3. Had a very prestigious occupation.
4. Seemed caring.
5. Had money.
6. Wanted a home.
7. Wanted my patient.

I am sorry to be so stark but these really were the criteria which came through; to the extent that sometimes these marriages and relationships went ahead despite the fact that the anorexic was fully aware of the other 'parts' of her partner's personality: parts that, frequently, later formed the basis for a divorce.

Whatever the case, even where a relatively decent relationship developed, it was seldom able to progress far because the anorexics inevitably chose men who were usually quite unable to open up properly to the demands of intimacy themselves. These men were, by and large, defensive, self-protecting and seemed drawn to a woman for what she could give him superficially rather than for any other reason. The partners I actually met were pleasant enough people but very like most of my anorexic patients: very socially aware, deliberate and intense. I found very little looseness or flexibility in them. They seemed, also, quite unable to cope with anger, be it their own or that of others.

What these relationships cover up is the naïvety and essential childishness of the anorexic. In her family, her parents, at least superficially, knew they had to care for their daughter. In many of the relationships of anorexics I studied, this minimal caring seemed absent between the partners; in the words of one of the husbands, it was "A no-holds-barred situation, me or her". In other words, the anorexic would soon find herself reduced to a dependent wreck with her partner or husband becoming a tyrant. Most of these men could not believe their luck — they found no resistance (of the interpersonal kind necessary for survival in a relationship) and were initially delighted to have such compliant women around. Howevei, this soon palled and a kind of chronic irritability set in — a mixture of boredom, emptiness and dissatisfaction. How stable the relationship was depended upon how long each could put up with this state of affairs. In one typical case I treated, the husband, kind, considerate and long-suffering throughout his wife's treatment, promptly walked out when she had recovered and was beginning to be more self-assertive; he wanted the old model back because it was less challenging.

The point is that hiding behind being married, behind a husband, the more prestigious, the better, and behind any children obscures the deeper unresolved anorexic problems. The longer the relationship goes on being used as a mask, the further these problems are buried.

In such relationships, both men and women usually have great trouble as they grow older — depression, phobias, sleep problems and other psychosomatic complaints being the most frequent. Both partners usually end up creating a cocoon of lies and contradictions behind which they lead their lonely lives.

HOW SOCIETY COVERS UP

It may seem as if we have covered most of what happens to an anorexic but we must look finally at how society furthers the duping process, so that later when we come to therapy, you are not taken in by slogans or explanations that seem socially acceptable and have the support of the community. It is necessary that you know precisely where societies err so that you can be careful where you place your trust.

At the simplest level, society is deeply involved in covering up what is going on in anorexic households by virtue of the fact that, as it is presently structured, it tends to support the myths created and fostered by parents and puts major obstacles in the path of the anorexic girl's attempts to find out what is really going on.

Note, however, that society is not a thing that can be seen or dealt with as a separate entity. We often refer to society as a kind of 'big brother'; we attribute to it a sense of knowing and direction as if it were a person — or a god. But it is neither. Society is a way of organizing human affairs, a way of institutionalizing or making routine, basic ways of doing things. Because of this and because our societies are so big, they tend to focus on problems of a physical or material nature before they look at psychological problems.

Societies focus on obvious and big problems — on whether or not people are fed, live in peace, survive and so on — and on whether or not law and order are being preserved and on whether war will break out or not. Societies' institutions focus in turn on the *appearance* of basic peace and quiet. If you have enough to eat, are well-looked after, educated and so on, they stop attending to you and turn to those obviously in need. It is a kind of morality that pervades society and is one of the reasons moreover that middle-class families do not usually attract the kind of scrutiny or attention that is given both to deprived or to rich families. Middle-class families have traditionally been regarded as the 'solid sensible' core of society. They tend to work hard, obey the law and apply themselves diligently to the task of keeping social and moral order. The children of these families are well-cared for physically, well-educated, and by and large, grow up with the same sense of duty and morality as their parents.[1]

One consequence of this is that there is very little awareness in society in general of the kind of difficulty faced by children growing up in these households, isolated in the manner described in the preceding chapters. Society is satisfied by the *appearance* of well-being and gives no directives to parents, teachers, doctors or children to think otherwise. It is thus easy for the basic isolation pattern to go unattended — a pre-anorexic's teacher for example is satisfied because he or she sees no overt problem and her family doctor and friends think likewise. They fail to notice the absence of essential reality-testing because they do not know how to look for it and too many of them, as we have seen, actually disparage play in favour of a premature maturity.

1 When I say 'middle class' I do not mean a specific middle class. I mean the concept of a middle class in general. There can be 'middle classes' in African tribes, in primitive settlements and so on.

A second consequence is that communities as a whole are not alerted to the fact that some children can be quite markedly neglected by their parents, even when they appear to take a tremendous interest in their children's lives. Consider the average anorexic girl: she is pre-occupied with schoolwork and often does a whole host of extra-curricular activities arranged by her parents. When do these children go out and play? When are they seen by, and played with, or fussed over by their busy parents? Seldom, if ever — as most anorexics will confirm. This is neglect obscured by the fact that society approves of the arrangement because the parents appear to conform with the values of middle class society. In reality these parents abrogate their responsibility to being with their children and raising them properly by handing them over to school teachers, dance teachers, drama teachers, nannies, maids, books, television and the like.

There is a third consequence of the absence of proper psychological and emotional perspective in modern social thinking, and it is, in my opinion, one of the most crucial. Both of the previous consequences apply to male as well as to female children of middle-class families and account in part for the fact that these children do frequently have psychological problems and do seek treatment for them (most psycho-therapy patients come from the middle class). Such children are isolated and neglected and pay the price through suffering anxiety and other mental symptoms. But if you think about it, you will see that the female children of such families are in many ways up against even more formidable obstacles than the male children: it is very much more difficult for them both to break out of the psychological restraints applied to them and to make real contact with the outside world. In each case, the social constraints against women help to reinforce the already isolated, neglected and submissive pattern laid down by the anorexic's family.

In an earlier chapter, I discussed how important it is for the growing child to be able to rebel against any particular perspective or idea that he or she is made to accept. This rebellion need not, of course, be a rebellion in a violent sense. It simply means being able, or rather, being free enough, to look at a situation (or think about it, see it or feel it) from a different perspective, one which originates in the child's real world. Middle class moralities tend in general to permit only very muted forms of rebellion to their codes of behaviour and in particular, they are extremely restrictive on the behaviour of their female children.

Male children in society are generally permitted a fairly large degree of freedom (within the standards set by their middle classness) from an early age. They are expected (and often encouraged) to be 'difficult', independent, rebellious, robust and to do more in the outside world, especially physically. They get valuable opportunities to meet reality head-on through scout movements, mountaineering, and other such activities. Sometimes this may have its own unfortunate consequences: the boys are frequently deprived of physical and emotional contact with their parents from a too-early age and develop a whole range of substitute-seeking behaviours (fetishes) that make it difficult for them to form proper relationships with women later on in life.[1] However, they are at least permitted room to breathe; females raised in the same society tend to be raised very differently. For a start, some parents (frequently the fathers in a misguided attempt to preserve their daughter's innocence) insist on near-angelic behaviour, keeping their daughters away from not only the people of whom they disapprove but also from the very essence of the growing child's reality, the rough-and-tumble of playing, getting dirty, hurt, excited, muddy.

Secondly, and by far the more damaging, female children in our society are committed from an early age to a servile and acolyte-like relationship with their mothers that I believe often literally smothers them. Girls have always been supposed, socially at least, to have a particularly intimate and symbiotic relationship with their mothers, often to the envy of their male siblings. However, this frequently works to their own detriment. Boys are supposed to have, in turn, special relationships with their fathers but this is a quite different thing from that enjoyed (supposedly) by mothers and daughters. Most boy-father relationships involve very little personal or physical

---

1 These usually take the form of too-early sex-orientated habits and a narrowing of consciousness about women in general.

intimacy. Boys accompany their fathers on such things as hunting trips and may be permitted an insight into the 'big world' of their fathers; a world often denied female siblings. But there is an essential distance between father and son that makes rebellion or breaking off or disagreement just that little bit easier. Boys are socially allowed to go against their fathers. It is a sign of 'manhood'. Not so with the girls. There is little social approval for a girl defying her mother; instead it is often taken as a sign of pathology, even today.

It is true that girls are permitted to remain as children for somewhat longer than boys. They are permitted a range of vital emotions and forms of breaking down (crying) for far longer than boys and their mothers are permitted to comfort them in this. But one of the reasons that these behaviours are permitted in society is that they conform with the centuries-old dictum that women are weaker and should supposedly be kept in a submissive or secondary role.

These role differences make a major difference to how girls and boys grow up. While girls' reaction patterns are somatically healthier (it is better to cry; children should be left as children longer) the symbiotic and submissive role they are conditioned to and taught to play means that rebellion against it is eventually extremely difficult; made more so in the face of neglect or isolation. To rebel as a normal adolescent girl in our societies is a major undertaking. To do so as an anorexic is a nightmare.

From my experiences with a large female practice, and through lecturing and discussing these issues with women in general, I have come to the conclusion that the question of female rebellion in adolescence is an extremely traumatic one for most women in our society and, I need hardly add, an area neglected by our society. What should be a normal, straightforward transition from childhood to adulthood becomes, I believe, fraught with emotional difficulties.

To grow up properly requires free contact with reality as a child experiences it. It also requires the ability to rebel and to think for yourself. All this must take place within a protected emotional framework in which the full brunt of outside reality is shouldered by the parents. The key to being a successful parent is knowing when and how to systematically unload this protection: growing up for a child means that he or she must be constantly watched and exposed to increasing levels of contact with reality as he or she requires it. Now this process is clearly a major undertaking if it is to be done properly; it almost amounts to a full-time occupation.

Ideally, both parents should be involved and I think you can see why: to give both levels of contact with reality — male and female. But in our society, we replace this careful bi-parental attention by the following: firstly, mothers are by and large charged with the task of childrearing from babyhood to teens. Most fathers are socially permitted to frequently be absent from the rearing process. Secondly, instead of a child's individuality being monitored, he or she is squeezed not only into sex stereotypes, but into age level stereotypes: he or she should be doing a particular thing at the age of six, and something else at the age of seven and so on — levels set not by the parent fully familiar with his or her own child but by society and institutions. Then, in free time, that is when the parents are at home together with the children, the responsibility of bringing up the children is shifted onto television, radio stations, pinball machines, anything but the parents who are usually — especially in the middle classes — busy with a myriad of social, family or political activities.

Let me say here, that I believe that, as a whole, we need to spend more time in looking after our children — *both* sexes — and that we need to spend much more time on our own personal difficulties as well than we do at present. We spend far too much time being busy, making money or performing other social tasks. Children benefit far more from proper attention than from having their own colour television in their bedrooms.

Female children suffer the most under this system. Firstly, they do not have sufficient contact with their fathers and with their fathers' world, and secondly, they are over-exposed to their mothers' world and to the symbiotic relationship. Although this symbiotic relationship is an absolutely vital part of growing up, it should be phased out systematically. However what happens in many middle-class families is that the female children are not only over-exposed to their mothers' world but they are cut off from male and physical reality at the same time. The stereotypes practised against females ensure that they fail to make physical contact with the real world. They are forbidden and perhaps even punished for getting dirty, being wild or tomboyish. They are also expected to be soft and gentle, clean and tidy, good, pretty and helpful. Further, they are expected to make the transition from childhood to adulthood without causing trouble and this is usually taken to mean without any trial and error.

Think about it. The male reality, the male experience that is not permitted to girls, is to get things wrong, to experiment, to play, mess around — in short, to learn by direct contact with reality. That is why men have appeared to be more creative and capable throughout history: they were allowed to be socially. Girls are permitted practically no freedom, no time to go through the clumsy, awkward, messy process of shifting from childhood to adulthood. Kept in place by their mother's symbiosis, they can only play within the incredibly narrow confines of dolls, clothes, fashion, makeup and the like.

It is this claustrophobic social and psychological matrix that does the damage. The adolescent girl has to fight her mother and society simply to get the right to live and grow properly. Few males are aware of just how oppressive and difficult this battle can be. It is, in my opinion, a massive one and one of which our male-dominated society is largely ignorant. I believe that most modern women go through this crisis, some more successfully than others. The anxiety involved is massive. Look at these typical statements made by women I have known:

> "The thought of challenging my mother tears at my stomach, it nauseates me." "Oh I couldn't leave home now, I'd die. What would my mother do?" "I try to fight her but in the end I just give in. I feel so vomity afterwards."

These are all statements made by normal women who had never been anorexic. Notice the similarity, the continual reference to nausea, vomiting, anxiety. Many of my non-anorexic patients and students reported episodes of stress and tension at home when they were unable to eat, had no appetite, nearly always arising from conflict with their mothers. Many more reported episodes — often brief and non-anorexic — of vomiting a meal when conflict between the mother's wishes and those of the girl became overwhelming.[1]

Because of the position held by the mothers in these families, they become the executive arm of all the injustice and prejudice that society inflicts on women. It is usually the mother who forces the rules and the necessity to conform with them, yet at the same time, she is the only source of love and affection. If a boy fights with his father, he is often able to be comforted by his mother (often with social approval too); if a girl fights with her mother, very often she has her father to contend with as well.

What I am saying is this; in our society, for a female child the task of growing up and rebelling creates as a matter of course a situation in which anorexia (loss of appetite), nausea, anxiety and vomiting arise.

This is a normal situation for most women and one that most women have to go through. I believe that every woman is forced to pass through this growth crisis and that the prime symptoms of anorexia, as described above, accompany this. In short, every woman in our society confronting the stereotypes it sets up, has to pass through an anorexic phase. This, I believe, is the only theory that adequately accounts for the fact that men rarely get anorexia, and that anorexia and bulimarexia are becoming major problems — to the extent that millions of women are now thought to be suffering from the condition.

To recap: growing girls are exposed to a restricted contact with the outside world. They are coerced by mothers into conforming to an inadequate pattern of behaving and thinking. In adolescence, this pattern becomes exposed as being inadequate (and with the increase in female consciousness, will become even more exposed).

The woman's fear of the outside world — a world she has not been permitted to investigate — comes through and she realizes in fright that her mother cannot protect her and that she can be wrong. Most women are trapped for a time, unable to cope with being overwhelmed by the demands of the

---

1 Loss of appetite and nausea are amongst the most central biological components of fear. Extreme distress often causes vomiting.

outside world and the contrary demands of their mothers. I can think of no more deeply terrifying stage in a person's life save war, perhaps. Biologically any person in the same circumstances will manifest fear symptoms — loss of appetite, nausea, vomiting. These are all signs that animals display if they are cornered and unable to fight. I think you will agree that if you are a woman, this is a familiar feeling, and a traumatic one. Many normal women can fight and escape the fear. The anorexic phase disappears and life goes on. If, however, all the other factors I have discussed that go to make the anorexic condition are present, the girl is completely unable to run and cannot fight. So she stays in a state of anorexia and tries to live with it, ritualizing it so as to try in her mind to cope with the cage that she really is in. She stays in a semi-permanent state of intense terror.

Women, in general, can choose to solve or avoid the problem: many women simply conform and grow up in reduced ways, conforming to stereotypes and never challenging their roles or the limitations placed on their personalities. Other women are lucky in that their mothers are aware of the problem and bring up their daughters to be *people* first and not *female* first. Many millions of women do not quite make it and continue to struggle throughout their lives; depression, sexual difficulties and psychosomatic symptoms being the more obvious signs of their stress. Many women survive by adopting one or other of the forms of anorexia or bulimarexia, never seeking help, hiding it from everyone and never knowing why they do it.

Summing up

What society has covered up, then, has been the whole range of conflicts experienced by women of which an anorexic crisis precipitated by conflict with the mother and the social roles behind her plays a major part. In other words, anorexia is one of the symptoms of rebelling. People who stay locked into it remain trapped and unable to move, with three choices open to them: to starve themselves to death; to enter the régime of bulimarexia, or to become semi-permanently anorexic.

Chapter 11

Becoming normal

At the simplest level you are very much a creature of your parents: you are literally their child — whether you are 14, 19 or 45. The isolation in which you have lived with your family has removed you from a normal contact with reality. Your personality has been developed, not out of a mix of life at home and increasingly greater contact with reality outside the home, but purely out of your family's reality.

This isolation ensures that you have not gone through several vital levels of learning about reality. Instead of knowing how to get on with other children and people of your own age, you know only to do what you have been taught in the home. So your views of life and the world is *doubly* biased. Firstly, your parents' view of life is biased through their own limitations and poor life experiences; because you are isolated, you are prevented from testing out their ideas — so you absorb them second-hand. Secondly, you have learned to exist in the only level of reality to which you have been exposed — you know how to coexist with your mum and dad and your siblings. You know little else but at this, you are expert.

Here is a sample list of things at which the anorexic is proficient and which arise out of these factors. The anorexic is generally:

1. Highly sensitive to the personal needs of people in a position of power and authority over her.
2. Tremendously willing to sacrifice self and personal needs, even personal status in order to help someone else,

to be a part of something considered important, to gain acceptance.

3. Able to smooth over problems and frictions — at great personal cost — to keep situations happy and conflict-free.

4. Extremely good at giving sympathy, insight — even guidance — at saying what is necessary irrespective of its morality.

All of these attributes are often seen as highly desirable socially and usually they attract a lot of warmth, affection and praise. They are also often hailed as signs of responsibility and sensibility. Certain institutions in our society fête these characteristics. For example, schools, universities, businesses and professions look for people with these characteristics — usually to fill helper, secretarial or assistant-type roles: in other words, secondary 'server' functions in which someone else's dictates or needs are attended to.

However, the following characteristics accompany those already mentioned. The anorexic girl generally possesses:

1. High sensitivity and manipulativeness towards anyone who threatens her role or status.

2. An inability to assert individuality, to be personally and individually responsible to her own needs.

3. A whole range of passive-aggressive activities that are built in to her behaviour to ensure some release from anxiety and frustration (anorexics can be clumsy, spiteful, devious and malicious).

4. A basic inability to function without the goodwill or attention of the person in authority — in short, little self-motivation.

5. An obsession with preserving her own status and position, not building, changing or developing.

Within the context of home, these attributes were necessary for survival. They ensured that the anorexic fitted in somewhere between mother and father and her other siblings. In adolescence, this basic personality learning — together with the learning of the parents' clichés and ideas (second-hand) — is all the anorexic has to deal with the outside world. As a child, this narrow training was initially ideal for contact with teachers, friends and so on. Teacher-pupil relationships, for example, are very similar to mother-daughter relationships, and the girl simply does what she has been taught. Similarly, friendships with both boys and girls follow the same pattern. The difficulty is that this is just not enough outside the narrow domain of being a child. When the anorexic becomes an adolescent, she meets a lot of people who do not fit into this mould. She reads or sees things on television that puzzle or frighten her. She does not know how to cope and how to behave and begins to sense how deep this goes. She knows nothing of equality, of give and take, of robustness — only what she has met at home. So what does she do? Two things.

She retreats into the home, living even deeper in the family, terrified of going out alone or of misbehaving and in constant dread of losing her parents and their protection. Secondly, she tries to make whoever she meets, or has to deal with, fit into the mould she is familiar with — that is, she seeks out friends or teachers who treat her and care for her as her mother and father do. When she cannot do this, she is terrified. The key to adolescence as opposed to childhood is that there really is no escape: you cannot turn your friends into your parents. You can block your inadequacies by *using* relationships but sooner or later, they catch up on you.

THE ANOREXIC'S LACK OF CONTACT WITH REALITY

Having received all her information second-hand, the anorexic girl, when exposed to reality by adolescence, is left only with an *explanatory myth* — that is, a set of ideas about life, about what to do, how to behave, what to discuss, think about — all set down by the family. Being second-hand, they are not only inaccurate, but they are also out-of-date. They are artificial, highly formal, highly stereotyped and highly simplistic. Of what possible value can the following be to an adolescent today?

Trust nobody but your family.
Suspect the worst of people — that way you'll never be disappointed.

Your family is all you will ever have.

You will never have such joy again as you have had at home.

Only we can look after you.

Only we want the best for you.

People try to cheat all the time.

Trust only people with a university degree.

Trust only people with breeding.

Trust only 'decent' people.

And here is a longer cliché — a very common explanatory myth found in families of anorexics:

"Your family is a very good one. It is superior. It is not only normal, it is supernormal and so is everyone in it, including your relatives, ancestors and unborn family too. You are very talented. You are not ordinary, you are special. You must not mix with common people; they will be jealous of you and try to steal your ideas. You are privileged, they are not."

The consequence of behaving according to precepts of this kind is that the anorexic will sound very adult, very grown-up and sure of herself, socially. She is fluent in her verbal behaviour. Of course, she will also have been taught how to be socially discreet about her superiority, but it will be there all the time. Teachers and many people of her own age will be taken in by her apparent confidence. However, she will trust no one and confide in no one but her family; her superiority outside will only exist as long as she has her family to turn to for daily support.

The anorexic will have been kept away from other children and taught not to copy their 'bad' or 'common' behaviour. However, this behaviour is precisely what the anorexic must experience to come into contact with ordinary reality and learn how to deal with it. These are some of the things the anorexic misses:

She will not have thought or acted for herself. We have already dealt with this at some length but to recap briefly, not only will she not have thought far beyond the confines of the family explanatory myth, she will not know *how* to think. She will only be able to repeat ideas and actions. She will not be able to originate them. Her critical thinking will be limited to the rigid pattern of the myth; she will be able to sneer 'put down' and repeat clichés but she will not criticize anything for herself.

Normal children have one important experience that anorexics miss: they are permitted to behave childishly and get away with it. They are allowed to make mistakes, to get things wrong. By testing reality as children, they have a whole backlog of approximations, of playing with reality, that anorexics lack. When, as older children and teenagers, they merge the play experiences achieved as individuals at home with the group experiences of school and semi-adult play, they form a contact with one another as partners in trial-and-error that anorexics never have. The anorexic's adult attitude separates her from other children who find her aloof and independent. Anorexics tend to cultivate the friendship of teachers, to do 'good' things and seek out other people who, like them, are also adult and mature. With them, they engage in the same kind of sterile watching, criticizing and self-boosting that they do at home with mother and father.

This may not sound a spectacular loss — the lack of contact with peers and normality. But without this experience, anorexics are unable to make contact with reality, both in the shape of dealing with peers (male and female) and in the shape of the world outside. This is the reason behind feeling so 'left out of things'. Let us take a closer look at this.

NORMALITY: THE MISSING LINK

It may seem very subtle, almost too subtle, to say that the lack of proper contact with peers is the missing link between leading a normal life and the life of distress that anorexics experience. But this is one of the few links in the long chain that shapes anorexia that something can be done about. In fact it will be the focus of the rest of the book: you can re-do your early learning with other people if you want to. It is possible when you are shown how. But you cannot change your family structure and in my experience, it is seldom possible to treat parents or to change them sufficiently to help you to correct deficits. Apart from anything else, they seldom see the point of the exercise — it is not they who need changing after all, in their view, it is their daughter; she is the one with the problem. Let us see what this missing link really is.

The logic of reality testing

No system of thought can ever be equivalent to the reality it describes — it is logically impossible. We can only conceive of a perfect match between theory and reality. Most science fiction does this and most of the common myths and fantasies about science and future societies are based on the conception or belief that there exists — somewhere — a perfect theory about reality. We cannot, however, achieve this in any real sense: to be perfect, to describe reality fully, a theory has to be capable of locking time into its own framework and controlling every variable in the reality it describes. If it does this, it is no longer a theory — it becomes real.

All this is an elaborate way of saying that no framework or idea about life or reality is completely correct. There will always be areas of weakness in any theory and areas in which the theory is wrong. This is true of even the most advanced theories in sub-atomic particle physics or mathematics. It is even more true of human affairs. In physics for example, to some extent the variables can be controlled — far more so than in society —by doing an experiment in a laboratory. Not so with human affairs. Even for psychologists or sociologists. Anyone with a smattering of knowledge of the history of science, and especially psychology in this century alone, will confirm that the essence of that history has been an endless stream of arguments about which theory is the correct one. Physicists, psychologists, chemists — all of them argue about which of many theories is the right one; there is no way of settling these things easily because most theories are right some of the time and in some aspects.

Now if this is true of the scientific world, how much more true is it of the ideas about life and reality that you learn in the family? In other words, what your parents teach you is based on their selection of many theories about reality and about how to behave in life. Some of your parents' theories may be absolutely true, but like the theories of scientists, they are inductive theories derived out of your parents' own experiences and limited by their own experiences. If a scientist never did new research or never exposed his theories to the criticism of his colleagues, if he lived in perfect isolation, and never listened to what his colleagues said, or read about what they had found, he would be a very limited, misled person. Imagine the terrible consequences of such a person getting into a position of power, being in charge of society and making it run entirely on his, partially true, theories. This is what actually happens in some societies. And this is, in effect, what happens in the anorexic's home. The parents become like the isolated scientist and they ensure that their children grow up in an isolated way.

The most disturbing thing about this is that normally, children automatically act like scientists: they take various theories and ideas which they are offered about life, both from their parents and their friends, and they test these theories out — loosely, robustly, roughly and experimentally — in games, in play, in feeling and so on. Not only does this childish experimentation put children in contact with life but it also creates in their minds and actions a sense of identity and privacy — a sense of being, of having a right to explore, experiment and, ultimately, to exist. How strong this sense is depends, of course, on their experiences but most normal children have in some degree or other their own sense of being. It is an essential element of individuality and uniqueness, but, more simply, it is vital to their survival: they learn that it is right to have ideas, feelings, thoughts and actions quite apart from and different from those of their parents. They learn that they have, in childlike ways, the right to be 'normal scientists' — to form their own theories about reality and to test or act them out. Being private means being able to think outside approved frameworks. It is the first step in learning the logic of true survival. While normal children are involved in this, the anorexic learns instead the logic of surviving only in her household.[1] (*see opposite*)

What does this all mean in practical terms? The central point about a normal child or adolescent is that he or she is basically *free* — not in the simple romantic notions of artists and novelists but in the sense of the child's experience. Such children are free of crippling systems, free of the need to live within them. They are free to explore and try things their own way, see things through their own eyes for themselves, without the burden of being tied to accepting and living out a particular ready-made theory. Let me detail what this means as this applies to various age levels.

Normal child behaviour

As a child, the normal person is brought up pretty much as an anorexic child would be. That is, normal children are also obliged to live in their parents' system as if it were the only way. There is no perfect system of reality (as I mentioned earlier) so normal children also grow up with 'flawed' systems. They too have to suffer the deficiencies of their parents. Being normal does not mean being perfect, nor does it mean being gifted, trouble-free or free of neuroses. Normal parents can be just as troubled as the parents of anorexics, and in fact often are. Normal children are also subject to neglect, even isolation. But they have one advantage: they have the missing link. They are free to modify their parents' influence on their own lives. They are free to use their own minds and behaviours outside to supplement any lacks from within the family. A normal growing child will disobey and be naughty. He or she will easily give up a parent's theory or dictate if it does not altogether work. Imagine a child playing with a ball. The ball goes into the road. The child wants to fetch it but remembers that mummy said: "Never go onto the road because of the cars". So the child leaves it. Her friend comes up and says ,"Don't be silly — just go and fetch it." That is a new theory for the child. The first child will not go against her mother's theory. Another friend

1 Normal children do not even know they are learning to survive properly: it is taught at such a deep level that they do not realize it is happening. Anorexics are taught in the same deep way and they do not realize that they have not learnt the same system.

says: "All right, I'll get it." She watches carefully for cars and when the road is clear, she retrieves the ball. End of experience. But the normal child learns from all this. She learns that rules are made to be broken, as long as the problem — the danger — of which the rule warns is carefully watched for.

By repeating this kind of reality experience several times, the normal child learns a whole range of behaviours and thoughts about her reality that add to and develop the theories of her parents. An absolutely vital part of experiences, such as the one mentioned, is the role played by friends in the experiment — their actions and their criticisms. In our example, the girl's friends said she was 'silly' not to retrieve the ball. These childish imperatives, not to be silly, should be and usually are powerful motives for new learning, for developing new specific-situation rules. The usual symbiosis and power of mother is broken, temporarily, by the need to be liked by the group and to play the game.

You can imagine over time how vital and important all of this is. The pathway to 'being' with other children, to 'normalizing' your dependency on and obedience to your parents is to let the symbiosis break down by being diluted. In the years of childhood, it must be diluted by friends as a prologue to your being able to emerge as a person who is not over-led by your needs to conform with your parents' notions. You see your own 'silliness' and the flaws in your parents' ideas as well as your friends' silliness (the one who wanted to run into the road for the ball without checking for cars first) and you are taught the solution in a rudimentary non-verbal way — the correct alternative to solving the problem. Moreover you also see the relative value to your parents' rules: that is that they are partly right.

Every time this happens you build on this awareness of relativity. You build your sense of relativity about emotions and symbiosis too. A child goes through whole sets of symbioses. The 'correct' theory (*watch* for cars in the road) supplied by the friend in our example opens up a new symbiosis: the friend knows more in the context than mummy. It is a child's way to be all or nothing, so the child worships her friend and her wisdom. She is still in symbiosis with her mother at home and for most things — but not in playing. Soon however, she will find that her friend too has flaws. The friend will be wrong about something and after the hurt and disappointment, the normal child will get over it and find someone else. Each time she does this she will have learnt more about real life and will be undergoing several symbiotic relationships, each of which will have diluted the power of her parents.

When a child does not go through these steps, this is what he or she misses:

(i) *Being silly* To start the whole process you have to be 'silly'. If you are not, you will not experience the power of your friends to change you, to modify the theory you are carrying. What happens to the anorexic is that she never learns how to be silly amongst friends where it is a 'quick-and-easy' learning experience. Everyone is silly now and then, teased about it, laughed at, and laughs and learns in turn. And we do it to others, as a right. Anorexics are exposed in their families to adult censorship for being silly or weak or useless and it cripples them. They vow to avoid being silly because they suffer for it. So they never learn how to accept being silly, how to see it as the first step in the creative process of learning about life.

(ii) *Being teased and feeling vulnerable* When you are silly and are laughed at it is normal to find it very upsetting. The first few times, the normal child runs home in tears and should be physically comforted by her mother or father. Wise parents comfort the child, let her cry and hear what it is all about then send the child back. The wise parent admits mistakes, sure in the knowledge that he or she is roughly right and that it is time for their daughters to learn new rules. The wise parent also trusts his or her daughter and her friends.

It is this being able to run home to seek sanctity that helps the child's individuality to grow. The wise parent accepts the need for his or her ideas, recognizes the role of childhood learning and is not threatened by being 'wrong'. The parent does not over-react or over-protect in the wrong way or at the wrong time. But what happens in the anorexic's home?

Inevitably there is no sanctity. Few parents of anorexics

offer proper *physical* comfort; they are afraid of holding and hugging, it is too stressful. They prefer a child who does not need such comfort. Moreover, a child coming home in these circumstances will likely as not distress and upset the whole household. This is the typical response of an anorexic's mother:

> "Oh God, what is the matter? What have you done? As if I haven't got enough to worry about...Keep quiet, your brother is doing his homework, your father is sleeping, or your mother has a migraine...Quick, tell me about it and stop crying...Oh, your friend went into the road, did she? Called you silly, did she? Stupid girl, who is she? Yes, I thought so — not a very nice little girl — no manners. And her mummy's a bit funny too. When will you learn not to play with children like that? They are not the same as we are — nasty people. You are not to see that girl again, see? It's a disgrace — we won't have girls like that laughing at you. Why do you want to go out and play — there's plenty for you to do at home. Have you practised your piano lesson yet? Or you can help me with the supper..."

Experiences like this are familiar to most anorexics. They learn not only not to take their troubles home but also not to go through experiences. They learn to avoid being silly or being teased and worse, they learn to justify their avoidance by a myth that stresses their superiority and specialness. This completes the chain. They avoid learning and, thanks to the great *explanatory myth*, they feel relatively happy about it.

(iii) *Being part of 'the gang'* Apart from missing the symbiosis dilution of which I spoke earlier, if you subscribe to the great *explanatory myth*, you will not go back out to play after an upset. Your friends will as a result be puzzled and a little afraid — perhaps they will get into trouble? They are only children and they cannot understand the logic of it all. When you do not come back to play, eventually you are cut out. Later, when your friends do see you, and you ignore them, they become hurt and angry and puzzled. They may even tease you more and thereby upset you again. You become known for being aloof, different. Nobody plays with you. You only attract people similar to yourself, people who will reinforce your family myths. Further, you have upset your friends and they have upset you — it only goes to confirm your parents' dictum, "They are nasty people, best to be avoided."

Unfortunately, in choosing not to get involved in life in the same way as a normal child, you cut yourself away from a vital support system without which you cannot survive growing up. Being part of 'the gang' is not just a childish phase — it is a developmental link on the road to being free, an independent person. It sets up emotional, physical and intellectual contacts which, in the tasks ahead during adolescence, could and should offer you constructive help.

(iv) *Not being lonely* When you only have your parents' ideas and company, or the company they choose for you, an incredible gap in your life occurs of which they are unaware. But you know all about it. Belonging to a gang ordinarily fills up a child's spare time and much of his or her emotional life. The normal child focuses on 'gang' things — whether or not so-and-so likes him or her, what the latest pop songs are and so on. Normal children take their parents for granted, they seldom worry about them or their affairs. Anorexic girls miss out on most of this — especially the thrill and excitement of it all. If any of this is done at all, it is done as an illicit pleasure, a guilty secret, kept from the family.

Childish things are disapproved of; your behaviour is supposed to be sensible and mature; you are not to cry, not to need physical comfort, you are not supposed to be a baby anymore and demand attention (much of which could be satisfied by a combination of home and the gang). You are neglected and cut off from any substitute for attention from the family, both of which make you lonely. You have to compensate by doing good deeds, working hard at family-set tasks and helping around the home. The trouble is that there is only so much a lonely child can do and so much she can take, before eventually she begins to pressure her parents. She demands affection, attention, demands to be noticed. In fact, the anorexic girl puts her finger on the heart of the matter; since her parents have made themselves responsible for her state, by rights they must do things for her. And they do: she is cut off and filled with their ideas, their behaviours, which do not satisfy her. When she complains, they become irritated and urge her simply to do more of what they have told her to do.

Not being normal means, in this context, having the basis of one's creativity and energy cut away and pushed into empty, superficial rituals that leave you lonely and disgruntled. Further, the anorexic girl hates herself for needing attention, for whining and for being a nuisance. She goes on protesting but she feels bad and ugly. There is no physical contact, no emotionality, no challenges, no childishness, no outside contact. The anorexic girl senses these things and learns (while her peers are busy enjoying life) that all these needs are signs of inadequacy or weakness. To the loneliness is added a deep sense of guilt and hurt: a massive and growing nausea and self-disgust. And no way to solve it.

Normal adolescent behaviour

Normal children pass into adolescence by intensifying their activity within their groups and by expanding these to include different sets of groups; one for dealing with boyfriends, another for girls, one for sport, one for work and so on. By the age of 13 or 14, most teenagers have a well-developed sense of their own systems of thought, feelings and behaviour, as being separate from both their parents' and from their sibling groups. They are self-seeking, and while they still cling to their groups for support, confirmation and emotional security, they are beginning to be self-directed, to think about what they want out of life and relationships. Their parents are still there as important components of their lives, but their ideas and morality are seen as separate, something to be argued with, probed, exposed and if necessary, modified. By late teens, most adolescents are very aware of their parents' failings and weaknesses in their systems of thought. It troubles them little, however, because by then, they are far too busy with their own lives to do much more than find ways of avoiding the pressures and constraints put upon them by their parents.

In childhood, the child learns to think for him or herself, to think out his or her own ideas and behaviours in minor but important ways, to dilute the symbiosis. All of this is, however, done within the confines of the formal existence set up for him or her by his family and society. That is, the child bends the rules, does things for him or herself while doing roughly what he or she is told. This privacy or individuality is a limited one. In adolescence, however, the sense of being personal and private deepens: formal systems are criticized and questioned. Growing adolescents set up and structure their own sub-cultures, their own private worlds. Further, the emotional-physical barrier, the key to cementing new symbioses, is finally broken in adolescence so that the new intimacy (boy-girl) actually offers an emotional and physical satisfaction and security of a quality superior to that of home. This is the keystone on which the tasks of adulthood are built: the one-to-one relationships that will be the basis of dismantling the power of 'the gangs' and the adolescent sub-system. The door is then open for adult intimacy and an exploration of both the new adult relationships and the world at large.

Adolescents need more than just the support of their groups to complete the tasks set. They need an ethic — a general social approval (or rather, a social ambivalence); they need books, movies and movements that direct them into experiments with relationships, in sex and in behaviour in general. It is no easy task for anyone to break parental rules or to tackle adult relationships. How do you learn to touch someone? How do you learn to kiss? To trust? How do you learn to be at ease, relaxed? How do you learn to be *any*thing? Most adults see these things as 'ordinary', forgetting how tough it was in the beginning; they forget about the massive need to be accepted, the terrible anxiety of being rejected, of being thought silly, that awful repulsion when it goes wrong the first time; the hurt and the loneliness. Teenagers have to learn all this and they need the teasing, the cajoling and the lightness of their groups in which to do it; 'the gang' sets it up, making it easier to go it alone. It helps to relieve the anxiety and above all, the sense of repulsion, the feeling (often intense and threatening) of awkwardness, clumsiness, foolishness, callousness, naïvety — the anger, hurt and frustration that always attends learning new things; the misunderstanding and insensitivity and so on. Even normal parents cannot help much in this. These experiences must be shared with others going through the same thing; a parent gives the wrong kind of help, tries either to over-protect or to brush off adolescent experience too easily. 'The gang' or a friend know how to help much more — a look, a touch, a word; all convey a feeling of sympathy shared by *equals* going through the same struggle at the same time.

The important learning task in adolescence is simple: keep going. Learn from your mistakes. At no other time in one's life is it so important to be free to be individual, experimental and to think for yourself. Only you can manage your life. In childhood parents are able to do things for you — they can protect you, do your homework, comfort you — they can even live for you because the needs you have are minor. Even in adulthood it is possible to get away with using others to hide behind: marriage, for example, is one way; careers and professions are another. Being married enables a person to avoid a whole range of problems by virtue of being socially and practically 'excused' by obligations to a partner. Society does not put pressure on its members to sort out relational difficulties, or personal inadequacies, especially not its married members. Add to this the power of a career or job and it is possible to get away with a great deal. I know so many doctors, for instance, top specialists, who are incredibly immature, who behave like spoilt brats and tyrants to their staff and families, yet face no stress or anxiety simply because their status guarantees that society will excuse their behaviour.

Adolescence is the one time in life when it is difficult to hide or to excuse failure. An attorney or a doctor who fails miserably as an individual can, and will, excuse himself or blame others. An adolescent who cannot get a girl or boyfriend knows deeply and immediately that he or she is failing — and so does their society.

The early training in private thinking becomes absolutely invaluable in adolescence because it is the framework on which personal relationships are built. Think about it: your parents and society teach you to behave and think formally and they check on this. At school, you succeed or fail according to how well you do the work. Later, it is the same with your profession or career. Your personal life, however, is left up to you. Your parents and society care that you stay within the law and that you do roughly whatever is expected of you, that is, you have a relationship with the 'right' person of the 'right' sex, get married and have children and so on. There are no public tests for sensitivity; for the correct expression of warmth, or for making your partner happy. We order people to 'cherish' and 'obey' but we do not teach it or check it. How do you learn to argue? How do you gratify your partner sexually? How do you give affection non-sexually? These are all vital issues and they form the crucible of most private and public human actions, yet we have the paradoxical situation, whereby we learn more about how to experience emotion from film fragments or novels than we ever get from school or university or from home. These things can only be learnt through private relationships.

The normal child's ability to think and to behave outside his or her parents' framework develops in adolescence into the ability to set up his or her own private world — a world that will eventually be shared with another person. This is central to the issue. If you have no private life, and no personal world, other people are seen or experienced simply as formal units. You cannot share their world, because to share, you must have your own private world to offer as an individual, and also, you must be able to recognize the private world of another beneath the formal and superficial structures. Developing these twin abilities is really what adolescence is all about; all the learning, the trial and error, the being silly, making mistakes, all these lessons of childhood set the individual up, ready to learn how to be a person in the individual, private sense of normal human intimacy. Just as the child has to learn to cross the road, learn to judge the safety factor for herself, learn to take the teasing and the goading, learn to keep going to keep the game on the go, so the adolescent has to learn a vast amount of new information about how to talk to people, how to make contact, to love, to balance self-needs with the needs of others and so on. The adolescent who runs away and who retreats from the first failure, the first teasing, the first feelings of ugliness and repulsion, the adolescent who uses these awful experiences to justify never trying again is the teenager destined to fail as a person. The key element is to keep going, not to run away, to keep trying, to keep on learning. Sooner or later, it works — not in the simplistic sense of once and forever but it works for the time being. Life is not a matter of solving problems once and for all; it is a matter of learning how to tackle problems and to keep going at them. Some you put aside, some you solve; sometimes you rest on your laurels too, but there are always other things to test, to excite you and to stretch you. There are no final solutions in life. You do not stop learning and challenging till you die. And I include in this learning such activities as learning to relax properly, to rest, to be properly lazy and so on. All of life is learning, and our bodies are physiologically programmed to accept learning. What you learn to achieve personally as an adolescent serves you for the rest of your life. It cannot be underestimated or dismissed as mere 'kids' stuff. Let us see now what happens to anorexics in this vital phase.

The adolescence of anorexics

Earlier, we spelt out how anorexia starts and what the consequences are that help cement the various forms into place in the anorexic's personality. What we will look at here is how the early childhood learning, plus the new anorexic rituals and the shock and distress that accompany them, jar and distract the anorexic from the normal tasks of adolescence. Once we have seen this, we will be able to pick out precisely what the anorexic has to do, both to get the childhood learning done and to get back on the proper adolescent rails. *Do not panic*. It seems a huge task — which it is — but it is possible; once the initial steps are taken it does become harder to keep going but I promise you it is a lot less frightening. Nothing is more frightening than living a fearful life in the dark, not knowing why, or how, or even what is going on. Once you have seen what it is, you will no longer be in the dark. And that really counts, believe me.

The anorexic teenager is spared all this adolescent learning; instead, she retreats from contact with her peers into the security of the familiar world of her parents. Her attempts to make contact outside are psychologically blocked, so that not only does she not go through the kind of trauma already discussed, but she learns with her family's help to regard it as 'beneath' her, a foolish and futile waste of time. Thus reassured and probably traumatized by her first few 'real' contacts outside the family, she switches her attention to learning how to do what her parents have told her to do to the best of her ability. Just as the normal teenager throws his or her energy into being a private person and trusts instinctively the new direction, so the anorexic puts her trust in her parents' ideas and ways.

It is not as if the parents of anorexics have no ideas for what they should be doing. Far from it. They have masses of clichés: "Find a decent boyfriend — get married — your studies come first" — all familiar slogans that parents use, but there is one significant difference. Normal teenagers laugh at their parents — especially at what they think constitutes a 'decent' boyfriend and their idea of marriage and studies and so on. The anorexic girl listens avidly as her mother and father lay out plans for her and tell her what to do, all their ideas and all to be done their way. She is told to be 'scintillating', to keep a man interested, to make him 'fall at her feet'.

But how do you find a 'decent' guy if you have never had any experience? How do you 'keep a man interested'? How do you be 'scintillating'? What do you do when he 'falls at your feet'? Do not laugh: anorexics — everybody — need to know these things. If the anorexic had had friends, she would have learnt far more from them than from her parents — "Make him come after you — ignore him," they would say. Parents fabricate, even the best of them; they tend to exaggerate their own charmed lives, blend romanticism with all the movies they have seen, and above all, they forget how terrifying it all was at the time. Kids need other kids. Anorexics get their parents' myths instead. When they push for more, the parents get angry: "Don't nag — just go and do it." Having failed to teach anything, refusing to allow their children to go through trial and error, they send them out to win gold medals with their first performances. And woebetide them if they fail or let their parents down in any way.

The result? The terrified girl goes out trying to remember every bit of advice she has ever been given, every half-baked cliché, and ends up being charming, sophisticated, seemingly mature, adultized, but a doormat, open to being manipulated by everyone. Let us take the example of going to a dance. If the girl is pretty, she is going to get attention anyway, especially from men. Everything may go very well to begin with — purely because of this fact. If she is able to talk about the weather in an adult way, fine, she will attract meteorologists who do not expect 14-year olds to know so much about these things. In short, she will attract all the wrong people for all the wrong reasons. Not that meteorologists are necessarily the 'wrong' kind of people or that being pretty is 'wrong'; the point is that the girl should be attracting people and communicating with people of her own age and experience. Nine times out of ten, the people attracted by the anorexic girl are not good for her because they fail to see beyond the superficial. Most of these relationships are doomed from the start, even if they happen to result in marriage, because there is nothing substantial to them.

What happens to anorexics is this: as responsive doormats, they co-operate and please their men too eagerly, are soon bored (and boring) because there is no follow-through, no proper shared personal lives (and sex, remember, can be as impersonal as yawning). They do not often even know how to hold a conversation. Worse, if the girl's parents approve, wedding bells (or thoughts of them) are immediately sounded and the poor girl is hussled into thinking "This is it! — this is the one and only" before the first week is out. No chance for experimentation, no chance to learn, to explore and to make mistakes.

When I say the anorexic is used as a doormat, I mean doormat. All the learning capacity, the anger, the stubborness, the energy, the caring and sexuality is locked away in the anorexic's secret world of fantasy and ritual. Publicly, she is an arrogant, over-sophisticated doormat. Privately, she is a stubborn, obsessive, frightened child. Untreated, these two worlds never meet, yet everything is there, just waiting to come out. Take all the anger in the anorexic's rituals, the force with which food is thrust into her mouth, the determination with which the same food can be resisted, the agony of vomiting, the discipline of lying, the pain of loneliness — take all these and put this energy into a relationship with another person, man or woman, and a personality will be born. It is what happens to every normal teenager. However, the anorexic's lack of knowledge, terror of being left alone (learnt from her parents and transferred to every other person she meets), her feeling of isolation and her rituals create a dread of loneliness, to the extent that she will literally give up everything to avoid it. Unfortunately, it is just this determination that results in her giving up her personality, her rights as a person and ultimately, her life.

As time goes on and the unfortunate anorexic settles into her long adolescence, her loneliness intensifies and she begins to split off from reality: she maintains her outside façade, but inside she begins to focus more and more on the physical limits of the only presence, the only reality in which she has an effect — with which she can play and at least have some satisfaction — her body. That she abuses. She pushes it any which way. Not only does she eat and vomit, not only does she starve it and then fill it, but she also masturbates excessively, uses suppositories endlessly, takes laxatives, scratches herself, mutilating, tugging, pushing, chewing, smoking, spitting and picking her nose. Her body is all she has to play with. All this fills in her spare time and helps to fight off the inner collapse and terror eating away inside her.

Outside, in the world, she throws herself into her parents' clichés with a total ferocity. As time goes on and she has been hospitalized once or twice, her parents become less glib, more frenzied in themselves, searching violently for any sign of alleviation or improvement. Many of my patients' parents confessed to me that at times, they wished their daughters had died — just to end it all. (Note, they did not wish *they* would die — which would also 'end it all' — only their daughter).

The stress grows intolerable, the girl works harder, goes out more, literally forces herself to find a solution. Anorexics explain their failure by arguing (as their parents teach them to) that somewhere they are not getting the system right, somewhere they are failing to perform the cliché properly. After desperately and obsessively trying to get it right, spending sleepless nights, they resort to a frenzy of compulsive repetitions of clichés. If mother says, "Wear more make-up", they virtually buy up a beauty shop. If father says, "Wear some jewellery", hey presto, they look like Christmas trees. If mother says, "Read more", they exhaust libraries. If father says, "You need to study more", well, two or three Ph.D.'s later, nothing has improved.

This is just one aspect of it. As adolescence wears into adulthood, any set of clichés given by anyone who seems 'caring' is followed and adopted. Causes, ideas, diets, religions, life-styles — all are tried and all have their use for a while but end up on the scrap heap of the anorexic's mind as just so many discarded skins, unable to fit her rampant needs.

They do not, however, disappear. Each fresh relationship —be it with a person, a book or an idea — ends in the same way, with the anorexic's genuine abilities — to please, to sense needs, to acquiesce and to sacrifice self and energy — being used to fulfil the demands of others.

Once a doormat, always a doormat. The anorexic is, however, grateful. She is at least needed to be that — a doormat. These crumbs, the basis of her relationship with her parents, are the familiar ones and the only ones she thinks she can get (because of her essential ugliness and uselessness, she thinks) so she hangs on to them even while she has lost hope of ever being properly cared for in a relationship. Each such relationship takes its toll on her energies since each has to be serviced to survive. This all leads up to the situation where the anorexic may build up a whole web of essentially crippling relationships that ensure she has no time left for her real needs at all. Usually her parents are at the centre of the web, followed by a boyfriend or husband, several girlfriends, perhaps a lover or two (or a boss who needs her body every now and then) and a handful of causes. Each sets her tasks to perform, gives her clichés, and locks her into a pattern that ensures that she will never find herself. Breaking these relationships, or deepening them to make them work differently, becomes an impossibility. As life goes on, they seem to be the only links left with the outside world and the only things between her and her main worry: the death of her parents (or husband or friends) and the loneliness that will ensue.

The tragedy of our time is that once adolescence is over, it is very difficult for the direction taken to be changed under one's own steam. Adulthood locks you in place; it locks your fears and how you cope with them into your personality. If you do not take the chances of learning a proper privacy, a proper reality-testing and a looseness and robustness in your personality, it becomes increasingly more difficult to get back to it; our society does not encourage regression or second childhoods. It does not foster the insight necessary to see what should be done, nor does it create the intellectual and emotional climate to ensure that re-learning does take place. As a child, if you had had a normal childhood, you would have been into other children's homes and you would have seen how they lived and how their parents related to one another; it would have given you an insight — another way of seeing or another picture of things, in the same way as throwing your lot in with 'the gang' would have. By the time adulthood comes along, if you have not made contact for yourself, these avenues are closed to you; children are geared and exposed to the alternatives, but all that adults get are movies and novels about other lifestyles and other kinds of relationships. Our societies trade on ideas but have no way of showing how they should be properly realized. Further, by and large, they censor the experimentation necessary for change to be achieved. They do not tolerate adolescent behaviour in public by adults; only in the privacy of a relationship is this tolerated at all. And this is exactly what anorexics have never learned how to form. The circle is complete.

Normal adulthood

For the normal adult, once the basis for forming relationships is made, these relationships then become the basis for a whole new world of experience. During adolescence, the private-personal world is extended from the child level of 'the gang' to close intimacy of a psycho-sexual kind. 'The gang' broadens into 'teenagers versus the older generation' and leaves the individual breathing space to satisfy deeper one-to-one relationships as well. This pushing back of society plus the new relationships broaden out in turn into the task of finding jobs, having an interest in and eventually taking an interest in society at large. The one-to-one sexual intimacy becomes played with, expanded or narrowed at will. Life is more complex, you begin to see things more clearly: having a job and running a career take more than just talent and hard work — there is a whole personal dimension involved. It matters how you get on with people, how you play their games. Success or failure, superiority or inferiority — they all depend on how you behave. You have to learn to preserve the child-adolescent parts of you with their uniqueness and individuality in the face of massive pressures and games applied to you by adult society. It is no fun and no longer just play — your survival depends on how you respond to the excitement and challenge of adulthood. You have to take on the older generation and the full weight of their hostility and affection and still keep your private and personal thoughts and acts intact.

A normal adult is thrown into the kind of world an anorexic experiences from birth but by then the adult is infinitely more equipped to cope and survive. Take for example the experience of having a job where your boss wants you to behave in a certain way, if you do not you risk losing his esteem, perhaps even your job. I remember the terror of going against my professor's ideas at university — my job was threatened, he pulled every emotional trick in the book to coerce me into thinking and behaving as he wanted. It was massive pressure but I was not a child; I did not need him that much — I had my own family, my own students, my own support. I was able emotionally to survive the pressure for long enough to call his bluff. On a couple of occasions, I gave in to him. The challenge and the exhilaration were distressing but I survived and learnt not to be put in such a position again — to choose who I worked for more carefully, to know that ideas have to be fought for at all levels (just like one's personality) if they are worth anything. It stood me in good stead later. When I could not create the kind of treatment programmes I wanted to have at the hospital at which I worked, I knew enough by then not to burn myself out in a useless fight against disinterested authorities (as I had done against my professor). I simply took myself and my patients into private practice. It is the kind of dilemma that many adults have to face sooner or later.

Anorexics cannot do this kind of thing for themselves because they are faced, in effect, with this situation at the age of seven, eight or nine when they *have* to give in. Normal children do not have to face this situation prematurely and so do not later feel that they have to give in to authority every time. Later, when they have learnt to be self-reliant, they can take on these situations; although it is still nerve-racking they can take it. In fact, this is what life is all about: the battle for yourself, your mind, and your own relationships.

Once you have formed the basis of your relationship to the opposite sex, to the older generation and to your friends, when you have survived a few tiffs with your partner, and withstood a few changes of partner, jobs and friends, then you begin to see that every situation provides grounds for exploration and for developing your own ideas, thinking, insights, abilities and so on.

Not all normal people do all these things. There are many people who get stuck along the way, who settle for less or hide behind relationships or careers and the like. As you go through life, you are free to get off at any point you like. There is no end of the road, no completely 'normal' person. But it is vital to be on that road. Anorexics and a whole lot of other people with problems do not get on the road. The key is not to stagnate in any relationship: keep your life growing and moving as situations and demands change. Life is not a matter of hiding behind clichés and formalities. To be married, to have kids, to live a decent life — these are all symbols of normality — easy to hide behind. To some people, to reach the age of 21 is to have done everything and all that remains is to settle down. Wrong. Every little task demands the same private creativity and existential thinking that you should have learnt in your teens.

Relating properly to people means being able to reach behind the formalities to their private and personal lives and selves. Every new person requires new ideas and new behaviours. Each new person stimulates or depresses you or demands things of you in new ways. Normal people should be aware of these things and be prepared to honestly appraise how they feel and not be content to use slogans or clichés. If you think you are happily married and a film star or a new man in the neighbourhood happens to excite you massively, shouldn't you find out why? If someone makes you so mad that you could scream, shouldn't you find out why? These are investigations that may be difficult and disruptive for normal people, but they prove impossible for anorexics.

SUMMING UP

It is important for the anorexic to realize that anorexia has held her back from proper development; there are plenty of other people who fail in life who take the easy ways out or who hide behind clichés and social formulae. Very often these are the very people who form the bulk of social opinion and who uphold the clichés because it helps them maintain their own evasions. They need people like anorexics to have as scape-goats; pointing a finger at them takes their minds off their own hassles.

I include myself in this accusation because once, while I was 'helping' people in need, I was in fact using it to obscure the fact that my own life, while overtly appearing very satisfying, was in fact a mess. On the surface, I appeared happily married, a successful academic with a successful practice, while in reality I was overweight, overworked and I had neglected my personal development and that of my family. And all around me were people doing the same: colleagues and friends. We all looked the same, had the same problems, and told the same double-barrelled lies, namely that we were successful and that we helped people. When I set about changing my life, I hit problems and pressures I barely knew existed. I went through hell to change my life and in the process nearly lost everything, including my life, but in the end, it was worth it. It was part of normal growing up, staying on the road. I do not know a living person who does not need to explore his or her life further.

So what you have to achieve is attainable. Would I ask you to do something I had not done for myself? You are not alone, so bear with me. Realize (using this chapter to help you) what is involved and try to understand the spirit in which it is written. Nothing is easy — not just for you but for everyone.

Chapter 12

How to survive
anorexia nervosa

The main task, I think, is clear. To survive anorexia you have to move from your present system of coping to a new one in which the kind of psychological tasks described in the last chapter are confronted. You have to do this not by trying to stop your rituals and taking on the appearance of normality by resisting your desire to diet or to gorge, but by using your rituals as a means of opening up the child-like needs inside you. The object of the exercise is to give yourself the freedom to attend to your inner self, the time to get to know yourself properly and to plan your life around it. Your personality has been cramped and starved of daylight. Keep your rituals, open them out, give them life, let your real needs have a say, a demand in your life. If, after reading through the last eleven chapters you remain unconvinced of your right to be the person you are, then, I think, you will never be. I am going to assume that most of the people who have read so far want to get better and are determined to go through whatever is necessary to do so. One word of warning: do not expect to 'make friends and influence people' while you are letting your 'child' grow. It is not possible.

The best way I know of explaining something of what it is that you have to do is to use a case study. So let me introduce Angela, one of my patients who went through the kind of survival course you will have to go through. Try, in reading her case, to identify the pattern of her treatment so that you can identify the essential features of the actions she took to get better. Do not try to do exactly what she did; every person is different and you must only use cases to give you ideas to apply in your own life. Do not copy.

CASE HISTORY: ANGELA

When I first saw Angela, she was a 28-year-old woman, married for several years and recently registered as a postgraduate student at the university at which I taught. She complained of being unable to control her anorexia nervosa and she had clear episodes of normal eating behaviour interspersed with bouts of anorexia. She is a very typical case:

"It would start slowly. That is I would be getting along just fine for a while — something that happened for brief periods — my work would be going well, things would be fine at home with Joe, my husband. I felt I was doing well, achieving well and so on. My parents were pleased with me. I felt good, quite powerful, in fact, clear. I was careful with my food, just breaking even — not dieting but not over-eating either. Then I started to worry for no apparent reason, about my weight, my body. I felt fat. I really wasn't. But especially after meals, I would get alarmed and upset by feeling bloated. Then I'd over-eat a little at one meal, and then a bit more, and each time I'd panic about not looking thin. I'd feel my stomach, weigh myself everyday, every hour, before every bowel movement, the lot. I also took laxatives after a meal or when I felt fat, to empty my bowels quickly so I wouldn't be panicked by the figures on the scales. This all seemed to come out of the blue — I didn't think that anything in particular had caused it. Then I would suddenly snap and start to gorge, I'd stuff in food with the attitude of 'Oh God, if I'm going to put on weight, I might as well do it properly'. By this time, my worry about weight had taken over my life — discreetly — I'd learnt not to show my obsession with weight (no one liked it, they thought I was crazy). I was trying to remain normal and calm on the outside all the while hiding my obsession. I would be polite, make small talk, then once Joe had gone to work, I'd rush and check my weight. I couldn't stand it. It was like living with a tiger, a monster inside me — two monsters, really: one daring me to eat and the other forever warning me not to. It was endless, these voices in my head. They never stopped.

"Then something would push me over. Someone might remark on my figure or something would go wrong: I'd fail an essay or someone would criticize me and I would feel so terrible. It dawned on me that I was getting dangerously out of control. I was near a breakdown. I couldn't concentrate on my work because I was too hassled with my weight and I wasn't eating properly. Suddenly I was in terror of losing control which meant that people would see I was inadequate; it was showing in my weight and in my body and now someone had criticized me — Oh God, what was going to happen?

"Then I would make the decision to diet. Simple. Control myself, control my eating. Like my father said: 'Self-control is the key to life.' So it was clear. I must get over this ridiculous obsession and I would be all right again. So I didn't eat a thing. It was very very hard but I was ruthless with myself. I made a little régime in which to stop being tempted, I would keep busy, doing this and that — usually out of home so that I would be on 'show' and too scared to eat. I'd allow myself little treats, like a piece of cheese if I got through a couple of hours. Not eating was just as much an obsession as eating. I had to work so hard at it, to programme my whole day. Again I constantly kept a watch on myself in case I was weak. Once, my hunger got beyond a certain stage where I just didn't feel it — it was such a relief. At last I could relax. It was a great weight off body and mind. I didn't have to fight myself any more. Being anorexic was heaven to me. I looked good. I wasn't tempted. I could get on with my work. The only trouble was that to keep it that way, I couldn't afford to eat. I just couldn't eat normally.

"After a while I began to feel odd. My periods were late and I felt dizzy on and off. I felt removed, cut off. Joe was concerned and tried to make me eat. My folks began to fuss too. I began to go through a different kind of hell — I was causing trouble, causing them to be upset — they wanted me to eat and I couldn't.

"When I was a teenager, on several occasions our doctor was called in, and twice I went to hospital. After that I was careful; I tried to eat something, not to go so far. But it has always been difficult. I seem to spend my life in either one or the other of these two states — battling with my uncontrollable urge to eat too much or with the terrible pressure put on me to make me eat. In recent years, the cycle has got more frequent so that every two months or so I seem to get into a crisis.

This is how I worked with Angela. When she came to see me in therapy, I went through the programme I mentioned earlier, the deepening and broadening of her cycles so as to expose and open up the feelings inside, and then we related them to her real life and she began to use her relationships (with Joe and with other people) to get the adolescent learning that she had missed. It took a long time and it was a detailed treatment which there is no room to describe here. So let me summarize the processes to show you what to do.

DEEPENING ANGELA'S UNDERSTANDING OF HER CYCLE

We broke her reactions into four phases and worked at each one. They were:
1. The breaking-even stage
2. The obsession with weight
3. The diet and anorexia
4. Coming out of anorexia

The breaking-even stage

Angela felt she was at her most normal in this phase; she seemed to herself to be in control and she felt as if there was nothing wrong. Looking more closely at it, we discovered (by checking on her life with Joe, her studies, her parents) that her 'normality' was not created by her own self control — her triumph over eating, but rather by the fact that people in her life seemed to be less demanding than at any other time. Angela never quite knew why she suddenly and briefly seemed to be all right. To her, it had always been a bit of a mystery. What I found when treating her was that during these times, she tended to be less anxious than at other times, was more sure of herself and less insightful. She began using a lot of clichés that I knew came from Joe or her parents (that she was happy, fine, even began to wonder why she was seeing me, her problems seemed so insignificant). Over time, I was able to 'plot' and predict almost precisely when she would enter phase 2. It was always preceded by a subtle build-up of pressure on her by either Joe or her parents or her work; she denied this initially but after several months, saw the connection. Take one set of pressures, for example. Joe, her husband, was a fairly conventional, quiet man — patient, loving but not particularly insightful. He had a fairly demanding job to which he was dedicated. Every now and then, though, he would find things too much at work and would come home irritable. This would upset Angela, but not obviously so. She would come in to see me and say: "Oh, I've been fine but poor Joe, he's got such problems at work." On her face would be a little frown and I knew that within a week, Angela would have slipped into phase 2. She could not manage Joe's distress and neither could he. He put subtle pressure on her to mother him, withdrew inside himself and withdrew affection. All this frightened her; she felt she was losing control. She became more clinging and tried to regain the feeling of security but in the process made him even more resistant. Upset, but totally unable to recognize it, she would promptly go and see her parents on some social pretext and then be very disappointed with them (in the way they treated her) but not admit it. They were also unable to cope with upset and became irritated in passive ways if Angela seemed needy. Later, she put it this way:

> "They seemed to be scared by the fact that I was upset. In my early days, I could never say I was upset or worried about Joe because they would have overreacted, I just knew. They would exchange worried looks and my mother would come and sit next to me, very serious. 'Tell me,'

she'd say, patting my hand, 'Is everything all right between you and Joe?' — as if we were on the verge of getting divorced. I didn't see it all like this before I came to therapy. Their reaction frightened me. I trusted my parents absolutely in those days. I used to think, 'Oh God, maybe they're right — maybe Joe's having an affair or something.' They made it all worse. Instead of just being relaxed with me so that I could feel safe for a while, they'd overreact and I'd get frightened. I might have gone there initially with a vague sense of unease about Joe, but by the time I left I was scared out of my mind. It was ridiculous. So I never told them. Then they would think I was putting on a brave front for them and they'd start to fuss about me and then get quite angry with me for making them worry and for not telling them the 'bad' news about Joe — Oh it went on and on, a real mess.''

This is Angela talking after she had developed insight about her condition and after she had kept a diary to prove to herself how things actually were. To continue the story; before her insight, she would simply go back home to Joe, convinced in a low-level way that something really serious was afoot; she would feel that dread she always felt — the depression, the expectancy that things always turned out 'messy'. Consciously unaware of this, she would carry on putting on an act to hide her growing dread. Joe would see her thus and think she was being, in his own words: "A bloody selfish person, totally insensitive to me and my problems", and he would begin to brood even more at home. Usually it would be only a matter of days before Angela would enter phase 2.

The obsession with weight

Angela was trapped. Her only means of getting at least some security (by Joe showing he loved her and by her parents loving her) were blocked. Note that everything we have talked about so far was happening below the surface, as it were. On the surface, everyone was still polite and civil, saying all the right things — "Darling, I love you" — just as before. It is just that, as every anorexic knows, underneath the real feelings are different. As we noted earlier, anorexics are trained as it were, to look beneath the surface and act on the subtext. Their problems occur because they are not permitted to act out openly on the subtext they perceive, but must behave in a subtextual way. Angela's bright and breezy façades to hide her feelings actually showed, (as we later learnt from Joe):

> "A kind of mad frenzy; she'd go to her parents and come back with a fixed smile on her face and promptly start to clean the floors or something similar. It was her way of being bright and cheerful but inside I knew she was freaked but I couldn't say so because she'd deny it. Also, to be honest, I'd never say so — it's not in my nature."

A digression on hyperactivity

Getting into phase 2 was in itself interesting. As Joe said, Angela seemed to become more frenetic with the housework and so on. We found in many anorexics that the obsession-with-weight phase was briefly preceded by a kind of hyper-activity that itself *keyed* in the obsession with weight. Eventually, as our studies went on, we realized that hyperactivity was an integral part of the anxiety about weight. Let me explain this in Angela's case.

We know she is trapped. Inside her is a dread; she fears the return of the semi-permanent depression-volcano that gnaws away at her somewhere in a low-level way. She has a permanent anxiety and worry that things are going to collapse. Now she has been trained to handle this in her family — she must, she tells herself automatically, simply do more of what is expected of her: try harder, work harder. In short, in times of stress, she applies her family's clichés and the new ones she has learnt in her marriage. She tries to please Joe just as she has tried to please her parents. She starts a mental chain of instruction: smile, cook a lovely meal, keep yourself busy, be a good girl and so on. She loads her conscious mind with her clichés and obsessively thinks about them without reflection. She busies herself by doing them compulsively. This mental and physical hyperactivity effectively blocks her from thinking about or feeling the dread inside. She tries to smother it with effort. However, her expected reward fails to materialize. Far from being nicer and praising her for her efforts, or reassuring her that everything is all right (which her parents would have done), Joe simply became more and more irritated. Thus her best efforts simply worsened the situation and actually increased her dread and insecurity. Do not forget that by definition, anorexics tend to choose partners who accord with needs of their *surface* selves. Joe, like many anorexics' partners, had problems of his own and contributed to the situation in his own way.[1]

Angela reacts by more hyperactivity from her social self and the addition of an increase in her obsession with weight. It is like a dormant ulcer. It is always there and now with environmental stress, it escalates. It is really her 'little' self, the emotions within her rebelling. Angela becomes terrified that she will break down, that her distress will show and that she will put on weight, horror of horrors. Being hyperactive helps to break up this anxiety, the tip of the dread that she is trying so hard to cover up. As she experiences it, it feels as if her 'other' self, her inner monster — the ugly fat child — is threatening to come through and ruin everything for her by showing distress to the world.

In truth of fact, Angela's 'ugly fat child' is a natural part of her personality, her way of being upset. We all have such instincts that come through to the surface when we feel stressed. Most people have a lot of experience in letting these feelings through, first as a child with parents, then with friends and then with lovers and so on. They are always there, these feelings, these 'ugly fat children' — they help us to survive, they protect us from the pressures of the environment and the pressures of our own social conditioning, the unreasonable demands of our intellect. Normal people learn to act on them, to take a break or to break down. In Angela's case her two selves met in the battle over weight. Her hyperactivity was only checked by her weight-gain threat: her 'little' self wanting space in her personality and in her body. Slowly Angela's

---

1 A 'normal' reader might wonder why Angela does not just simply ask for reassurance. To ask, however, simple though it may seem, is a terrible task for the anorexic. It is part of what she used to do as a child and has long since repressed because of the violent way in which her baby pleading was treated.

focus shifts. She begins to battle against her impulses to eat and the other signs of what she calls 'self-indulgence'. Those are important too.

Angela has other 'fat child' behaviours which, until her therapy began, she was unaware of as links in an important 'little girl' chain within her. She would find, for example, that her rebellious 'other' self wanted to do things that her social self hated and which, of course, threatened her hyperactive 'good girl' coping self. She would be tempted to daydream, fantasize about a 'better' life, a better relationship, a better man. She found herself wanting to masturbate, to read romantic books, to laze around and do nothing, to spend hours in the bath. You see, the worry about being fat was only the tip of the iceberg; all these other behaviours threatened to disrupt her life too. They were all part of her 'bad child' self. They broke into her 'good girl' image and into her hyperactivity; they stopped her working and being active. She fought her 'bad child' side to the point of exhaustion where she could no longer trust herself and had to watch herself all the time. She felt she had no self-control, no discipline, she was weak, she would let herself down and everyone else. She had to keep busy, to keep hyperactive, to try to crush the voices inside telling her to give in, to rest, loaf around, eat and have fun. She desperately needed to stifle the child inside her.

You can see why Angela wants to eat, laze around, give in to being a child; it is the only form of release, of escape, of pleasure even, she has ever known. She exhausts herself with the struggle and slowly, bit by bit, she begins to give in, to laze, skip an essay, eat a chocolate. Once that step has been taken it is only a matter of time before the temptation to gorge, to go the whole hog, follows "It's so nice, so enjoyable". Bit by bit she begins to put on weight, to slip behind in her housework, to slip behind in her studies.

The diet

Although Angela thought of a diet as simply controlling her weight, it was in reality far more than that to her. It was her way of controlling the runaway child she felt was on the loose inside her. As she slipped deeper into eating and loafing around she felt increasingly more paranoid and realized she had to do something about it. A diet was always her last resort. And it always worked.

> "I felt I was being overwhelmed from within, eaten away, like a country being invaded. I had to make a stand, a last ditch battle. I chose to diet. It's always hard but I know I can do it. I diet and I win. I stop the gluttony in its tracks. Hurrah! I yell, onwards men, I say to myself and slowly but surely I drive through my body to my mind. I bring myself under control. I stop being bad. I win."

True. She wins. In order to keep her control, Angela has to put a tight corset on her personality; she becomes an occupying power, ever-vigilant to ensure the invader does not come back. The diet, the kingpin of her victory has to be rigorously enforced. Angela has become anorexic.

A digression on the anorexic personality

Unlike bulimarexics, whose rituals are usually much more a daily occurrence and whose personalities accordingly are more volatile and more flexible, 'pure' anorexics tend to have separate personality structures of a more rigid nature. That is, they have, like Angela, one personality that runs normally for a brief period and that is more 'human' and 'normal', and then another that is hauled into place, as we have seen, to discipline the other. It is like the return of the Ice Age after an all too brief and watery spring. It is more permanent, more formidable and more pervasive than the other personality. Where the bulimarexic goes through two major personality swings in the space of a day or even in the space of a few hours, the anorexic does so over a period of months.

You may remember earlier we talked of teenage anorexics who built a romantic literary world to support their anorexic personalities. Well, this is a very common occurrence amongst weight-loss anorexics like Angela. Once the diet victory is won, a higher order of aesthetic personality has to come in to control the rebellious depths of her personality and to overcome the anxiety about her reality (Joe). She has to withdraw from feelings of anxiety, and to do this she uses whatever help she can get from the outside world. This could be the movies, art or books and so on. Angela inevitably withdrew into being a 'perfect' student. She was doing a post-graduate course and as her diet progressed, she switched from being a hyperactive housewife to trying to be 'the best architect in town'. She had a very close relationship with the department secretary, a lady who confided in her and needed her, and with her professor. She began to improve these ties with the vague, unexpressed notion of finding in her department and in her professor, her salvation. She transferred her symbiosis onto the professor, doing just what he wanted and began to model her personality on his needs. This all helped her anorexic personality to take shape and control her 'lower' feelings.

This is a fundamental point. Anorexia is not just a problem of not eating — it is a movement in the personality to split off and control the basic personality, in favour of the safer, more 'adult' mode. In many respects, this mode is a more serious form of the illness because of the huge movements in personality needed to contain the internal struggle. It means that putting the two together again later is very much harder because of the lack of contact with the two levels of reality vital to the person's survival as a whole personality: her internal 'fat child' state and her immediate surroundings, and the problems contained in them. To use Angela as an example, when she slipped into anorexia, into her anorexic personality, she *first* cut off from her struggle inside ("When I stopped eating it was as if I went dead inside — it was a relief, like the end of a war."); *secondly* she cut off further from Joe and her life with him. In their place Angela focused on her world at work and her fantasies about it.

> "I kind of loosely fantasized about the professor needing me, about he and I going to congresses, falling in love, having a beautiful relationship and so on. It was unreal, I see that now, but I became totally absorbed in it as if I would die without it."

This focusing on fantasy served to block out Angela's perception of the other two levels and led to a narrowing of consciousness of her body's needs.

Coming out of anorexia

Most people use anorexic rituals like Angela's in a surprisingly similar way. The final phase of anorexia itself, the massive weight loss, is preceded by a change in personality and thinking that causes — through avoidance of demands of the two levels previously described — an all-encompassing anaesthesia of the internal sensations of need or feeling. Stopping eating silences more than hunger: it stops the perception of internal warning signs. There is a lack of attention, first to emotional stress, and then to signs of physical stress. Once this latter occurs, the person is in danger, because without environmental interference, the body can do no more.

The body uses many ways of expressing distress or overload. What happens in anorexia is that the anorexic person learns systematically to ignore the body's natural warning signs and to override them. Once this is achieved, the person — locked in her fantasy world — cannot regain them: she is committed to a slow death. How then, are people like Angela brought back to reality?

Angela was lucky. She had a husband who reacted long before her body had wasted away too much. I treated a number of married anorexic women whose husbands had learnt to tolerate them in states of severe emaciation before doing anything about it. Some people, after being hospitalized or otherwise, were shocked into doing something, or just plain intelligent enough to want to help themselves, set themselves weight ceilings that they will try to achieve. Sometimes they are successful, sometimes the temptation to push below that limit becomes a game in itself, a ritual with occasionally fatal results.

Angela's husband was the key to her coming out of her dangerous ritual. Joe started drinking as a means of coping with Angela (remember he did not know she was anorexic) and in an inebriated state, he would say and do things that he never normally did. These inevitably shocked Angela and she would collapse, weeping, and go to bed, sometimes even becoming physically ill (her 'child' coming through) and the two would slowly become reconciled. Joe was a caring person at that level.

Unpleasant and personally traumatic as the experience was, it served to break the cycle and provided — through crying and collapse — the necessary outlet for the deprivations actually occurring within. It saved Angela and she could start again. It in itself was a cycle, a perennial cycle of cutting herself off from the child inside her and then re-contacting it. The question was really how much strain her relationship would take.

The *deepening* process in therapy allowed Angela to begin to see what lay behind her rituals and behind the anorexia. The task was now to broaden her personality to put the two sides of her together.

BROADENING THE RITUAL

Realization and understanding help a lot but the actual changing process is much harder. The rituals and cycles, whatever the cost to the sufferer, are much safer to her than crying, wanting, getting angry, caring and needing.

Angela had been conditioned not to recognize or express these things. She considered them to be *selfish* needs — the word her mother had taught her. My job was to teach her to be selfish. This involved doing something about these feelings inside her, letting someone else see and feel them too. Simply saying to Joe that she was not coping was an enormous strain for Angela because there was, in her words:

> "Just so much inside. I wanted so much. What good did just *saying* do? And what was he supposed to do? Joe just nods and goes on reading. He's uptight too."

So I asked Angela: "Is that going to stop your recovery? Are you going to give up at step one? Try to get Joe to react; really *be* upset, break down if you have to. And if he won't respond, find someone who will. You are not bound by rules, you know — you can choose to do what is good for you."

Angela got nowhere with Joe. He listened, but he too was a pretty clichéd guy. So she did find someone else — not another man — the secretary of the department of architecture. She found that she could talk to her and be upset in a way she just could not with Joe or with another man. In fact, I found this was an important point and where self-help groups come in. I found that lots of women unwilling to enter therapy but needing to open out, would do so in the company of other women. And this can help tremendously in pulling through this broadening phase — especially when it comes to the gentler emotions like crying and being comforted.

In Angela's case, she also worked with me and gradually began to use people in her life when she needed them — even if she had to force herself on them. Doing this, taking the first steps to shifting the frenzy and fear locked away in 'being anorexic', opened up a lot of private experiences for Angela that we will look at in the next section. Let me conclude this one by pointing out that all the time these new steps were being made, Angela was still going through cycles of anorexia. Her dependency on Joe and her parents' world was very deep and it was essential to let them remain and to make changes slowly over time. This I think is a general rule: do not rush it and do not make massive changes suddenly because if you do, you simply transfer your dependency and do not work through the problems contained in it. Angela wanted to rush it, believe me, and once, when her professor made an advance to her, she very nearly threw in all the good work she had done. It takes a lot of discipline to stick it out and Angela and I had weeks of arguments and fights over this. There is a terrific temptation to take the easy way out. Do not do it. There is no substitute for a slow careful tackling of the tasks of normalizing yourself.

Talking of fighting, this was a vital part of Angela's recovery. Again, a simple task — *say* all the things that come into your mind when you are cross with someone. You need practice, and half the battle for Angela was to find ways of practising without destroying her relationships at work and at home. Naturally she used me a lot but she also began to fight with other people — policemen, shopkeepers, anybody. And these fights proved interesting.

She would come in to see me feeling very angry with someone in the electricity department, say. So I would ask her why she didn't tell the person in question. And she would reply: "Oh Lord, you can't argue with those people — I mean, they're just petty little bureaucrats, not really worth the trouble."

"That," I told her, "is one of your family's clichés. Go out and fight with the man and start to explore your prejudice. You are really scared, humiliated and very wary. Now face it and find out if he bites and if it really *isn't* worth all the trouble."

Reluctantly, she went back and tackled the man. Naturally, she made an ass of herself and behaved like a toffee-nosed snob, and naturally, everyone in the office hated her. But she had done it, and she could go on from there to discover more about all sorts of people and her fear of them.

There are lots of other instances but the pattern is clear. Expose the shallowness behind your clichés, your sneers. Discover the *real* world, make mistakes, face up to being disliked and resented, but keep going until a balance occurs where you are less frightened and as a consequence more yourself. I found that many anorexics like Angela had large areas of their lives that were 'no go' areas because of such prejudices and fear. Nearly always, these areas are just the areas that should be explored. Let me give you one more example from Angela's life.

Angela tended to approach what she did in life very narrowly and very intellectually; she had her marriage, her studies, her anorexia and very little else. How did she account for the fact, I asked her, that she did no 'fun' things? She did not dance, did not like rock music, did not play sport; she only did things that fitted into her social and public image. She would not dream of going to see a 'bad' film, for example, only the intellectual ones. She went to sensible cultural parties, never to wild ones. She wore sensible clothes, never outrageous or daring ones, and so on and so on.

To each question she had a plausible answer — each denigrating or putting down the unconventional, or the wild or, as she put it, the unstable. She did not like wild parties or rock concerts or the people who went to them, on the grounds of their being insensitive and noisy. But what she was actually hiding from, was the fact that she had never actually done any of these things, never tried them. She was frightened and unnerved by them because they did not fit into her image and because they had an element of the 'uncontrolled' in them. I suggested that firstly she should try a few of these wild things and then evaluate them. She did. Her opinion remained the same. But for a few weeks after going to a rock concert, for example, she would talk of nothing else and it was not long before she went along to another. She found, in short, that once over the fear threshold, she broadened her perception of the way in which she had reacted. She began to recognize needs inside herself, needs to share things like laughter, enjoyment, music, art, needs that she had always sneered at in others and in herself. She began to become a person like everyone else — and this she found distressing:

> "I don't want to be like everyone else. I want to be *élite*, an intellectual. But I like being in a crowd, on a dance floor too. I get confused, it's like fighting a battle inside myself."

My job was to keep her going so that the inner conflict between herself as a child and adolescent, and herself as an indoctrinated adult was intensified. Behind the stereotypes lay fear — fear of liking what she despised and in turn fear of being despised (by her parents). She was terrified of opening up the child in her and her adolescent parts. Once she saw this, it helped her to direct herself better but it did not ease her conflict until after quite a while. The reason? She had never done these things, never danced, played, sung, had belly-laughs and so on. When she did do them, it was done self-consciously, clumsily, badly and in her own words, she hated herself for being "clumsy, ugly, silly, childish, stupid, inept". Like many anorexics and bulimarexics, she used her 'sneer' and stereotypes to prevent herself from going through that trial-and-error learning she should have gone through years before; and it is very difficult to start at the age of 28, 29 or 30. But she did, and slowly, inch by inch, the locked-in part of her began to open up and she allowed herself to learn about proper living.

When you start this broadening process, you must keep going and face that self-repulsion time and time again, until it eases. Do not run away into safe options — if you do, you are cheating. The self-repulsion and insecurity is your key. If you are experiencing it and keep trying, you know you are opening yourself up inside.

DEVELOPING RELATIONSHIPS

Of course, all this is made much easier if you have good relationships. If you go dancing, play games or whatever, it helps if you go with someone you can lean on, someone who understands and can help you through with the right measure of tolerance and comfort. Angela found Joe unhelpful because he himself had difficulties in much the same areas. Angela's departmental secretary, though, was helpful, being herself exploratory and in fact, recently divorced. The two became good friends and did a lot of exploratory work together. They played sport, went to concerts, parties and self-help and feminist groups together and so on.

In most cases, I found these relationships of the utmost importance in helping the patients do the things they needed to do. They had a deeper significance too.

Digression on symbiosis
How do you break out of a close bond? A bond, say, with your mother? Well, it is not easy. What normally happens, is that symbiosis has to be broken through a series of dilutions, as I mentioned earlier. Thus, the adolescent's first few bonds (with males or females) are incredibly intense symbioses, that usually hurt a lot and cause a lot of distress and anger. The same needs felt towards one's mother or father are the needs governing these early relationships. We learn first in life how to *be* with our parents and in the first relationships we make outside the home, we use the same behaviours. The trouble is, of course, that Mike, Jack or Jill just are not mummy or daddy; they are in fact equals and make demands too. They are not as perfect as mummy or daddy, not as apparently caring. After several attempts at achieving the same gratification and being disappointed, the dilution begins. The adolescent begins to learn limits and to treasure the new, more equal relationships, for what they are. Besides, in most cases, mum and dad are still there in the background anyway.

Now in Angela's case, when she married, she turned Joe into a mix between mum and dad, a symbiosis based, exactly as she had been taught, on his needs. When she met the secretary, she formed another symbiosis in the same way. Rosemary (the secretary) was more dominant. After a while,

Angela found that she was treating Rosemary "almost like a lover". She watched her obsessively, just as she had with her mother and Joe; she became jealous if Rosemary did not pay attention to her and was upset if she talked to other people and so on. All these were vital new challenges that could now be properly worked on, whereas her relationship with Joe and with her mother could not be. Here was a chance to break symbiosis properly, just as the healthy adolescent does, by competing, by not being a doormat, by forcing herself to be an equal. Or, as in the case of most adolescents, Angela was learning to have other friends in case one let her down. It takes time and practice to stand up for yourself. Rosemary was an excellent challenge for Angela because, in fighting for herself with Rosemary, Angela had to learn first to show her feelings (to herself) and then to confront Rosemary with them. This would ensure that her new 'self' would be referenced into her relationships as well.

As the relationship went on, Angela became more and more upset, just as she had done with Joe. If life was running smoothly with Rosemary, she would be fine. If not, she began to become obsessive about her weight — the first sign of her cycle. When this happened, I climbed in. "No," I would say, "Don't use that as a sign of distress. Be scared and show it. Tell Rosemary."

Angela did not want to do this. "She'll think I'm silly, I'll be just like a whiney little girl, she'll despise me."

"But," I would tell her, "That's just what you are right now — why hide it?"

Eventually Angela did go off and tell Rosemary and Rosemary was delighted and delightful. She hugged Angela and the moment passed. I pointed out to Angela that a whole anorexic phase had been aborted by this 'little' act. It was a good sign.

There were also a lot of 'downs'. Rosemary was not a perfect 'mummy' by any means and she had some nasty traits too. But these were valuable: when she was insensitive to Angela, for example, and Angela got upset, I was able to point out to her that there was no good in her being 'a little girl' with Rosemary then — Rosemary would not be able to respond. Now was the time to use depression or to be upset with Rosemary. Angela had to learn when to be 'little' and when to be depressed, when to be angry and so on. She learnt that when she was feeling upset and depressed it was best to *be* so for a day or two. If Rosemary was being insensitive, it *was* upsetting so Angela was not to block the feeling by seeking quick comfort. She had to learn not to take her mind off her upset by fixating on eating or making love to Joe or working harder. She had to *be upset*.

With a struggle, Angela was able to do this. She was not used to being upset or depressed out in the open, she had always been so afraid of this — like being lonely. But if you have to face it, it is not so bad and sometimes (as I was able to show Angela) it has to be faced in order to avoid doing more damage to yourself in the long run.

After such a period of depression or upset, I encouraged Angela to do something else — to find someone else to spend time with when Rosemary was being insensitive. Note that this was not to avoid the depression or the upset, but after having had time to be upset, she had to learn to be *less dependant* on Rosemary and to make Rosemary attend to her properly. She did find another woman, and while at first she became dependant on her instead, it was less intense and she also had Rosemary and Joe and me to spread the load.

SUMMING UP

You can see the relevance of all this. Relationships help to broaden your personality base and serve as the testing ground for building up a proper learning of personal intimacy. Unfortunately, I just do not have enough room to do more than sketch the roughest of outlines of this here, but there is enough, I think, to show you what is necessary. What must be stressed, in my opinion, is the importance of getting all this done while the rituals are going on. Only when Angela had had two years of therapy and had been through several very intense relationships with women, had left Joe, and had gone through an intense relationship with a man; only then was she in a position to stop her cycles. In fact, they stopped naturally. She had got so 'into' relationships that she had barely noticed that the extremes of her cycles had fallen away. She did diet every now and then and she gorged every now and then but no one could have called it anorexia.

It did not always happen to work like this. However, in every case where the individual really worked at the stages of therapy I have outlined and built up relationships under my guidance, I found that the momentum of going through normal tasks was so great that the anorexia gradually fell away. Where there was too much resistance or where a patient's family, friends, career or community were too supportive of her pathology, the re-learning could not take place and the anorexia stayed.

The key is the re-learning. If you will do it, you will recover. Angela became, in the opinion of her family and her professor, 'a bit of a disappointment', to say the least. Her marriage broke up, she never finished her post graduate course, she was accused of being a lesbian, of being immature, even psychotic. She was none of these things. She was just a person trying to find herself — which she did. She went through a healthy, proper growing period, in my opinion, and today is a vital and healthy person — with problems of course. But she is *not* anorexic and she *is* a person. Societies and families put up massive pressures in order to maintain the status quo. If you can resist it to do what is right for you, you will survive.

Chapter 13

How to survive bulimarexia

Most of the bulimarexics I have treated tended to have episodes of 'pathology' on a much more frequent basis than Angela. While Angela slipped slowly into an anorexic episode over weeks, most of my bulimarexics tended to go through their complete cycles very quickly, often several times a day. Because of this, I think bulimarexics are frequently more in touch with their feelings than ordinary anorexics, and more aware of the links between the pressures of the outside world and their inner reactions. They are, in short, more labile, more immediate people and this I think is a big help in therapy because of their awareness of need. Many of the people I have treated who suffer from anorexia nervosa tended to be dissociated from how needy they really were. Bulimarexics know they need comfort and know they need it fast. In this they are absolutely right — the trick is to make use of these immediate feelings and get the right help in the right way. In a nutshell, this means breaking your cover and opening up inside to show what is really going on instead of simply using a bulimarexic's ritual. Let me outline roughly what most bulimarexics experience subjectively so that we can then go on to examine how best to change things.

The two of you

Part of you thinks, feels and behaves in a way that allows you to cope with your outside world and with everything you should be doing. The other part of you tends not so much to think as to do — usually an eating-vomiting ritual. As you progress from adolescence into adulthood, your consciousness will have separated into two parts. The *thinking* part, the way you deal with the outside world, is flat, unemotional, passive, agreeable, reasonable, insightful, intelligent, calm, mature, clean and so on. The *feeling* part is greedy, needy, piggy, ugly, vicious, messy and so on. Your personality feels as if it is in a continual state of cold war, with the 'social' you despising the 'piggy' you, refusing even to acknowledge its existence. Your piggy side, in turn, does not bother thinking much —it leaves your social side to pick up the pieces after it has been satiated. Unlike ordinary anorexics, with bulimarexics, the two 'you's' battle continually on a daily basis.

The problem in starting on the road to recovery is that even as you sit reading this, only your 'social' part — your mind, if you like — is reading it. Pigs do not read. So we have to appeal to your intellect, the thinking part, to do something it finds repugnant — admit the existence of its other half, to think about the pig in you, examine it, turn it over, contemplate it — as if it were an essay to prepare, an exam you must pass.

Organizing your thoughts:

At any given moment you will be aware of three basic systems of pressure which cause you distress:

1. Your parents: Whether you see them a lot, or live with them or do not see them at all, your parents in one way or another dominate your life. You will constantly feel obliged to worry, think or focus on them, their values and their problems. Your entire thinking pattern will be geared to them, to doing what they want and what they have set out for you. How you relate to everything will have its roots in how they feel about you and what you do. This will form the biggest single pressure on you. Most of your social life will be taken up with them or their values and ideas. These form the basis of the 'social' you.

2. Your own world: Quite apart from your 'social' you, you will also be aware of an underlying dimension to everything you see or hear or relate to. You will know your parents' weaknesses, you will know their faults and where they hurt you. You will know that you are a doormat, used by people. You will see how people really function — you *do* have insight. While you are going about your daily life, this part of you operates consciously, parallel to your other part: it is like a little voice in the back of your mind — very small, and very wary. It will never speak, but it is there. Somewhere you know what is happening to you; this is the 'new' you we hope to build up.

3. Your ritual: This will not be a little voice in your mind — this is a big savage animal that rampages through both of the other two states. It forces you to break all the rules, to do everything you feel you should not.

The three systems are all involved in your day-to-day existence. The first task then is to start thinking about what happens to you during your ritual and in the time preceding its onset. That is, you must use your 'social' you to analyse and examine your 'piggy' you. Then like an algebraic equation, we will put the results together with the feelings and ideas that the 'new you' thinks about and see what comes up. It may sound complicated but it can be done.

DEEPENING THE RITUAL

Let us again use a case study, someone you have already met, Jane. Here is a normal day in her life at the time she came to see me:

"I would come home from work — feeling really shit — usually because the guy I worked for was trying to avoid me — he'd been making advances to me and I fell in love with him. So I decided that he was crazy about me and started pursuing him. And then he started avoiding me —and I felt awful. So I would go home — feeling ashamed. And I would want to eat. So I'd go to my mother's cupboards and start rummaging through her drawers for chocolates and start stuffing one after the other into my mouth — Then I'd go to the fridge and inside would be last night's left-overs — cold mashed potato cold peas, stew — anything, and I would gulp that down —

one or two platefuls — with huge chunks of bread — frantically buttering more to have ready once what I was eating was finished. Then, three or four glassfuls of cool drink, another cup of tea or two so as I wouldn't have too much solid inside me and too little liquid — because it might make bringing up more difficult. Then, I knew I wasn't satisfied. So I'd go off to the supermarket. I'd buy two tins of canned fish, three packets of sausages, baked beans, a cake, two litre bottles of orange juice, another loaf of bread and a couple of dozen eggs. On the way home in the car I would open up a packet of biscuits that I'd bought, and by the time I'd got home, a couple of minutes away — it would be finished. I'd be watching all the time to see if anybody could see that I was eating. Because no one must see me eating. But by then I would be so frantic that nothing seemed to matter. I would be stuffing food into my mouth heedlessly, watching in my rear view mirror, trying to drive and feeling completely horrible — guilty, dirty, uncontrolled but I couldn't stop — because nothing else was as nice for me as eating — nothing. And even if it meant vomiting whatever I ate up into plastic bags and having to keep them in my room for a day, because I couldn't go to the toilet, because the drains were blocked, I would carry on eating. I would eat until my stomach was so distended that I couldn't move. I would have to drag myself to the toilet to vomit. And after a while I would start eating all over again.

"I could eat a loaf of bread, two packets of sausages, six eggs, five slices of cake and two bars of chocolate — vomit and start all over again. Some days, when I managed to get the house all to myself I could go through the same procedure, up to 25 times and by the end of the day I'd feel as if I could just lie down on my bed and cry for ever."

Let us break the ritual into stages:
1. Getting the food 2. Ensuring privacy 3. Eating 4. The bloated feeling 5. Vomiting 6. The aftermath. In Jane's case, we examined each of these in depth; do the same for yourself if you can.

1. Getting the food

Jane, as with a lot of bulimarexics, began originally when she lived at home by raiding the fridge; then she moved on, significantly, to her parents' private store of goodies and then later, if these were not enough, (and when she left home) she went to the supermarket and loaded up. Let us look at the feelings and examine what went on inside her mind at each phase. Again, if you try to block the ritual as a form of therapy, you will not be able to find out what you feel inside nor be able to open it out.

Jane's 'raiding' expeditions
Basically, here, her feelings were of doing something very wrong, of taking food that did not belong to her. There were two elements to the feelings however, a feeling of giving in to gluttony, of actually eating her mother's food, and a feeling of being naughty. And inside this was a secret glee: "Especially if I took from my mother's secret store" said Jane. Her mother had chocolates and sweets and toffees hidden all over the house. Sometimes she would lock them away and Jane would find the key. When she first began, Jane would take only one or two sweets but then when nothing was said ("How could she?" said Jane. "My mother prided herself on never eating sweets and staying thin.") she started to take more.

We interpreted this strange conflict very carefully because it marked a kind of secret contact, a secret battle between the two, mother and daughter. Was Jane taking food as a substitute for affection? Probably, but there was more. In a way, she had trapped her mother in her own dishonesty and what is more, her mother knew. It was, I think, symbolic of Jane's whole relationship with her mother.

Her mother knew it was Jane taking the food so she changed the locks. Jane simply had keys made and so the battle went on. Jane felt a kind of cold anger — a ruthlessness — come over her when she started this phase of her ritual. By thinking about it more, she was able to identify her anger at her mother, her bewilderment inside, and her blind determination to go on doing it. Once, I said to her: "Well, maybe you shouldn't take your mother's things." She almost wilted and

felt guilty but then immediately there was an inner light, a
viciousness, and when I asked her about it, she launched into
an attack on her mother that came as a surprise to her. These
two reactions, the guilt and the bitterness, seemed to coexist
very comfortably in her mind and it was very easy for her to
swing from the one to the other.

Going through these feelings and talking about them were
the first steps in building up a new understanding of the
emotions and their rationale. This loosened the force of the
guilt.

Shopping at the supermarket
This had a slightly different feeling about it. Jane used to take
a wad of money and go and buy large quantities of everything.
When asked why, in the shop, she used to say it was for her
family. Then she used to make up a game to ease her anxiety,
whereby she would really believe that she was shopping for a
family. She also used to choose supermarkets where she felt
"The world was at my feet, I could take what I wanted, there
was so much — it was unrestricted food. I used to rush around
grabbing this and that in a frenzy of excitement — it was nice."
Here it was like a wish come true, a fantasy — always having
enough to eat, never worrying. It was a loose fantasy for Jane
— barely felt in the rush to get at the food, but it was there.

Was Jane doing for herself what she wanted her mother to
do for her? I wondered a lot about this because a great deal of
the behaviour contained in bulimarexic rituals seemed to me to
be self-caring behaviour; that is, the girl tries to help herself by
ritualizing what she needed as a child. When she is frightened,
she wants to eat food, the family substitute for comfort and
warmth, so she either takes it from her mother (the source of
love?) or goes out and buys it *as if* she were a mother. I am not
being Freudian here: the links seem straightforward and
uncomplicated; the bulimarexic is looking after herself in the
only way she was taught. Just as a normal person would seek
out warmth and comfort through being held, not sexually, if he
or she were afraid or upset, so the bulimarexic seeks out food
in a warm and comforting way. You can see, incidentally, how
realizing this can help you try to seek out a better way of
comforting yourself than resorting to food. Jane had to learn

to be open and needy to me first and then with other people so she could be 'childish' and run to them instead of to food. I found that she knew all along what she really wanted and on several occasions before she had started therapy with me, she had really tried to get what she wanted but had always been misused.[1]

2. Ensuring privacy

This, I would have thought, would prove to be a bit of a problem for many bulimarexics, but it is not the case. It was also the way I discovered something about quite how many of my patients were neglected. Basically, most parents were either at work or at some social function; if they were in the home, they never noticed what was going on.

> *Marian*: "My father locked himself into his study and you weren't allowed to disturb him."

> *Tina*: "My mother was often lying down with a headache and couldn't be bothered."

> *May*: "It was like a dare. When I lived at home I used to sneak food out of the fridge, almost under their noses; in fact, I think there was an element of sneering in this for me; I was cheating them by pretending to be on a diet but in reality I was moving food to my room all the time. I think they knew but they said nothing."

When Jane left home and ate in the privacy of her own flat, she reported a kind of *loss* in some way; she felt a new hopelessness in her eating as if, as she put it: "I was really alone now — they wouldn't be able to find out even if they wanted to."

To me, it seemed as if the whole question of privacy was a very fragile one, that it was a reluctant privacy, as if the girl had

---

1 Remember, comfort and warmth do not mean sex. Many bulimarexics try to get warmth but do it solely through sex. There is a difference between affectionate physical contact and sex. Nothing is wrong with having sex, but in our culture it can be very distracting to someone who needs something more. The bulimarexic needs childlike, safe relationships first and so it is sometimes better to turn to a female friend initially if you cannot resist the heavy male emphasis on sex. Care and love should come first whoever you choose, then sex. Women's groups can help here to make you more conscious of the need for friendship.

always been left with too much privacy; in other words, the girl was kept isolated at home and left alone in it. Eating in secret, for people like Jane, definitely served a plea-for-discovery function; a game she played, half-hoping that things would change and she would be noticed. When I broached this possibility with her, there was again, a two-sided reaction — an understanding and a self-effacing guilt as well as bitterness. "When I left home, they never once came to visit me. I mattered so little, I could have died and they wouldn't have known." The problem was that her bitterness had no bite, no real awareness; this all came later. It was important though that she *voice* her feelings and keep voicing them. These thoughts of hers were so seldom voiced and only vaguely felt in the 'little' voice mode. It was central that she talk to someone about them and build up a familiarity with them.

3. Eating

There is a tremendous violence in a bulimarexic's *secret* eating. Jane describes her two modes of eating:

> "Socially, I eat like a dainty lady. Which is how I try to portray myself. I pick tenderly at my food, eating a little bit of this, a soupçon here, a soupçon there. It's a terrific kick for me to say 'no' to the most tasty food while secretly dying to wolf the lot. In secret though, when I eat, you've seen nothing like it. I'm an animal. I cram as much into my mouth as possible without giving myself a chance to swallow properly. While I'm gulping down a huge chunk of bread, thickly spread with butter and cheese, I'm cutting the next wedge. My hands fly to the litre bottle of orange juice and I gulp down three glasses quickly and while I am doing this, I'm heating up a huge pot of stew — I'll eat five or six platefuls till my stomach's so full I can't move and the skin across my stomach is taut."

Look at the feelings in this: "I force the food in — slobber, spit, burp, swallow whole," it is like a breakdown, a terrible act of self-humiliation. Here there is only hurt, anger, self-punishment, a massive upheaval in which all the food is forced down and through the body. This is the core of the bulimarexic's feeling: the only time in her life that she taps the real distress inside her — her 'baby', if you like. The tragedy is that as it is carried out, her child self and her social self clash. Stuffing food down is a self-mutilation, a giving-in to the 'baby' need for attention (food) but in such a way as to hurt the need. We are all familiar with the person who uses an essentially natural act (feeding a baby with a spoon, say) but does it in such a way as to hurt (thrusting the spoon into the child's mouth, banging it against the mouth and so on). Well, this is how the bulimarexic feeds herself, hating herself for needing it.

Over time, I discovered that many bulimarexics repeat in their rituals a pattern they learnt from their parents; that is, irritation expressed through doing something in an angry or hurtful way. It is one way that Jane's parents, for example, gradually controlled her and made her wary of asking for things outside the home, like food. It was much safer, we learnt, for her to ask for a sweet when she was upset, than to run crying and clinging to her mother or father. A sweet at least tasted nice — wanting a hug always hurt. The same pattern is carried through by the bulimarexic in the way she handles herself and her own needs.

A digression on getting attention

Think about something for a minute. Food is a very easy commodity to dish out (provided you have enough of it). It is easy to give material things — like food, cars, presents — but it is much more demanding to give attention and affection. A child who is crying or upset needs a lot of *physical* attention: you have to listen, take time off from your own world to comfort him or her, wait till the crying stops, let the child cling, wander around with you, be reassured, be fussed over. Above all, you have to hold the child. All of this takes time and mental attention. Ideally, you should give the child your attention and in this way, make him or her feel important enough to distract you from all else; that is security. A preoccupied adult, unable to shift from his or her world to the child's, fobs the child off with easy solutions — sweets, clichés about not crying — 'be a man', 'grow up' and so on; or worse — 'be quiet, mummy isn't well' — these all help to set a pattern which, if continued for long enough, ends up forming the basis for something similar to the way in which anorexics treat their own child-like needs.

4. The Bloated Feeling

Once her stomach felt ready to burst, Jane vomited. This was really a waking nightmare for her and also the key moment because apart from the contact she had with her fears of actually being seen to be what she was (fat, ugly — in her mind), she was aware for a while of the terrible conflict in her and the cruelty of her own personality. She scared herself and rushed to escape from those feelings. This is the red-hot core of the volcano inside, an instinctive rushing away from the terrible thing felt within. It is a paradox: no one but the girl herself has made her fat and bloated — it is almost as if she is desperate to be fat; and then the moment it is achieved, it is so horrible it must be removed. It is like a play within a play: she plays with getting fat, which she has learnt is symbolic of all the 'bad' childish ways she has tried to leave behind (by being anorexic, by being thin). Those childish feelings still intrude, however, so she lets them in, under her control, and allows herself to get fat (to show emotions); then she promptly terminates the game at the first feelings of revulsion and self-disgust and the trauma buried in it.

5. Vomiting

If you look closely at the way in which vomiting starts, or the way in which normal people experience non-medical vomiting, it is an inevitable reaction to deep fear or anxiety. The person is so afraid that he or she wants to be sick. It is in fact a very common reaction in children: motion or travel sickness, head-aches and nausea are all ways in which children express distress. Stomachaches are another example. They arise when the child's normal outlets of expressing fear (crying, running to mummy or daddy) are blocked: they are fear symptoms. It is my opinion that the vomiting in bulimarexia does not occur simply as a means of removing food in the girl's stomach, but is discovered in *panic* early on when *fear* of being fat induces nausea. It is then that a queasy stomach, eager to be relieved, makes itself felt and vomiting occurs. Sit back and think for a moment: imagine you have a distended, swollen stomach right now — what is your most immediate feeling? Fear, I bet, followed by a mild wave of nausea.

Vomiting on its own does not preoccupy the anorexic much, I believe. It is over quickly and feels unpleasant but there is too much relief and reduction in the panic to allow vomiting to be obsessed on for its own sake; it does not form an important part, *psychologically*, of the ritual. What is important is the relationship of fear to vomiting and the need to identify other fear-related situations outside the ritual. Thus with Jane, by thinking about the feeling of nausea, she was able to note that she felt it quite often at home, during dinner, in public when she ate with someone, whenever she felt nervous or frightened by a situation and so on. Others, like Tina, found that waves of nausea seldom ever seemed to be far off.

6. The Aftermath

Once vomiting is over there is a feeling of asceticism, as if everything had been a dream. Normality returns. Your body feels sore and bruised as if you had played a game of rugby, but otherwise you feel calm and relieved as if you had gone through a great emotional upheaval — which, of course, you have, in more ways than one. Immediately, however, the memory of what you have just done fades and you focus on your 'social' self. Within moments, your 'young' emotionality is transposed to the other side of the wall. There is no time for reflection or for other feelings lingering on, primarily of sadness and loneliness. In fact, once the frenzy of the ritual is over, loneliness and a certain softness can be detected but most bulimarexics push these feelings down. They are worth looking at, however, because at that time, the sadness itself can lead very easily to tears, tears of self-pity. This distresses the bulimarexic so she busies herself to avoid feeling this. Guilt and anxiety are turned aside by settling down to doing something conventional: working, homework, needlecraft — all indicating a certain nostalgic need for mother's comfort and reassurance that she is loved. This is the lowest ebb of her life.

Here we have examined Jane's ritual in order that you can see how to look at your own. We have broken the ritual into six parts and we will look back over them, broadening them as we go, showing you how to think about them and how to begin the detective work of linking what happens in your ritual with your life in general.

BROADENING THE RITUAL

It may seem as though we have simply described the rituals rather than probing them but going over them like this is absolutely necessary to the process of self-help. I found in therapy that it was necessary to keep going over and over again the kind of analysis we did for Jane and Angela in the last chapter. The insights were only that — without action, they lost their meaning. Also, old patterns die very hard and very slowly and all my patients had to be constantly pushed initially to *think* about what they were doing all the time; to re-interpret it along the lines of explanation I have offered here and not to slip into the easy old patterns of either non-thinking (in the ritual state) or of selective, superficial thinking. In the rest of this chapter, we will concentrate on how to go about taking the initial probing deeper to start to link the new thoughts to new actions.

I am sure that anyone with a bulimarexic ritual reading Jane's pattern would find plenty in it to think about. When it came to broadening her ritual, though, I made the mistake early on of focusing on the eating and vomiting aspect instead of appreciating that each phase serves an important function. After spending hours discussing how she felt during her gorging state, Jane looked across at me and said:

> "I don't know why you're so bloody obsessed with my gorging. Just on instinct, I'd say that the *worst* time for me is the first phase — the looking for food, for something to stuff into me. *That* upsets me the most."

Well, Jane was right. When we started looking at how she felt going to the supermarket or searching her parents' room for hidden chocolates, she began to look very miserable and soon started crying.

"Christ, it makes me feel so bloody sad. I just see myself searching the whole house for something — like a refugee. Just me in this big, empty house, looking for tit-bits, anything."

I asked why it upset her so, still thinking that the stuffing and vomiting must be the central thing.

"Because it was so humiliating, so degrading, so childish."

It was this word *childish* that gave us the clue we were looking for. It was the key for opening out Jane's ritual: what she was actually seeking out, we found, was childish. She wanted to be loved, to be comforted. She was frightened and upset and frantic about it. When she actually performed her ritual, all these feelings were quickly swamped by the franticness, the need to actually get comfort, to get something to stop the fear and anxiety inside her and to prevent her breaking down and showing the upset. When she had to think about the ritual in the safety of my office, she had time to linger on all the important little things underneath and so deepen her pattern. The following is an excerpt from a session we had probing this:

Me: Why do you feel childish?
Jane: Because it feels silly; I was upset over nothing. I was being hysterical.
Me: What did you want? Picture yourself searching your mother's cupboard, what are you going through inside?
Jane: Sweets. I want sweets.
Me: Forget the sweets. You said you felt childish.
Jane: (Stopped to think) I think I would like to be held. Like when I was a child.

She stopped there and refused to go on further, saying she felt too upset and had gone blank.

Me: O.K. Leave it now — but next time you start rummaging, try and deepen your feelings — go slower, feel more first, before you start gorging. Try to find out a bit more about what you feel inside.

Jane did this. Two days later, she was back.

Jane: I think I've got something. I went home after our session and as soon as I was there, I felt I wanted to gorge. So I started going through the cupboards. I did slow down though. I felt very very miserable inside, I just wanted to cry. I wanted to throw myself on their (her parents') bed and howl and howl and smell them, my mother, and cry in her pillow. But I didn't. That's all I could get to. Then I just had to eat. But I think it's important because I felt it so deeply and it frightened me.

Me: Why?

Jane: In case I actually did it.

Me: And then what?

Jane: Oh God, I can't even think about it. I just wouldn't do it.

Me: Why not?

Jane: You know why. We don't do it in our family. You know why. Why are you being so stupid? You know our rules.

Me: No listen. Why won't you cry. Or throw yourself on the bed? What *actually stops* you at the time? What thought or feeling?

Again Jane got blocked and had to watch out for the next time to try and uncover the feelings. This time it led to a whole chain of other feelings which I will summarize here because it took several months to work it all out.

Jane wanted to be childish. She wanted to run to her mother (or climb onto her bed) to feel safe and reassured. What stopped her was the thought of the immediate physical consequences:

"My mother's room is always spotless; if I got upset I'd mess it up, she'd freak out, perform, get a migraine, be hassled etcetera — it depresses me. It wouldn't be worth it. Much easier just to take her chocolates — no hassle, no fuss."

At this point Jane would begin to hate herself, feeling angry — both with her mother for not being there (her 'little' self) and with herself for ever needing her mother (her 'grown-up' self). In her ritual, she found her mother's chocolates initiated a kind of mental scenario in her head. Her one voice would say, cold and hard (like her mother):

"O.K., you want to be a child, you want food, here — make a pig of yourself — stuff your hot, dirty little mouth..."

The other voice in her was more a feeling than a thought:

"Eat, eat, eat, eat, — the warmth of the chocolate, the sweet explosion of it in my mouth, the beautiful taste — it was a thrill, I needed it so much, and then the tears, the horror of it all, the full tummy, the nausea and then the vomiting..."

The door that Jane discovered and opened up led to her wanting her mother. Long ago she had learnt not to go to her mother and to substitute chocolate instead. The thrill of her mother's touch and the joy of being loved, comforted and made to feel safe were all lost, forbidden and replaced by the feeling of chocolate in her mouth. And this had become vital in Jane's ritual:

"No other chocolates would do. She used to buy really super ones and I was addicted to them — I'd tried eating others but it wasn't the same and didn't have the same sensation."

Were there other similar sensations, I wondered. This set off a hunt. And in fact there were, but again it took time to trace the links. For example, Jane would sometimes masturbate on her mother's bed with very much the same satisfaction and anxiety:

"When I sat down and started thinking over everything, I realized that there were a lot of things I did all related to the same thing — to being a child. It started by us thinking about what feelings were going on underneath my ritual. We figured I wanted comfort or security because I was frightened, we worked out that I ate *her* chocolates because that's all I ever got; that I stuffed them into me because it was all I had and then vomited them up to keep my figure, to stop it from showing. Why was weight and thinness so important? Simple: my new 'super' adult image demanded it. It kept my father interested in me.

And that was all I had going for me, right? So now I think, forget about all that adult stuff, what do *I* want (the 'little' me)? I'll tell you. I want my fucking mother! I don't want to be grown-up, I don't want to be a fashion model. I don't even want men to touch me. I just want to be a baby — in bed with my mother. I want my mother to love me. She is the only one who can give me anything.

"Suddenly I realized how much I needed my mother, how many little things I did to stay close to her. I used to masturbate in her bed. I used to bathe for hours in her bath. I stole her perfume — I loved doing it. I played with her things and I took my pleasure — masturbating, the thrill of her chocolate, her sheets, her bath — from her. She wouldn't give it to me so I took it."

So what started off as an examination of the eating-vomiting ritual for Jane ended up with a very full appreciation of a whole mass of needs; feelings and actions never before linked together in her mind. The acceptance of all this severely disturbed Jane because she had avoided thinking about it or facing what was happening to her:

"I have started to use my rituals with far more feeling now that I have begun to see things. It doesn't stop me gorging or vomiting but it helps me gain access to a new world inside me."

Here are some of the new insights and feelings that emerged as Jane began to deepen her feelings:

"I used to think that going to the supermarket was just to buy food and rush home and gorge. That was partly true but there was something else. My mother would never buy food for me, only for my father and herself — special food. I used to whine in the supermarket with her, 'Oh buy me this, buy me that — jam, sweets — she never would, just told me to be quiet. So my going to the supermarket was me trying to make myself happy inside. I was doing it for myself."

There were other things too:

"My mother used to get very irritated with my wanting

things but my father actually encouraged it, but only after I had lost weight and looked more attractive. Before that I was just a fat ugly duckling who he barely noticed. After I lost weight he actively enjoyed taking me shopping — he used to buy me clothes, make me model them. He got a kick out of being like a sugar-daddy. Later I used to go and buy myself clothes and jewellery and make-up to make myself feel nice. It was a ritual on its own. I used to buy it all in the same way as I used to eat. I bought for the sensation of owning it, of having it all. Consequently, I have a huge collection of useless cheap jewellery and make-up.

"Like eating, it was all so useless. I would be walking along, feeling depressed and empty and suddenly I'd just have to buy something, just to stop the emptiness inside. Just like my eating-vomiting ritual. I would buy two or three pieces of jewellery, lipstick, eye make-up or whatever and then rush home to try them all on, excited. Then nothing. But I knew I would do it again the next day. In between gorging and vomiting, buying clothes, food, and jewellery, there was little time for anything else."

Anger and related feelings

Condensed within each ritual, within each behaviour pattern for Jane was a whole range of feelings that were not permitted to see the light of day. Upset or fear precipitated ritual and anguish; emptiness and calm followed its completion. Within each ritual was the whole range of normal human emotion, cramped up as if in a pressure-cooker. Exploring Jane's *anger* feelings during her gorging-vomiting ritual helped to uncover what it was like in there.

Initially, it appeared that all anger was self-directed along a kind of closed internal circuit. Jane's 'older' self got angry with her 'baby' self for being a baby; then her 'baby' self became angry with her 'older' self for being so hard and controlled and so on. She stuffed herself in anger and vomited in anger, to punish herself. She bathed in anger, scratched in anger, bought clothes, lazed around, all in anger to spite herself. There was no outlet, it was useless endless anger that went nowhere. I asked Jane to slow down and to think about these feelings more:

> "When I began to work on this I was amazed to find that I was really a very very hostile person all the time. But only inside. I never actually said anything. When I thought about it, I found out that when I was eating I was very angry with my parents, especially my mother, for not being there. I found it was easy to get angry with my mother and to pretend to make her do things, like be my slave, cook for me, buy me things — in fantasy. For instance, I would eat a chocolate and along with the taste, savour the thought that it was one less for her."

These thoughts ran through Jane's mind most of the time and in fact she later realized that a lot of her rituals were aimed at her mother; the 'little' part of her was doing these things — demanding, eating, buying — to spite her mother.It was however all extremely passive. Jane attached little importance to her anger and resentment. She called it her 'silent voice' — it was there but carried no weight. The simple act of talking about it to me caused her great anxiety and it was some time before she would spontaneously say she was angry. For her, the ritual *was* her anger — she did not consciously think angry thoughts or say or do angry things, she only did her ritual. It was her way of being angry, of protesting.

You can see the importance of the concept of *broadening* the ritual. Not only does the ritual cover a multitude of feelings and block out fear, it in itself is a form of protest, of anger. By looking at it, it becomes seen as such, as a statement about anger and hurt. It is a rebellion, covered up under the self-deceiving camouflage of explanations like 'weight-loss', 'being thin', 'eating' — all of which give it a non-rebellious status. I have talked often here about the volcano inside. Well the ritual itself *is* the volcano and once the enormous anger inside is felt, by looking and feeling around inside the ritual, the bulimarexic can go on to open it all up and let the anger take shape.

RELATIONSHIPS

Most of the problems involved in broadening the ritual can only really be worked out and sorted through in the context of ongoing relationships. It is hard to get comfort alone, to be angry, volatile, excited and so on when you are on your own and, of course, the basis of getting better depends on the repetition of patterns with other people.

One of the first things I used to say to my patients was:

> "If you really want to get better, you will have to change and be a whole lot more ugly a person than you are now. This means that some of the people around you won't like the 'new' you and you will therefore lose some friends. But if you want real comfort, real companionship and want to become a real person, you will have to find people who will accept you for what you are. In short, stop being polite, stop being a doormat, stop being snide and bitchy, stop hiding behind things and stop being 'nice'. Be hostile, angry, silly, childish, 'little' — be all the things you are inside."

The key is to find relationships that will help and again I want to quote from the advice I gave to my patients, in this case Jane, once more:

> "O.K., we have deepened your ritual, right? You have been and are much more openly upset in your rituals now. You are feeling a lot of self-pity and weeping a lot and getting angry too. Mostly though, you are still doing this alone — or with me, here in the safety of this office. Now the time has come to deal with your relationships outside. We will look underneath the perfect image you present to your friends and start to change it. That is, we want to see where you actually get upset, where you have problems, where you curb your personality. Then we want to link those problems back to your ritual and the emotions that are in there which relate to your 'outside' self, your outside life. We are looking for pathways, roads to broaden out your ritual and link the inside with the outside. Not to destroy either nor to swamp the one by the other, but so that you can learn to put the two together, so that you

can — in the several years that it will take you to achieve this — normalize yourself and go through the proper stages of adolescence. The trick is not to suddenly act out your needs, your ritual and the things we are finding underneath — that would be useless. You cannot become normal overnight. To try and do this would precipitate real mental distress — it is what actually happens in psychosis. There is nothing wrong with your inside feelings (they are not 'sick' or 'mad') but you have not got the social or emotional support you need yet. Also, if you change your behaviour too rapidly, people around you might believe you to be 'crazy' — remember society is not an all-seeing, all-loving parent any more than your own parents are. People in society create problems as much by their reaction to mental distress as to the problem itself. Society is scared of emotions, just as you are, and just as scared of reality. Further, and most important, recovery does not consist solely of putting the two 'you's' together — that is just the logic, the direction, the code, if you like. The act of learning to put them together is what actually constitutes the recovery — taking your life and everyone and everything in it and learning bit by bit to put the two together. What matters here is that this all has to be done slowly and carefully with your trying hard to choose friends and relationships that will help rather than hinder you.''

There were two factors that mattered in the lives of people like Jane. I want to conclude this by exploring these a little to show you how to tackle them. The first concerns self-awareness and the second, men.

Improving your self-awareness

You have got to try to assess yourself more competently and identify specific things or challenges to work on. Jane, for example, managed very well the deepening and broadening parts but did not know where to begin with relationships. She described her relationships in a very bland, soap-opera way and was quite unable to see beyond the surface with many people; she was, in short, amazingly stereotyped along one or two simple dimensions. She saw men, for example, as being superior, women as being a threat, new friends as being exciting and fun, old friends as being a drag and so on. This is how Jane explained her relationships, firstly with men and then with friends:

> "I'd never really gone into why my relationships broke up or why they never satisfied me nor gave me the kind of thing I wanted — nor stayed with me for long. I began asking men what they thought of me (and I asked my girlfriends) and I was quite shocked. They found me, it seemed, shallow and unemotional. It wasn't something they could define exactly but they felt that I 'wasn't there', I didn't share things with them the way other people did. Chris (an old boyfriend) said he thought I pretended a lot, especially in sex. I never thought he knew — he was such a drip — but he was dead right. I had never orgasmed with him or anyone else. But there was more — it wasn't just sex, they felt somehow that I wasn't to be trusted. In fact, unbeknown to me, I had the reputation of being loose and easy. I'd never thought of myself like that but when you add up my men and my affairs, it could be seen like that.
>
> "My girlfriends, those who had been at school with me, said that I didn't really have friends because everyone thought I was too spiteful and jealous; I was very possessive with my friends and wouldn't share things. If someone had a new boyfriend, I tried to get him; whatever they got, I would want. This was all true but I thought everyone was like that too. They complained that I talked about nothing; that I was too fixated on me, too ambitious; at work, people felt that I was very calculating, not to be trusted. I used things and people."

What really surprised Jane though, after being very hurt and angry, was that in spite of all this, people actually liked her:

> "It took me a while to realize and to work it out but even though they said all those nasty things, they also said they could see through them, that inside, they could see I was a nice person, could be soft and caring. They kept saying, if

only I would relax and just be me, act normal, things would be different. Chris said that the trouble with me was that I was too close to my parents, that I had no one else and when anyone got remotely close to me and really liked me, I seemed to run away, to get nasty and put them off. A crazy-mixed up kid.''

Jane's real surprise though was that she had never thought that other people could see all this. She thought she came across as being mature, sophisticated and 'together'. The very things they liked her for were the parts she kept hidden — the 'baby', vulnerable, needy parts.

I hope there is enough data here for you to work on. The point is that you have got to get a more realistic perspective of yourself operating so that you can build on it. When you have got this far, in realizing that you are quite a messy person and that you are neither all good nor all bad, then you can go on to linking these insights into your ritual.

In one of the early cases, one of my assistants (female) had to live with one of my serious bulimarexics for a month to observe and check on her and her eating and vomiting. The data she got helped us to build up a rich perspective of just how to make the patient begin to change her relationships. Here is an excerpt from the report:

"To begin with, Ann behaved very considerately. We both felt awkward and she really tried to make me feel at home; she was very sociable — 'My home is yours, my food is yours' and so on. Throughout the month that I was there, she didn't change this openly or verbally. But the reality changed. The reality was completely different. She acted out with unbelievable selfishness at every opportunity. I'm exaggerating a bit because it got me down eventually and also because I really didn't know what to expect. I'll give you some examples of how she lived and how she was with people:

"On the phone, she was like several people. She was always phoning home to speak to her mother and father. Every night, every time, something was wrong. And she was 25! When she spoke to them, she was like a child, whiney, weepy, pleading — she would ask them to come and see her and they never did. After she had phoned them, she would go and get something to eat, because she had found them 'cold'. Then, her boyfriend would phone. Immediately she'd change. Cool, then warm, game-playing, teasing, like a scene out of a movie. They'd been going out for ages yet she was unreal with him, playing a role. After this call, which was full of long silences and awkwardnesses, she'd freak because she was scared that he was going out with someone else. Later I found out that this was a permanent preoccupation, a permanent worry. Then someone from work would phone, a woman. Ann would become like a queen, really power-tripping, being bitchy, putting the woman down, finding fault quite openly as if she were implying, 'we're friends and can be quite open with each other' — except she never applied it to herself. After the phone call, she'd come through and start talking about her friend, mocking her, imitating her, sneering at her and so on. It turned out that this woman was really devoted to Ann and saw her as a real friend to whom she told all her troubles. Ann pretended to like her but really despised her. There were other phone calls and Ann seemed to have as many moods as there were callers. It was quite unreal.

"She was very passive-aggressive. At first she cooked for me then she would come home early and eat for herself then there would be no food and she would say she was ill and could I please go and fetch some. Then I would find a full shopping bag in her room which she'd got for herself. She was very often clumsy, breaking things, often had a headache or stomachache, drawing attention to herself. She was permanently insecure and inconsistent. For instance: she was having a scene at work with her boss and continually plotting how to get this or that man as well. I tried to relate all this to her deep relationships with her boyfriend and her own anxiety about him. She just shrugged. She didn't think about it. She was two people, one terrified of losing her boyfriend and *all* her friends, the other never actually being a friend and constantly manipulating and plotting with other people. She was hard and soft and all mixed up. Her only allegiance was to her parents. She had no sense of being a friend, of personal commitment and responsibility.''

I am not suggesting for one moment that all bulimarexics are like this. I am giving you instead an example of what happens in an extreme case so that the consequences of a lack of self-awareness can be seen. It requires discipline to be honest, to be vulnerable, to trust and to be an ordinary friend. Too many bulimarexics try to get above this kind of self-honesty and ordinariness to avoid the anxiety and frustration involved in learning to be normal, to be involved, to be committed and to being a part of an ordinary relationship.

You are frightened of it and this fear urges you to be aloof and to run away. If you can face the fear, you will find you have less inclination to run away. You will see that other people get afraid too and are just as child-like, clumsy, awkward and so on. Then you can become part of the team.

Men

One of the main stumbling blocks to proper self-awareness in bulimarexics and to developing proper working relationships is the fixation most of them have on men. I believe this is started by the kind of attention their fathers give them and continues with their tendency to venerate men and treat them as the givers of affection and attention. Many of my bulimarexics clung to the idea that only a man could really help them and while I, as a man, was acceptable as such, the help I offered them, in their view, was unacceptable. The main reason for this was that I did not treat my patients as their fathers had and as they wanted to be treated in fantasy. I treated them as people and as equals when they expected to be 'used' for their bodies or for the help they could give — the subservient role they could follow.

Many of my patients hid their child-selves from their male partners; they had one persona for men and another for women — and they truly believed that the next man to come along would be the solution to everything. They were looking for their own private version of their fathers so that, free of mother, life would be lived happily ever after. There might be nothing wrong in this if you were to actually get involved with the personality of the man in your life but I found that this seldom happened.

So, one important point: try to turn the men in your life into people first and men second. To show you what I mean, let me cite one last case, that of Tali, a young married woman with two children who could not escape from her roles:

> "The thought of changing things with Danny (my husband) was very daunting. Especially the idea of making him see me as a person or of me standing up to him. However, I found a way — in sex. He liked it every day, like clockwork — whether I wanted it or not. And over time, during my therapy, I had tried to withhold it or play at being sick but I had always lost my nerve when it came to the push. So, one day, I decided to talk to him about my sexual fantasies, just casually, because talking, for me, was easy. Anyway, he liked what I was saying (about my dominating him and being in charge) and he let me try it.

> "Now it may seem strange and I know there was more to it than this but this single little act of role-reversal began my whole change-over. We played, he liked it, we talked some more and I found out a bit of what he goes through in his life and he found out about me. It started with sex but it ended up with much more. Today, I feel we have got a real relationship. I don't vomit or gorge anymore because I don't have to — I feel more of a person and, in a way, I feel his support behind me. I know he likes the new me. But I have never told him about my vomiting and I never will."

Tali may be right or wrong in this, I cannot say. What I do know is that while she did not do her therapy quite as I had suggested (I had wanted her to become more conventionally assertive first), she had found her own way within the limits imposed on her by herself and the man in her life. This then is the basic message: *find your own way* — both with men and with being a person. Do not hide.

LAST WORDS

Once again, I have to say it, if you go through the process of normalizing yourself, and meet the real challenges of living, then gradually, over time, you will feel less like going through your ritual to ease the anxiety inside. Do not expect overnight success; do not expect your ritual to disappear quickly nor your anxiety, depression or despair. They will stay as long as they need to be there, to register the distress in your mind. When you find the right way for you to ease that distress, then you will have beaten your problem.

Chapter 14

Finale

Of course, I have left the really hard part to you. You must take the clues in this survival guide and apply them to yourself and your world. And of course, it will be easy to say: "Oh that is not really like me, at all" or "I couldn't possibly do that" and simply carry on as before. The key to using this book, however, lies not in trying to identify with any specific case nor to get out any specific set of rules that you can use, but to think about *you* and what *you* can do. There are no grand rules in life, no formulae save those that I have spelt out in the chapter on normality.

Each of us has a life that is unique, thank goodness, and what you do with yours is all that matters. Let yourself be open to ideas, let your interest be attracted by some of the things I have said here but, in the final analysis, do it your way, with your own best interests at stake. If something I have written does not fit in with your life, or if you do not happen to agree with me, prove me wrong by finding out what does fit and what you do agree with, then test it out in your world. Tell me about it (by writing to me) or tell anyone who will listen. We are all of us living experiments, and arguing, talking and testing help each of us find out how to live. The trick is to keep on going and not to hide.

Bibliography

What to read? If you're going to read about Anorexia or Bulimia it's vital that you don't just pick up a book or article and follow religiously what it says. You will help yourself much more by reading around the subject and trying to get an awareness of the problems involved both in understanding the anorexic syndrome and its treatment. Reading is a useful adjunct to active therapy or self-help, but remember; *what* you read is not only a distillation of what an author or authors think, but often only describes only a fraction of what she or he does in reality. Academic studies for example are supposed to be truly objective accounts of reality but often tend to be bland and superficial because authors (to get published) have to frame their reports in a set style or orientation. Similarly, personal accounts, while containing more 'meat' than textbooks, tend to flog or push set ideas and in the process often miss out a lot of valuable and thought-provoking ideas buried in the text. The thing to do, I think, is to get an overview. Even if you have no medical or psychological training, there is nothing to stop you looking at all sides of the literature. Get a good dictionary and plough through academic or medical tracts as well as the more popular medical and personal accounts. If you must read, do it properly. To help you I have prepared this fairly comprehensive list of articles and books. Most of them I have found helpful at one time or another and as you will see, they should land you fair and square in the middle of the controversy.

GENERAL STUDIES

Blitzer, J. R., Rollins, N. & Blackwell, A., Children who starve themselves, *Psychosomatic Medicine*, 1961, 23, 369-74

Bruch, H., Perceptual and conceptual disturbances in anorexia nervosa, *Psychosomatic Medicine*, 1962, 24, 187-94

Bruch, H., *Eating disorders*, Routledge, London, 1974

Crisp, A. H., Clinical and therapeutic aspects of anorexia nervosa, *Journal of Psychosomatic Research*, 1965, 9, 67-78

Crisp, A. H., Premorbid factors in adult disorders of weight with particular reference to primary anorexia nervosa, *Journal of Psychosomatic Research*, 1970, 14, 1-22

Crisp, A. H., *Anorexia nervosa*, Academic Press, London, 1980

Crisp, A. H., Palmer, R. L. & Lacey, R. S., How common is anorexia nervosa? British Journal of Psychiatry, 1976, 128, 549-554

Dally, P., *Anorexia nervosa*, Heineman, London, 1969

Duddle, M., An increase of anorexia nervosa in a university population, *British Journal of Psychiatry*, 1973, 123, 711-712

Erikson, E. H., *Childhood and society*, Penguin, London, 1965

Erikson, E. H., *Identity: youth and crisis*, Faber, London, 1968

Gomez, J. & Dally, P., Psychosometric rating in the assessment of anorexia nervosa, *British Journal of Psychiatry*, 1980, 136, 290-6

Grinker, R. R., The poor rich: the children of the super rich, *American Journal of Psychiatry*, 1978, 135, 913-6

Halmi, K. A., Anorexia nervosa, *Psychosomatic Medicine*, 1974, 36, 18-30

Halmi, K. A. *et al.*, Pretreatment prediction of outcome in anorexia nervosa, *British Journal of Psychiatry*, 1979, 134, 71-8

Holt, S. *et al.*, Abnormal gastric emptiness in primary anorexia nervosa, *British Journal of Psychiatry*, 1981, 139, 550-552

Hsu, L. K. G., Crisp, A. H. & Harding, B., Outcome of anorexia nervosa, *Lancet*, 1979, 1, 61-5

Hsu, L. K. G., Meltzer, E. S. & Crisp, A. H., Schizophrenia and anorexia nervosa, *Journal of Nervous and Mental Disease*, 1981, 169, 273-76

Jones, D. J. *et al.*, Epidemiology of anorexia nervosa in Monroe county, N.Y., 1960-76, *Psychosomatic Medicine*, 1980, 42, 551-58

Kellett, J., Trimble, M. & Thorley, A., Anorexia nervosa after the menopause, *British Journal of Psychiatry*, 1976, 128, 555-8

Lacey, J. M., Sexuality and body weight in normal, anorectic and obese young people, *Journal of the Institute of Health Education*, 1978, 16, 73-5

Mechanic, D., *Mental health and social policy*, Prentice Hall, Englewood Cliffs, 1980

Palmer, R. L., *Anorexia nervosa*, Penguin, London, 1980

Rasper, R. C. *et al.*, Disturbance in body image estimation as related to other characteristics and outcome in anorexia nervosa, *British Journal of Psychiatry*, 1979, 134, 60-6

Russell, G. F. M., The nutritional disorder in anorexia nervosa, *Journal of Psychosomatic Research*, 1967, 11, 141-9

Russell, G. F. M., Psychological and physiological mechanisms contributing to amenorrhoea in anorexia nervosa, In N. Morris (Ed.) *Psychosomatic medicine in obstetrics and gynaecology*, Karger, Basel, 1972

Sours, J. A., *Starving to death in a sea of objects: the anorexia nervosa syndrome*, Jason Aronson, New York, 1980

Smart, D. E., Beaumont, P. J. V. & George, G. C. W., Some personality characteristics of patients with anorexia nervosa, *British Journal of Psychiatry*, 1976, 128, 57-60

Vigersky, R. A. (Ed.), *Anorexia nervosa*, Raven Press, New York, 1977

Winnicott, D. W., *Playing and reality*, Tavistock, London, 1971

HISTORY

Gull, W., Anorexia nervosa, *Transactions of the clinical society*, London, 1874, 7, 22

Janet, P., *Les obsessions et la psychasthene*, Félix Alcan, Paris, 1903

Kay, D. & Leigh, D., The natural history, treatment and prognosis of anorexia nervosa, *Journal of Mental Science*, 1954, 100, 411ff

Lasegue, C., De L'anorexie hysterique, *Archives Général de Medécine*, 1873, 1, 385-403

Le Roy Ladurie, E., *The history of the historian*, Routledge, London, 1979

TRADITIONAL MEDICAL APPROACHES

Benady, D. R., Cyproheptadine hydrochloride (Periactin) and anorexia nevosa, *British Journal of Psychiatry*, 1970, 117, 681-2

Bernstein, I. C., Anorexia nervosa treated successfully with electroshock therapy and subsequently followed by pregnancy, *American Journal of Psychiatry*, 1964, 120, 1023-25

Boyar, R. M. *et al.*, Anorexia nervosa: Unmating of the 24hr luteinizing hormone secretary pattern, *New England Journal of Medicine*, 1974, 291, 861-5

Carmody, J. T. B. & Vibber, F. L., Anorexia nervosa treated by prefrontal lobotomy, *Annals of Internal Medicine*, 1952, 36, 647-52

Dally, P., Anorexia nervosa — long term follow up and effects of treatment, *Journal of Psychosomatic Research*, 1967, 11, 151-5

Dally, P. & Gomez, J., *Anorexia nervosa*, Heinemann, London, 1979

Dally, P. & Sargant, W., A new treatment for anorexia nervosa, *British Journal of Medicine*, 1960, June, 1770

Garfinkel, P. E. *et al.*, Hypothalamic-pituitary function in anorexia nervosa, *Archives of General Psychiatry*, 1975, 32, 739-44

Maloney, M. J. & Farrell, M. K. Treatment of severe weight loss in anorexia nervosa with hyperalimentation and psychotherapy, *American Journal of Psychiatry*, 1980, 137, 310-14

Moore, D. C., Amitriptyline therapy in anorexia nervosa, *American Journal of Psychiatry*, 1977, 134, 1303-4

Nemiah, J. C., Anorexia nervosa, *Medicine*, 1950, 29, 225ff

Pierloot, T., Wellens, W. & Houben, M., Elements of resistance to a combined medical and psychotherapeutic programme in anorexia nervosa, *Psychotherapy and Psychosomatics*, 1975, 26, 101-17

Stein, G. S. *et al.*, Lithium in a case of severe anorexia nervosa, *British Journal of Psychiatry*, 1982, 140, 526-8

Walsh, T. *et al.*, Adrenal activity in anorexia nervosa, *Psychosomatic Medicine*, 1978, 40, 499-506

Weller, R. A. & Weller, E. B., Anorexia nervosa in a patient with an infiltrating tumor of the hypothalamus, *American Journal of Psychiatry*, 1982, 139, 824-5

LEARNING THEORY AND BEHAVIOURAL APPROACHES

Agras, W. S. *et al.*, Behaviour modification of anorexia nervosa, *Archives of General Psychiatry*, 1974, 30, 279-86

Bhanji, S. & Thompson, J., Operant conditioning in the treatment of anorexia nervosa, *British Journal of Psychiatry*, 1974, 124, 166-72

Bianco, F. Rapid treatment of two cases of anorexia nervosa, *Journal of Behavior Therapy and Experimental Psychiatry*, 1972, 3, 223-4

Bruch, H., Perils of behavior modification in the treatment of anorexia nervosa, *Journal of the American Medical Association*, 1974, 230, 1419-22

Eckert, E. D. *et al.*, Behaviour therapy in anorexia nervosa, *British Journal of Psychiatry*, 134, 55-9

Garfinkel, P. E., Kline, S. A. & Stancer, H. C., Treatment of anorexia nervosa using operant conditioning techniques, *Journal of Nervous and Mental Disease*, 1973, 6, 428-33

Geller, J. L., Treatment of anorexia nervosa by the integration of behaviour therapy and psychotherapy, *Psychotherapy and Psychosomatics*, 1975, 26, 167-77

Halmi, K. A. *et al.*, Treatment of anorexia nervosa with behaviour modification: Effectiveness of formula feeding and isolation, *Archives of General Psychiatry*, 1975, 32, 93-6

Hallsten, E. A., Adolescent anorexia nervosa treated by desensitization, *Behaviour Research and Therapy*, 1965, 3, 87-91

Lang, P. J., Behaviour therapy in a case of nervous anorexia, In L. Ullman & L. Krasner (Eds.) *Case studies in behavior modification*, Holt, Rinehart & Winston, New York, 1965

Leitenberg, H., Agras, W. S. & Thomson, L. E., A sequential analysis of the effect of selective positive reinforcement in modifying anorexia nervosa, *Behaviour Research and Therapy*, 1968, 6, 211-18

Lucas, A. R., Duncan, J. W. & Piens, V. V., The treatment of anorexia nervosa, *American Journal of Psychiatry*, 1976, 133, 1034-8

Mawson, A. R., Anorexia nervosa and the regulation of intake: A review, *Psychological Medicine*, 1974, 4, 289-308

Pillay, M. & Crisp, A. H., The importance of social skills training within an established in-patient treatment programme, *British Jokrnal of Psychiatry*, 1981, 139, 533-9

Schnurer, A. T., Rubin, R. R. & Roy, A., Systematic desensitization of anorexia nervosa seen as a weight phobia, *Journal of Behaviour Therapy and Experimental Psychiatry*, 1973, 4, 149-53

Stunkard, A., New therapies for the eating disorders: Behavior modification of obesity and anorexia nervosa, *Archives of General Psychiatry*, 1972, 26, 391-8

PSYCHOTHERAPEUTIC APPROACHES

Barcai, A., Family therapy in the treatment of anorexia nervosa, *American Journal of Psychiatry*, 1971, 128, 286-90

Becker, H., Korner, P. & Stoffler, A., Psychodynamics and therapeutic aspects of anorexia nervosa, *Psychotherapy and Psychosomatics*, 1981, 36, 8-16

Binswanger, L., The case of Ellen West. In R. May *et al.* (Eds.) *Existence*, Clarion, New York, 1958

Bruch, H., Psychotherapy in primary anorexia nervosa, *Journal of Nervous and mental Disease*, 1970, 150, 51-67

Bruch, H., Psychological antecedents of anorexia nervosa, In R. A. Vigersky, (Ed.) *Anorexia nervosa*, Raven Press, New York, 1977

Bruch, H., *The golden cage*, Open Books, London, 1978

Caille, P. *et al.*, A systems theory approach to a case of anorexia nervosa, *Family Process*, 1977, 16, 455-65

Conrad, D. E., A starving family: an interactional view of anorexia nervosa, *Bulletin of the Menninger Clinic*, 1977, 41, 487-95

Groen, J. & Feldman-Toledano, Z., Educative treatment of patients and parents in anorexia nervosa, *British Journal of Psychiatry*, 1966, 671-81

Hall, A., Family structure and relationships of 50 female anorexia nervosa patients, *Australia and New Zealand Journal of Psychiatry*, 1978, 12, 263-8

Jessner, L. & Abse, D. W., Regressive forces in anorexia nervosa, *British Journal of Medical Psychology*, 1960, 33, 301-12

Masterson F., The role of maternal identification in 4 cases of anorexia nervosa, *Bulletin of the Menninger Clinic*, 1977, 41, 475-86

Masterson, F., Primary anorexia in the borderline adolescent, In P. Hartcollis (Ed.) *Borderline personality disorders*, International University Press, New York, 1977

Minuchin, S., Rosman, B. L. & Baker, L., *Psychosomatic families: Anorexia nervosa in context*, Harvard University Press, Cambridge, 1978

Norris, D. L. & Jones, E., Anorexia nervosa — a clinical study of ten patients and their family systems, *Journal of Adolescence*, 1979, 2, 101-111

Rosman, D., Minuchin, S., *et al.*, Input and outcome of family therapy in anorexia nervosa, *Adolescent Psychiatry*, Volume 5, Jason Aronson, New York, 1978

Solomon, A. P. & Morrison, D. A. R., Anorexia nervosa: Dual transference therapy, *American Journal of Psychotherapy*, 1973, 28, 480-9

Szyrynski, V., Anorexia nervosa and psychotherapy, *American Journal of Psychotherapy*, 1973, 28, 492-505

Thomae, H., Some psychoanalytic observations on anorexia nervosa, *British Journal of Medical Psychology*, 1963, 36, 239-48

Wold, P., Family structure in 3 cases of anorexia nervosa: The role of the father, *American Journal of Psychiatry*, 1973, 130, 1394-7

Yager, J., Family issues in the pathogenesis of anorexia nervosa, *Psychosomatic Medicine*, 1982, 44, 43-60

CONTROVERSIAL ISSUES

Boskind-Lodahl, M., Cinderella's step-sisters: A feminist perspective on anorexia and bulimia, *Signs: The Journal of women in culture and society*, 1976, 2, 342-55

Boskind-Lodahl, M. & Sirlin, J., The gorging-purging syndrome, *Psychology Today*, 1977, March, 50ff

Button, E. J., Fransella, F. & Slade, P. D., A re-appraisal of body perception disturbance in anorexia nervosa, *Psychological Medicine* 1977, 7, 235-43

Casper, R. C. *et al.*, Disturbances in body image estimates as related to other characteristics and outcome in anorexia nervosa, *British Journal of Psychiatry*, 1979, 134, 60-6

Casper, R. C.*et al.*, Anorexia and bulimia, *Archives of General Psychiatry*, 1982, 39, 488-9

Chodoff, P., Hysteria and women, *American Journal of Psychiatry*, 1982, 139, 545-51

Dowling, C., *The cinderella complex*, Fontana, London, 1981

EDITORIAL, *British Journal of Psychiatry*, 1981, 138, 164-6

Ehrensing, R. H. & Weitzman, E. L., The mother-daughter relationship in anorexia nervosa, *Psychosomatic Medicine*,1970, 32, 201-8

Eichenbaum, L. & Orbach, S., *Ouside in Inside out*, Penguin, London, 1982

Frunsella, F. & Crisp, A. H., Compassions of weight conceptions in groups of neurotic, normal & anorexic females, *British Journal of Psychiatry*, 1979, 134, 79-86

Friday, N., *My Mother Myself*, New York, 1977

Garfinkel, P. E. & Waring, E. M., Personality, interests, and emotional disturbances in psychiatric residents, *American Journal of Psychiatry*, 1981, 138, 51-5

Hsu, L. K. G., Is there a disturbance in body image in anorexia nervosa? *Journal of Nervous and Mental Disease*, 1982, 170, 305-7

Katz, J. & Sitnick, T., Anorexia nervosa and bulimia, *Archives of General Psychiatry*, 1982, 39, 487-8

Lawrence, M., & Lowenstein, C., Self starvation, *Spare Rib*, May, 1979

MacLeod, S., *The art of starvation*, Virago, London, 1981

McCrindle, J. & Rowbotham, S. (Eds.), *Dutiful daughters*, Penguin, London, 1981

Morgan, H. G., Fasting girls and our attitudes to them, *British Medical Journal*, 1977, 2, 1652-5

Naish, J. M., Problems of deception in medical practice, *Lancet*, 1979, ii, 139-42

Nicholson, J., *What society does to girls*, Virago, London, 1980

Orbach, S., *Fat is a feminist issue*, Penguin, London, 1978

Phillips, A. & Rakusen, J., *Our bodies ourselves*, Penguin, London, 1980

Rampling, D., Abnormal mothering in the genesis of anorexia nervosa, *Journal of Nervous and Mental Disease*, 1980, 168, 501-4

Schwartz, D. M. & Thompson, M. G., Do anorexics get well? *American Journal of Psychiatry*, 1981, 138, 319-23

Selvini-Palazzoli, M., *Self-starvation: From individual to family therapy in the treatment of anorexia nervosa*, Jason Aronson, New York, 1978

Schatzman, R., *Soul murder: Persecution in the family*, Allen Lane, New York, 1973

Stamey, H. C., Anorexia nervosa: A psychiatric symptom with many faces, *Psychosomatics*, 1971, 12, 174-8

CURRENT TRENDS

Beaumont, P. J. V., Further categorization of anorexia nervosa patients, *Australia and New Zealand Journal of Psychiatry*, 1977, 11, 226-38

Beaumont, P. J. V. *et al.*, The onset of anorexia nervosa, *Australia and New Zealand Journal of Psychiatry*, 1978, 12, 145-9

Beaumont, P. J. V., George, G. C. W. & Smart, D. E., 'Dieters' and 'Vomiters' and 'Purgers' in anorexia nervosa, *Psychological Medicine*, 1976, 6, 617-22

Bemis, K. M., Current approaches to the etiology and treatment of anorexia nervosa, *Psychological Bulletin*, 1978, 85, 593-617

Bhanji, S. & Mattingly, D., Anorexia nervosa: Some observations on 'Dieters' and 'vomiters', cholesterol and carotene, *British Journal of Psychiatry*, 1981, 139, 238-41

Branch Hardin, C. H. & Eurman, L., Social attitudes towards patients with anorexia nervosa, *American Journal of Psychiatry*, 1980, 137, 631-2

Cantwell, A. P. *et al.*, Anorexia nervosa: An affective disorder? *Archives of General Psychiatry*, 1977, 34, 1087-93

Casper, R. C., *et al.*, Bulimia: Its incidence and clinical importance in patients with anorexia nervosa, *Archives of General Psychiatry*, 1980, 37, 1030-5

Ceasar, M., Hunger in primary anorexia nervosa, *American Journal of Psychiatry*, 1979, 136, 979

Ehrenreich, B. & English, D., *For her own good: 150 years of the experts advice to women*, Pluto Press, London, 1979

Garfinkel, P. E., Moldofsky, H. & Garner, D. H., The heterogeneity of anorexia nervosa: Bulimia as a distinct subgroup, *Archives of General Psychiatry*, 1980, 37, 1036-40

Halmi, K. A., Struss, A. & Goldberg, S., An investigation of weights in the parents of anorexic patients, *Journal of Nervous and Mental Disease*, 1978, 166, 358-61

Hudson, J., Laffer, P. S. & Pope, H., Bulimia related to affective disorder by family history and response to the dexamethasone supression test, *American Journal of Psychiatry*, 1982, 139, 685-6

Kalucy, R. S., Crisp, A. H. & Harding, B., A study of 56 families with anorexia nervosa, *British Journal of Medical Psychology*, 1977, 50, 381-95

Katz, J. L. & Walsh, B. T., Depression in anorexia nervosa, *American Journal of Psychiatry*, 1978, 35, 507

Kron, L. *et al.*, Hyperactivity in anorexia nervosa: A fundamental clinical feature, *Comprehensive Psychiatry*, 1978, 19, 433-40

Lacey, J. H., Dietary chaos — a compulsive eating syndrome, *Proceedings of the 13th European Conference on Psychosomatic Research*, 1980, 73-77

Martin, J. E., Anorexia nervosa. A disorder of weight, *Occupational Therapy*, September, 1978

Mitchell, J. B., Pyle, E. & Eckert, E. D., Frequency and duration of binge eating episodes in patients with bulimia, *American Journal of Psychiatry*, 1981, 138, 835-6

Morgan, H. G. & Russell, G. F. M., Value of family background and clinical features as predictors of long term outcome in anorexia nervosa, *Psychological Medicine*, 1975, 5, 355-71

Orbach, S., Anorexia in women, *British Journal of Sexual Medicine*, 1981, July

Palmer, R. L., Dietary chaos syndrome: A useful new term? *British Journal of Medical Psychology*, 1979, 52, 187-90

Pyle, R., Mitchell, J. E. & Eckert, E. D., Bulimia: A report of 34 cases, *Journal of Clinical Psychiatry*, 1981, 42, 60-4

Russell, G. F. M., Bulimia nervosa: An ominous variant of anorexia nervosa, *Psychological Medicine*, 1979, 9, 429-48

Spencer, J. A. & Fremouw, W. J., Binge eating as a function of restraint and weight classification, *Journal of Abnormal Psychology*, 1979, 88, 262-7

Stonehill, E. & Crisp, A. H., Psychoneurotic characteristics of patients with anorexia nervosa before and after treatment and at follow up 4-7 years later, *Journal of Psychosomatic Research*, 1977, 21, 187-93

Stober, M. *et al.*, Validity of the bulimia-restricter distinction in anorexia nervosa. Parental personality characteristics and family psychiatric morbidity, *Journal of Nervous and Mental Disease*, 1982, 170, 345-51

Stober, M., The significance of bulimia in juvenile anorexia nervosa, *International Journal of Eating Disorders*, 1981, 1, 28-43

Stober, M., The relationship of personality characteristics to body image disturbance in juvenile anorexia nervosa, *Psychosomatic Medicine*, 1982, 43, 323-30

Van Buskirk, S. S., A two-phase perspective on the treatment of anorexia nervosa, *Psychological Bulletin*, 1977, 84, 529-38

Wardle, J. & Beinhart, H., Binge eating: A theoretical review, *British Journal of Clinical Psychology*, 1981, 20, 97-109

Winokur, A., March, V. & Mendels, J., Primary affective disorders in relatives of patients with anorexia nervosa, *American Journal of Psychiatry*, 1980, 137, 695-8

Yager, J., Rudnick, F. D. & Metzer, R. J., Anorexia nervosa: A current perspective and new directions, In E. Serafetinidese (Ed.), *From research to practice: Biobehavioural contributions*, Grune and Stratton, New York, 1981

THEORETICAL AND CLINICAL BACKGROUND TO THIS BOOK

As mentioned earlier, I believe that each clinical problem requires attention in its own right and that also includes each individual patient. This is essentially a phenomenological-existential view but it need not be either unscientific or go against experimental research on grouped data. In essence, each clinical problem must be confronted afresh with the investigator/therapist being fully aware of all the research available (behavioural, psychoanalytic, existential, personal, experimental) using this, together with the person in situation, to construct hypotheses and theories about that person. In short, we need, as patient and doctor, sets of alternative ways of viewing a problem in order that the individuality of a specific person at a specific time can be described and worked upon. This very briefly is a condensation from my doctoral dissertation (A theory of existential psychology: The role of values in psychology and psychotherapy. University of Cape Town, 1971) which contains a full treatment of the theoretical background. You can read a shorter version in *Humanitas* 1974, 2, 419-24. I've written a number of papers detailing the theoretical and clinical implications of this perspective which might be of interest:

Psychology and epistemology: operationism revisited, *Psychological Record*, 1970, 20, 229-34

Authoritarian trends in contemporary psychology: The dominance of the paradigm, *Psychological Reports*, 1970, 27, 575-82

Psychology and socio-political reality. Apartheid psychology and its links with trends in humanistic psychology and behaviour theory, *International Journal of Psychology*, 1973, 8, 73-9

Scientific status of technical eclecticism. A critical note, *Psychological Reports*, 1971, 28, 169-73

Behavior modification techniques and the treatment of psychosis: A critique of Alumbauch, *Psychological Record*, 1973, 23, 93-7

The dangers of therapy without assessment. A case study, *Journal of Personality Assessment*, 1974, 38, 263-5

Treatment of transvestism and subsequent coital problems, *Journal of Behaviour Therapy and Experimental Psychiatry*, 1974, 5, 101-2 Reprinted in N. Houserman (Ed.) *Symptoms and syndromes*. Baltimore: Williams and Wilkins, 1978

Differential effects of psychotherapy and behavioural techniques in a case of acute obsessive-compulsive disorder, *British Journal of Psychiatry*, 1974, 125, 181-3

Psychotherapy and race. Inter-racial therapy under apartheid, *American Journal of Psychotherapy*, 1975, 29, 179-84

Treatment of a severe case of encopresis by a system-based operant method, *Psychotherapy: Theory, research and practice*, 1976, 13, 286-9

The use of assertive training and psychodynamic insight in the treatment of migraine headache, *Journal of Nervous and Mental Disease*, 1976, 163, 61-4 Reprinted in Marmor, J. & Woods, S. M., *The interface between the psychoanalytic and behaviour therapies*, Plenum, New York, 1980

A multiple-paradigm treatment programme for migraine headache, *British Journal of Medical Psychology*, 1978, 51, 103-10

There are many texts you can read in this area in addition. The Marmor and Woods book (above) is quite useful, but there are a number of books and articles dealing with complex ways of thinking about psychology and psychiatry. Some that influenced me are:

Back, K. W., Decisions under uncertainty: Rational, irrational and non-rational, *American Behavioural Scientist*, 1961, 6, 14-19

Bannister, D., Psychology as an exercise in paradox, In D. F. Schultz (see below)

Berner, P. & Kufferle, B., British phenomenological and psychopathological concepts: A comparative review, *British Journal of Psychiatry*, 1982, 140, 565-85

Bridgman, P. W., *The way things are*, Harvard University Press, Cambridge, 1959

Feather, B. W. & Rhoads, J. M., Psychodynamic behaviour therapy, *Archives of General Psychiatry*, 1972, 26, 496-502

Feyerabend, P. K., How to be a good empiricist — a plea for tolerance in matters epistemological, In B. A. Brody (Ed.), *Reading in the philosophy of science*, Prentice Hall, Engelwood-Cliffs, 1970

Greenspan, S. I. The clinical use of operant learning approaches: Some complex issues, *American Journal of Psychiatry*, 1974, 131, 852-7

Gunther, P. A., The philosophy of science: Its functions, *Main Currents in Modern Thought*, 1968, 24, 68-74

Hine, F. R., Werman, D. S. & Simpson, D. M., Effectiveness of psychotherapy: The problem of research with complex phenomena, *American Journal of Psychiatry*, 1982, 139, 204ff

Hill, O. W., *Modern trends in psychosomatic medicine*, Butterworth, London, 1976

Kuhn, T. S., *The structure of scientific revolutions*, University of Chicago Press, Chicago, 1962

Lipowski, Z. J., Psychosomatic medicine in the seventies, *American Journal of Psychiatry*, 1977, 134, 233-44

Polanyi, M., *Personal knowledge*, Routledge, London, 1962

Polanyi, M., Logic and psychology, *American Psychologist*, 1968, 23, 27-43

Rosenhan, D. L., On being sane in insane places, *Science*, 1973, 179, 250-8

Schultz, D. P. (Ed.), *The science of psychology: critical reflections*, Appleton Century Crofts, New York, 1970

Schwartz, G. E. & Weiss, S. M., What is behavioural medicine? *Psychosomatic Medicine*, 1977, 39, 377-81

Shapiro, M. B., The single case in clinical-psychological research, *Journal of General Psychology*, 1966, 74, 3-23

Shapiro, M. B. *et al.*, A clinician's approach to experimental research, *Journal of Clinical Psychology*, 1973, April, 165-9

Taylor, J. G., The role of axioms in psychological theory, *Bulletin of the British Psychological Society*, 1968, 21, 221-7

Turner, M. B., *Philosophy and the science of behavior*, Appleton Century Crofts, New York, 1967

Unger, R. M., A programme for late twentieth century psychiatry, *American Journal of Psychiatry*, 1982, 139, 155-64

Von Bertalanffy, L., An essay on the relativity of categories, *Philosophy of Science*, 1955, 22, 243-62

Woody, R. H., Toward a rationale for psychobehavioral therapy, *Archives of General Psychiatry*, 1896, 19, 197-204

Index